TEST
CRICKET

TEST CRICKET

THE UNAUTHORISED BIOGRAPHY
JARROD KIMBER

hardie grant books

Published in 2015 by Hardie Grant Books

Hardie Grant Books (Australia)
Ground Floor, Building 1
658 Church Street
Richmond, Victoria 3121
www.hardiegrant.com.au

Hardie Grant Books (UK)
5th & 6th Floor
52–54 Southwark Street
London SE1 1UN
www.hardiegrant.co.uk

A Cataloguing-in-Publication entry is available from the catalogue of the National Library of Australia at www.nla.gov.au
Test Cricket
ISBN 978 1 74379 019 9

Cover design by Josh Durham/Design by Committee
Text design by Patrick Cannon
Typeset in 11.5/15 pt Adobe Garamond Pro by Cannon Typesetting

Printed by McPherson's Printing Group, Maryborough, Victoria

CONTENTS

Chapter 1

A DEATH IN THE FAMILY

A HAPPY BIRTHDAY BALLOON is floating at the front of Adelaide Oval on day one. It's the ground's 130th Test birthday. The balloon isn't for that.

It is for the birthday that Phillip Hughes never had. It floats above the spontaneous fan tribute to Hughes.

Underneath it is a Christmas tree. Radios. Beer. Sunglasses. Portraits. Headbands. Flowers. A toy cow. And cricket gear. So much cricket gear. Bats with rosary beads. Tear-stained balls. Kids' bats. Signed gloves. Well-used bats. Pads with stories. Illustrated bats. Bats. Bats. Bats. All put out.

Team hats from clubs all around Australia are there. One from Orange. Another from the Bowen Barracudas. And the Brothers Cricket Club. There is also one from Merlynston Hadfield Cricket Club. Probably one of the hardest cricket clubs in Melbourne, a club famous for men, and boys, who batted without gloves. Their home ground seemed more frightening than the cemetery next door. One of them has donated his hat. Even the hard men are crying.

Then there is a helmet. It's hard not to think it should be on someone's head instead of sitting in this tribute. On the peak is a photo of Phillip Hughes.

The condolence book is full. 'Bat on forever.' 'We love you mate.' 'Hope you're smashing them in heaven.' It has far too many RIPs written in kids' handwriting.

A fan walks past, takes a quick look and says it's 'too morbid'. Hughes' promotional photo smiles back at him from the wall. The sort of photo that all professional athletes have to have taken has been turned into a shrine.

A memorial to a man who played cricket – and was killed by cricket.

Hughes wasn't the first cricketer to die in first-class cricket. Players had died of natural causes. Club cricketers around the world have died in almost every way imaginable. Former Indian Test player Raman Lamba died when struck fielding in close. But something about Hughes, and the way cricket was now consumed globally, meant everyone remembered Hughes playing. Everyone could go online and talk about it. Everyone could, if they wanted, find the video clip of Hughes being struck.

Our game had killed someone, and no one could really handle it.

The game had been beaten, abused, choked and cheated. It had been used to racially segregate, or to keep the natives in their place. When certain players of darker skin have excelled, they have been accused of cheating. The very game itself has laws based on betting. The game has been used to exploit women, sometimes sexually or financially, while mostly mocking or ignoring them. Cheating in cricket has resulted in people going to jail. People on the way to cricket matches have been killed by terrorists. Players have been shot.

'Cricket civilises people and creates good gentlemen. I want everyone to play cricket in Zimbabwe. I want ours to be a nation of gentlemen,' said the brutal dictator Robert Mugabe. Mugabe and men like him have abused this sport from the day they started organising, and betting, on it. Cricket has grown into a billion dollar business. It has been commoditised and trademarked. It has been taken further and further away from where it began: just a bunch of kids bowling a ball, hitting a ball.

That was the part Phil Hughes liked. He wasn't in it to be a millionaire. He wasn't trying to build a brand. He just liked to hit the ball.

Then Hughes played his hook shot too early. The ball struck him. He went into a coma. He passed away. And the cricket world realised it was a billion-person community. A community in mourning. Remembering that little guy with the homespun technique.

One fan, Paul Taylor, had been so moved by Hughes' death that he had put out his bat, took a picture, and then urged Australia to do the same. Soon, everyone did it. Millions around the world saw the pictures, took the pictures and shared the pictures. Fans put their bats outside their house, work, car – all in honour of a man almost none of them had ever met.

It went viral online and it infected homes around the country – and the world. People stopped while driving just to cry at the tribute. Billy Bragg put out his guitar. Google Australia put a bat leaning on its logo. Viv Richards put out his bat. Families put them out. Clubs. Factories. Everyone. Bats were bought by people just to be placed outside.

That's cricket. Not some imaginary spirit, but something real.

Mostly the spirit of cricket is like a huge, heavy, imaginary version of the Bible. You can use any part of it to prove you are within the spirit of the game, and any part of it to prove your opposition is not. It is a magical cape that you can wear in order to tell others they are dirty cheats.

It was in the late 1990s that the MCC stuck the spirit of cricket at the start of the laws of cricket. An amendment referred to 'the game's traditional values'. It didn't say those values included class distinctions, racism and sexism. They even trademarked the term.

Months after that day in Adelaide, I was lost in the Victorian country-side looking for a wedding. There were no houses around, no one I could ask for directions. But on the corner of a fence, there was a cricket bat. I got out of the car, ran over quick enough so that snakes wouldn't bite me, and saw that the bat said, 'RIP PHIL'. It'll be there until the wood rots.

Australia was due to start a series against India. New Zealand and Pakistan were halfway through a Test match. That Test was paused. Australia's series was paused.

Cricket needed time to heal.

Out in the middle, Phil Hughes was all about batting. Whenever he thought his partner was faltering, or losing concentration, he would say, 'Come on, let's dig in and get through to tea.'

Cricket had spent its entire history overcoming the very worst of humanity. Now it had to overcome a tragedy it created.

Cricket had killed one of the men it helped create. This time, it would be tough to get through to tea.

Chapter 2

ARM TWISTERS

YOU ARE IN LONDON; it is another millennium. You don't have enough money for the Tube. You walk across London. It's crowded and cold on this summer day in June, 1899. You travel through Hyde Park. People stand on soapboxes shouting about God and Charles Darwin. You see the recently moved Wellington Arch. You hurry down past Queen Victoria's Buckingham Palace. You cross the Vauxhall Bridge, where men who don't want their faces seen scurry. You stop and give a young boy some coins as he performs a comedy routine in oversized clogs. You continue down Harleyford Road until you get to Kennington Oval.

You pay for a ticket; the price is higher than usual. You make your way into the ground, where you stand down near the pavilion. In front of you is the Oval cricket ground, behind it the gasometers. You see the two opening batsmen walk to the middle. You only smile at the thought of one of them. You are at a first-class cricket match.

Gentlemen and players. The gentlemen are amateurs. High-class men, well educated, and the cream of the crop of English society. Rather than do anything crude like ask for money, they play purely for the love of the game. The players are professionals. They are good cricketers – of common birth. They are invited onto hallowed grounds to make a bit of cash for themselves, and even more for their betters.

But none of that matters: you aren't here for class warfare, nor even the game itself. You are here for one man. The one you can recognise from a hundred yards. There is a thick layer of tobacco smoke around the ground. Every man wears a hat of some kind. The square-leg umpire squats awkwardly; the leg slip twitches. The bowler takes the ball. The man you have come to see is the most famous man in Britain – and perhaps the world.

He is cricket's Big Bang.

The umpire says, 'Gentlemen, play.'

The ball comes down to this man. Everyone takes a gasp of air. His beard reaches down to his belly; the two seem almost joined in perfect unathletic harmony. He shuffles forward before easing backwards. He wafts, he chats, he waddles. He scores. You clap.

He scores again. You clap again.

He keeps scoring. You keep clapping. They call him The Nonsuch. It means excellent, perfect, like no other. WG Grace, William Gilbert Grace. Cricket's first God.

Well before Grace, cricket was a child's game. Some historians have tried to claim that Jesus played a version of it. But the idea of hitting something round with a club has probably always been with us.

A small boy, not yet two, holds a cricket bat. His father grips his arms while his mother gently lobs the ball at him. He plays an ungainly push; the ball takes the inside of the bat and hits his tricycle. He looks at his father. He looks at his mother. He smiles. He doesn't know what this is, but he likes it.

This is cricket. From the first moment that someone picked up a rock and threw it at someone who had a club, people have had that look, that feeling.

Cricket moved on from the small children having fun. At first it was the wealthy landowners who asked their esteemed gentlemen friends to play and then topped up their teams with skilled professional players – butchers, bakers, bricklayers – who needed the money.

It was then that the laws of the game were written in accordance with as many bets as you could make. The moral code of cricket was born and the grounds were fenced in. And the traditions were transcribed for future generations.

Cricket became a business in the 1700s and by the 1800s the best grounds made you buy a ticket for entry.

But cricket was a gentleman's game. They owned it.

Kids were playing cricket all over the UK well before anyone had heard of Hambledon. But Hambledon is where cricket started being narrated. That makes it the game's cradle.

The Hambledon Club was formed around 1760. It is in rural Hampshire, south of London. The noblemen and country gentry flocked to it. They charged spectators to come in and everyone had a bet.

It was here Tom Walker, a professional player, would bat as the first man in and, often, last man out. They say he once faced 107 balls off one bowler, and scored a single from him.

His nickname was 'Old Everlasting'. John Nyren, who is responsible for all the credit Hambledon now receives, wrote in *The Young Cricketers' Tutor* that Walker had 'a hard, ungainly scrag-of-mutton frame; weird, apple-John face; long spider legs, as thick at the ankles as at the hips, the driest and most rigid limbed chap; his skin was like the rind of an old oak, and as sapless. He moved like the rude machinery of a steam engine in the infancy of construction and, when he ran, every member seemed ready to fly to the four winds.'

Walker did something even more amazing than move like rude machinery or score 1 from 170 balls. He made an attempt to introduce a new form of bowling – round-arm – in 1788. There is a school of belief that outside the Earl of Winchelsea's entourage and Hambledon's other elite, in the streets and parks, kids and adults had been doing it for years. But their games were never reported unless someone died, used a dog as a player or it ended in a brawl.

At Hambledon, such disgusting bowling would never be allowed, and instantly Walker was called for a no-ball, and told by the council of the Hambledon Club that it was considered foul play. Batsmen were on this committee; batsmen of nobility and pedigree. Walker's rudimentary round-arm was fast and scary, and no-one wanted to face it. So the authorities said no thanks.

Walker didn't have the social standing to argue his case. By bowling that way he was putting his earnings in danger, so he just never did it again.

At the same time, William Fennex, a professional of Buckinghamshire, stretched forward to play a ball while remaining in his crease. It is what we would call a forward defence today. At the time they said, 'It's just not cricket.' It's doubtful that this was the first time someone had ever played forward to a ball whilst remaining in the crease, or accused someone of doing something 'not cricket' despite them playing within the laws of the game. It was just that this was recorded. Batting was evolving.

Walker kept playing as a batsman and a lob, or underarm, bowler. Almost 20 years later he played in a match where John Willes Esquire was playing.

Willes had a sister named Christiana who loved playing cricket. According to an article by her son, written almost 100 years later in 1907, 'It was my mother's skill in throwing the ball to him [John Willes] for practice in the barn at Tonford ... He then trained a dog to fetch the ball, and there was a saying that Willes, his sister, and his dog could beat any eleven in England.' That article gives Christiana the credit for round-arm bowling, as she couldn't bowl underarm due to her hooped crinoline dresses. That has been the common story about round-arm bowling's invention – even if fashion historians doubt the evidence, as does former UK prime minister and cricket historian John Major.

Cricket in 1800 wasn't anything like today's game. The bats had only just become the bats we know. Before that they were like boat paddles, and before that hockey sticks, back when the ball was rolled along the ground.

Back then they had stumps, but only two, and consequently one bail, not three and two. They had runs, but they were called notches. They had innings, but a long innings would be called a hand. Underarm was how you delivered the ball. By the start of 1800, bowlers came in two kinds: lobbers, who tossed the ball high in the air, even over a batsman's head, and softball-style bowlers, who tried to bowl a bit quicker.

So the bowling of John Willes, possibly Christiana's as well, and even that of Tom Walker was quite different. With the arm coming around the body (but not over the shoulder like today) the ball came out faster. Dangerous. Outrageous. Cheating.

But underarm bowling was kind of rubbish. It was fine for your three-year-old nephew, but not really a demanding athletic endeavour that would captivate millions of people, as it does today.

Willes bowled round-arm in high-profile matches. Although he was the main proponent, others bowled as well. The conservatives (virtually everyone important in cricket) hated it. William Ward, the man who bought Lord's from Thomas Lord to stop Lord from putting a property development on it, also hated round-arm bowling. Probably because he couldn't play it. It was ruining the game. It would ruin batsmen. It could cause injury. It was throwing. It was horrid. It was 'repugnant'.

Pads weren't yet being used. That only happened 20 years later, in 1841, not long after a batsman had his leg broken against Eton when facing a round-arm ball. There was even a story that one bowler had bowled so quickly that his wicketkeeper had missed it, and then the ball had gone through the jacket of his long stop and killed a dog. The message was clear: round-arm bowling broke legs and killed dogs.

But Willes kept doing it – for 15 years. Cricket never completely outlawed it, even if he wasn't always invited to play because of it.

Willes opened the bowling at Lord's on 15 July 1822. The umpire called him for a no-ball. Legend has it that Willes threw down the ball and left the field, jumped on a horse and was never seen on a cricket ground again. This moment forced the game's hand.

The Sporting Magazine ran pieces by a Mr GT Knight and a Mr Denison. Arguing in favour of round-arm, Mr Knight uttered a truth that still haunts cricket to this day: 'It is universally admitted that batting dominates bowling to an extent detrimental to the game.'

Mr Denison's main three reasons against were that round-arm was throwing, was dangerous, and was 'fatal to all scientific play, putting a premium on chance hits, and placing scientific defence at a discount.'

Mr GT Knight was actually George Knight, son of Edward Knight, who was Jane Austen's brother. So he had a family right to the phrase 'universally admitted'.

Knight was also the proponent of the experimental cricket matches to win over the MCC and people like William Ward to the benefits of round-arm bowling. The games were between Sussex and England; Sussex had two bowlers who were following the current cricket law of raising your arm as high as your elbow. They beat England easily in the first two of three matches.

A decade later, in 1835, the Marylebone Cricket Club, better known as the MCC, and based at Lord's, was fully in charge of the laws of cricket. It changed the law so that 'the ball must be bowled, and if it be thrown or jerked, or if the hand be above the shoulder in the delivery, the umpire must call no-ball'. But bowlers kept raising their arms higher and higher.

Still cricket fought evolution. Overarm bowling, as it is practised today, was not legalised until 1864, only 13 years before the first-ever Test – and a good 50 years after Willes.

In 1884, Alfred Lyttelton, England's keeper in a Test match, lobbed underarm with his pads on, and took 4/8. In 1910, George Simpson-Hayward played five Tests bowling underarm lob. He was the last lobber.

Willes had made cricket take the first step towards the game it is today. Underarm bowling meant cricket was only slightly more interesting than croquet. If it had stayed as underarm only, there would be no Ashes, no World Cup and Don Bradman would have been just a grumpy accountant. India, Sri Lanka and Pakistan would never have been swept up in leg-glances and doosras – and the English language would be all the poorer. The West Indies would never have come together as one. Without overarm bowling, there would be no cricket in the world today.

Overarm bowling is the single most important thing that ever happened to cricket. It is typical that the officials tried to stop it, that we really don't know how it started, and that a gentleman gets the credit for it.

Chapter 3

BY THE GRACE OF GOD

WILLIAM GILBERT GRACE was 'born in the atmosphere of cricket'. As a young man, he and his brothers (not his sisters, who had to field with the family dogs) were coached to play straight and point their left shoulder at the ball. From a young age, Grace, by his own words, threw stones at birds, which he believed made him a great fielder.

Grace studied medicine in Bristol. He was a poor student, but a gentleman and a cricketer. Given that he spent almost every possible minute of his life playing cricket (or telling people about how he played cricket), he would have been an awful doctor, even by the horrendous standards of the 1800s.

As a batsman, no cricketer before him had ever spent as much time simply working on his game, perfecting the technique – and inventing batting as we knew it.

Grace was athletic early in his life, playing football for the famed Wanderers. But he grew up in a period in which the underarm bowling was as good as it ever was, the pitches were vicious, round-arm bowlers were perfecting their craft and overarm bowlers were coming in.

So Grace did something so natural to modern cricketers and so alien at the time. He moved according to where the ball was pitched. If he needed to move forward, he would. If he needed to move back, he would. Grace invented footwork. He gave cricket a Fred Astaire and Ginger Rogers moment.

According to the Indian cricket author and maharajah Ranjitsinhji, Grace 'turned the old one-stringed instrument into a many-chorded lyre'.

Not according to Grace – for him, it wasn't about art, it was about runs. He didn't want to be remembered as a great artist. He wanted to be remembered as the greatest batsman of all time. From the time he first arrived as a teenage first-class player, until the day he died, he did everything he could to make that happen.

In 1866 Grace made 224 not out. He then missed the last day of the match to compete in a 440-yard hurdle race. He won. The 224 against Surrey was his maiden first-class hundred. According to cricket historian Harry Altham, he was 'thenceforward the biggest name in cricket and the main spectator attraction'. He had just turned 18. He was already known as either The Champion, or The Nonsuch.

Grace was so good, he created new stadiums. They put extra seating up everywhere he went. And then they charged extra to see him. Grace made the sport bigger. Grace was a megastar before the term existed.

When Grace was dismissed he was known to say, 'Play on. They've come to watch me bat, sir, not you umpire.' He was right. That's what they did. The game of cricket was just a stage; they came to see the world's best sportsmen.

Most sports were still sorting out their rules in the 1860s, and international travel was uncommon. WG Grace had played in Australia, Malta, Ceylon, Scotland, Ireland, New Zealand, Canada and the US.

Besides Queen Victoria, Grace had the most famous face in Britain. He was the face of Colman's mustard – one of the first sports advertising deals. So every time you see a sportsman mumbling his way through an ad, you can thank Grace. 'Colman's Mustard, like Grace, Heads the Field' was the tagline.

Grace being a gentleman also helped the sport, because as a gentleman, his deeds were reported on. Grace and his fellow amateur players were chronicled and pushed far more than any old professional player. People know where he was born, where he went to school, his family history and where he was coached. We have records of him playing as young as 11. Had he been some kid from Manchester with servant parents, we would have known little about him. He wouldn't have had specialist coaching. He wouldn't have been rushed through to first-class cricket.

His every move wouldn't have made the papers. His name definitely wouldn't have been advertised outside cricket grounds.

Yet his class was for the benefit of cricket. His class brought attention to the game. His class helped make cricket the most important sport in the world at that time. And as big as cricket was, Grace was bigger.

Many of the gentlemen took a beautiful game and tried to own it, monetise it, sell it. Grace was no different, but he spread the game to everyone.

Cricket was also international. The Parsees played it in India. Australians became obsessed by it. George Washington played a version of it. A Paris cricket club played a German one. Soccer giants AC Milan were founded as the Milan Cricket and Football Club. Cricket was being played in Chile. It was like a cute 19th century viral sporting infection. The English carried it with them, infecting the world.

Grace deservedly gets much of the attention in what were the first days of cricket. But other things were going on. Teams from England had started touring.

Across the other side of the world, in Melbourne, a couple of rich men wanted Charles Dickens to visit Australia and read from his books. He declined, so in 1862 they booked a cricket team from England instead.

It was largely for betting purposes. Knowing that the game might not be entertaining, as the Australians were still a long way behind the English, the promoters organised for the first Australian hot air balloon to drop in. There were 500 crates of beer on hand. Hot air balloons back then; fireworks and cheerleaders now for T20.

The third tour of Australia by an English team included Grace, who, despite playing as an amateur, was the highest paid player on the tour at £1500, which is around $300,000 today. In England, Grace's cheating, hustling and general bullying were accepted as streaks of character in a great man. In Australia, he was seen as a great player, and a great big cheat.

The Sydney Mail had a columnist, Square Leg, who wrote that it was an accepted fact that Grace wagered on the games he played in. 'The play of Grace and his team is looked upon with utter disgust,' he wrote. But Grace also inspired and praised the locals. The Victorians beat his team. Anything Grace did, the good and bad of it, was copied by the Australians, who had Grace in their papers almost every day of his tour. When he said that Victorian bowlers could do well in England, it was seen as royal approval.

With teams travelling to and from each country, things were moving towards proper organisation and national contests.

Nothing demonstrates how random the early Test matches were than the fact that Grace didn't play in the first one.

The crowd flocked in to the Melbourne Cricket Ground at 10am, on 15 March 1877. Unfortunately, the match was actually starting at one. At 1.05pm Australia went out and batted. Badly. Only one batsman went past 20. The largely rubbish English bowling was taking wickets in between grubbers and full tosses.

England would have swept Australia aside easily, had it not been for Charles Bannerman. Bannerman faced the first ball in Test cricket. He also made the first century, scoring 165 out of his team's 245. He was not dismissed, but retired hurt, when a short ball ripped the flesh from his hand. He was a pretty batsman who played all the shots and hit them hard. It would be the only Test or first-class hundred that Bannerman ever made.

After four days of cricket, Australia had beaten the best team that the leader of the Empire could muster in the first-ever Test by 45 runs.

The match attracted 20,000 fans, so it didn't take a genius to work out that another match should be played. The English were offered a bigger slice of the pie.

England got home in the return match by four wickets. Rumours circulated that they lost the first match just to cash in and have a second match.

In May, more than two full months later, *The Times* in London ran a piece about this match. It praised the Australian play, especially Bannerman, who it suggested batted better than any player before him, including Grace.

'Too fond of diddling an innocent colonial, and of looking upon the girls when they were bonny, and the wine when it was red – even more so when it was sparkling,' *The Times* reported, starting a tradition of the English press bagging their cricket team.

THE MAN WHO CREATED TEST CRICKET

The 22 men who played in the first Test at the MCG in 1877 did not know they were doing so. No matches were officially Tests until a man who held no official post called them that. Clarence Moody was a cricket writer from South Australia, who dedicated a section of his 1894 book, *South Australian Cricket*, to drawing up a list of the matches he believed were Tests. Moody didn't work for the Lord's MCC or even the MCG MCC.

He went back through the records of all the major matches ever played, and he alone decided which ones were Tests. He was a hard bastard. Most notably he didn't make Australia's win over the MCC in 1878 a Test, so national pride wasn't making the decisions. If two England tours were in Australia at the same time, then none of those games were Tests. And just because others called the matches Tests didn't mean he was going to agree. It was after a very long-winded, and yet still kind of wishy-washy description, that he finally announced that the first Test was 1877. His entire list became Test match canon.

It might seem odd that a sport could function like that. But cricket hasn't changed. When the umpire Decision Review System (DRS) came into cricket, it was untested by the cricket authorities. They simply believed that the TV gadgets must work. Because, as we all know, TV never lies.

Chapter 4

WHEN CRICKET RULED THE US

For many years the first international sporting match was barely talked about. The America's Cup has long been supposed to be the first international sporting contest. But another contest predates it by seven years.

The first international sporting match was a game of cricket between the US and Canada, played in September of 1844 in Bloomingdale Park, Manhattan. The game was actually between two clubs, but then again, of course, so was the America's Cup. The game was advertised as the United States of America versus the British Empire's Canadian Province, even if the players were mostly from the St George's Club of New York and the Toronto Cricket Club. A crowd of 5000 attended – and reportedly bet more than $100,000.

At that time cricket was the biggest sport in the US. It was played all over the country. It was played by all men, regardless of social standing. An English team toured there in 1859. Yet cricket barely outlived the American Civil War, which broke out two years later.

Philadelphia, the city of brotherly love and home of Rocky Balboa, was cricket's sacred land in America. In the 1830s Haverford College hired an English gardener by the name of William Carvill. He made them cricket grounds, introduced the students to the sport, and it just took over.

Later on, baseball was as strong in Philadelphia as anywhere else, but cricket remained important. Even the Americans were confused by it:

in 1903 the *New York Times* wrote, 'it has often been a problem for the psychologist or sociologist … why Philadelphians play cricket and why they are the only Americans who do play it.' When they played it, they were also serious about it. WG Grace played in Philadelphia. Australia toured there, too.

The Philadelphians also toured, as the Gentlemen of Philadelphia, and when they did, they took with them one of the greatest and most underrated cricketers of all time, John Barton King. Bart.

David Mutton, writing for the cricket quarterly *The Nightwatchman*, talked of visiting the Magill Library at Haverford College, which has America's only public cricket library. 'King's achievements are celebrated throughout the library. A bat commemorates his 38 centuries and highest score of 344, still the highest knock in North America. Under a glass case is a lighter that Ranjitsinhji gave to King – replete with a ruby and the Jam Sahib's royal insignia – after he had been dismissed for a golden duck by a delivery that he later said "sprang in at him like a tiger". Next to it is King's monogrammed cigarette case, emblazoned with a bat, stumps, and a ball.'

King took up cricket as a young man and was instantly good at it. By 18 he was playing for the American national team. Like a pitcher he covered the ball with his non-bowling hand as he came to the wicket, and swung it a lot.

The Australian squad to England in 1893 stopped in Philadelphia on the way back home. They played two matches. In the first they were hammered. First when they bowled, Philadelphia made more than 500, then King took five wickets. Everyone was shocked that a city from America could beat the Australians.

King would tour England in 1897 and take 72 wickets at 24. In 1903 it would be 78 at 16. And by 1908 it would be 73 wickets at 12. He did all of this while averaging 20 with the bat, and making a first-class hundred against Surrey. King was a player. Had he been born in Australia, England or South Africa, King would have been a Test player. In 1908 he was the best bowler in England.

Esteemed player and author CB Fry said he was 'the best swerver I ever saw in my life'. King took 415 first-class wickets at 15.66, which was 42 per cent of his side's wickets, according to David Mutton's calculations.

But cricket in Philadelphia was for the megawealthy, who in time preferred golf and tennis. There was no working class involvement in the game, so the game withered. Consequently, the extraordinary story of John Barton King, and of the US defeating Australia, has been all but forgotten. Sadly, American cricket has virtually been unsighted ever since.

Chapter 5

THE DEMON SPOFFORTH

THE FIRST TWO Tests in Australia had been a great success. So much money was made from them that Australian entrepreneurs chose Dave Gregory, captain in the First Test, to pick a team to tour England. Skill was important – and whether they could find the £50 fee to join the collective. This wasn't a team of amateurs or professionals in the traditional English sense. Australian cricket never really took up England's class system, but finding £50 was no easy task.

When they arrived in England there was general surprise that they weren't Aboriginal. An indigenous team had toured before; in 1868 a team from regional Victoria had travelled to the UK and played at Lord's and the Oval, where 7000 people saw them play. They played for Australia – but weren't citizens. Had they lived another 99 years, they would have been – just.

When Gregory's Australians took on the MCC at Lord's in 1878, 4742 people turned up to watch. This MCC team was seen as stronger than the team that Australia had beaten. Grace was in it to start with, and so were Alfred Shaw and Fred Morely, two of the best bowlers in the land. They were out to teach the Australians a lesson, to really humiliate them at the home of cricket.

The pitch was wet, and Grace decided to bat. He was out pulling to leg, as Gregory had told the fielder to move into that space as the bowler moved in. The crowd cheered, happy the underdogs had started well. At 2/27, Fred Spofforth came on.

First-change bowlers usually give respite. Not Spofforth. He changed cricket forever.

The Demon Fred Spofforth was a bank clerk from Sydney. He had been born in Balmain to a bank clerk father from Yorkshire. He had started out as a lob bowler, but like many Australians, had been inspired by the round-arm and overarm bowling of the early English tourists. Spofforth had an obsessive personality. He learned everything he could about bowling, and then practised it until he conquered it.

Batsmen said that looking into his eyes was like looking into death itself. Batsmen would stare at him, then look away, only to look back and find he was still staring straight through them. He looked like a theatre demon, and he acted like a real one. His giant hooked beak nose flared. His moustache bristled with blood lust. Richard Hodgson, a vicar, said he reminded him of the spirit of evil in Faust, with 'his hair parted down the middle, to give the impression of horns'. He might as well have had fangs and a cape.

This was just how he looked. His bowling was scarier.

His run-up was simple: a slow run of 10 to 12 paces. Not a fearless charge; more a polite jog. At the crease he had a maniacal action that would summon up hellfire and unleash it on his enemies, turning from comic villain to bringer of the apocalypse. A giant mutant, half-man, half-octopus, standing well above you, limbs flailing in every direction, and the ball spitting out of him at a pace quicker than any human had bowled before.

And the Demon had swerve.

By swerve, read swing. Spofforth might have looked like he was about to tie a woman to the tracks and twirl the end of his moustache. But he was also a bank clerk – a fire-breathing, mutant octopus bank clerk, of course. Spofforth had studied baseball pitching. He looked into articles on aerodynamics.

As overarm bowling had just been invented, it makes sense that no one had bowled with swing before. Spofforth told people he could swing the ball out, in, up and down. The batsmen must have believed the ball was possessed. Later in his career he would also develop slower and faster balls that looked the same to the batsmen. He couldn't have worried batsmen more if he'd told them he sold his soul to the devil at midnight.

And on a Lord's pitch with rain, on 27 May 1878, he was a monster.

His first over went for two runs. He would go for two more runs in that innings. And in giving those two additional runs, the MCC had gone from 2/27 to all out for 33. The Demon had eaten their souls. His figures: 5.3 overs. 3 maidens. 4 runs. 6 wickets.

Australia didn't do much better with the bat, but compiled a lead of eight runs. The talk around the ground was that Grace would fix the Demon. He would tame him and destroy the others. This was The Nonsuch, in the home of the sport he built. He wouldn't allow this colonial freak to torment them any further. Spofforth beat him first ball. Spofforth yelled, 'Bowled!' second ball. The MCC would lose, within a day, by nine wickets, to a bunch of blokes who paid £50 to travel there. The Demon took 10/20 and sent one off retired hurt. Spofforth had screamed at the home of cricket.

Two sides, both of whom thought they could win. One wanted to teach the colonials a lesson. The other wanted to rip their masters down. Had Spofforth or Boyle (who took 9/19) had bad days, the MCC would have charged ahead and the whole tour would have been little more than a decent money-maker for those involved. But gauntlets were hurled down. And an instant rivalry was born.

England had God. Australia had the Demon.

Not that Grace acted as a kind and gentle creator. It was his way or nothing. At one stage on the tour, he tried to poach the 'Sandhurst Infant' Billy Midwinter. Midwinter was born in the UK, but considered himself Australian. He had played in the UK with many of Grace's teams. And when Australia was due to play Middlesex, Midwinter was padded up and ready to open the batting with Bannerman. Grace spent 15 minutes arguing that he should be honouring his deal to play for Gloucestershire with him.

Grace was yelling and screaming, and shocked even the Australians with his language. Midwinter was bullied into leaving (although both sides claimed that bribes were involved) with Grace. Grace left the Australians an opener down, put Midwinter in a hansom cab and said, 'You haven't got a ghost of a chance against Middlesex.'

John Conway, the entrepreneur who'd set up the tour, was now seeing his 12 men turn into 11. He followed them to the Oval, in some sort of hansom cab chase over the Thames. When Conway arrived, he and Grace got into a screaming match. But nothing Conway said would change Grace's mind. Midwinter was under his control. With all his scheming, Grace's Gloucestershire lost to Surrey, and Australia easily beat Middlesex.

Chapter 6

BACK TO THE COLONIES FOR A RIOT

LORD HARRIS, OR George Robert Canning Harris, as his birth certificate said, was given a very weak amateur team with two professionals for him to overbowl on the tour of Australia. They played a Test at the MCG and Spofforth took a hat-trick; Australia won easily. There was to be another Test, but first a match against New South Wales. For that match, which was captained again by Dave Gregory, each team had to provide an umpire.

New South Wales took this very seriously and they picked Edmund Barton, at the time a barrister and an aspiring politician – and 22 years later, Australia's first Prime Minister. On the recommendation of the Melbourne Cricket Club, England picked George Coulthard, a 22-year-old who played Australian rules football for Carlton and bowled in the nets: a Victorian. As this game was to be played in Sydney, on what is now the site of the SCG, and with the rivalry between Victoria and New South Wales at its peak, young Coulthard was put in a horrible position.

On the first day, with England doing well, Coulthard gave Lord Harris not out caught behind – to the crowd's dismay. Coulthard was umpiring against the guy who was paying him, who also happened to be a Lord. His error was written about in all the papers. The whisper was Coulthard had bet on England.

The next day the crowd turned up again and New South Wales collapsed in their innings. Only Billy Murdoch did well, carrying his bat for 82. But he couldn't do enough and New South Wales were forced to follow on. In the second innings Murdoch was run out. The crowd decided it was a bad call, as did NSW's Dave Gregory, who refused to send out the next batsman. Instead he asked for Coulthard to be replaced as umpire.

Gregory was one of those sportsmen who in every single circumstance was wronged by umpires. Lord Harris refused. And then a riot broke out. Harris sent a letter home saying, 'I found the ground had been rushed by the mob, and our team was being surrounded, I at once returned to the wickets, and in defending Coulthard from being attacked was struck by some "larrikin" with a stick.' Harris and the English team stayed out on the ground, as they were petrified of leaving the ground and having the game forfeited.

Edmund Barton backed Coulthard and said it was a good decision. But there was so much hate brewing – at the English, at the Victorian Coulthard, at the treatment of their hero Murdoch – that it seemed nothing could stop the riot.

The game continued the next day, but after a rest day on the Sunday it was eventually rained off. Harris was so upset he called off the scheduled second match against Australia.

Lord Harris would become a spectacularly unpopular governor of Bombay. His letter, and his many retellings of the story, heightened the rivalry between the two countries.

The fall-out from the Lord's letter was that when Australia toured England the next year, 1880, few teams would agree to play them. Not one match was scheduled for London and they even had to advertise for opponents.

The Oval broke the London ban and asked Lord Harris to put together a side. Harris may have been won over in part by the fact that Spofforth would not be playing after being injured.

The England side was very strong. It included not one, not two, but a hat-trick of Graces. It also included professionals. It would be the first Test ever played in England, and the best attended match in memory. It was also WG Grace's first Test, and with the help of Spofforth being out injured, Grace also made his first Test hundred.

Before the game, he and Murdoch had a bet, for one sovereign, on who would achieve the top score out of the two. Grace made 152 out of his side's 420. Australia made 149 in their first innings. Murdoch didn't score. Australia was asked to follow on, and at 8/187, it wasn't looking good, but Murdoch was still there. He batted for another 140 runs with the last two wickets.

In doing so, Grace said he played one of the best innings ever, and Murdoch beat Grace by a run, winning the sovereign. He wore it around his neck for the rest of his life. Australia lost, but the heroics of Murdoch healed the riot wounds forever.

Australia won the next tour at home 2-0. George Coulthard, Dave Gregory's favourite umpire, had been picked for Australia. He batted at 11, made six not out, and didn't bowl a ball in his only Test. Both teams caught the same boat back to England to play in the next series, in 1882.

The tour started well for Australia. Hugh Massie kicked off with a huge 206 against Oxford, one of the strongest teams in England. They beat almost everyone, although they did lose against Cambridge at Fenners. Cambridge had the majestic Studd brothers. Against Lancashire, the county champions, Spofforth took 16 wickets.

Australia had only ever faced one team from England that could be called full strength: that at the Oval in their only previous English Test. At best, they were Graceless, at worst they were a collection of struggling pros or overrated amateurs. Australia had put together as close to the strongest teams they could, without taking players from the west coast, or from up north.

The England team for the Oval match was far better on paper. Australia had Billy Murdoch as their star batsman and captain, but their batting was weak, as it had been since the beginning. They had Spofforth and Boyle with the ball. But they had to bowl to a batting line-up of Grace, and others who had scored more than 10,000 first-class runs. England was a better team, in better form.

Australia won the toss, and their innings lasted 80 overs, bearing in mind that an over was four balls at the time. They made 63 runs. By 3.30pm England was batting. Spofforth, who was disgusted with his batsmen, took it out on England and got rid of Grace – and practically everyone else. On the verge of stumps England was all out for 101. Spofforth had taken 7/46.

Hugh Massie would play nine Tests for Australia as a batsman. He would average 15, and make one score of over 50. It just happened to be that this was the day. Massie clearly decided that he might as well hit out.

Australia was scoring at quicker than a run a minute. Bannerman was hardly hitting it off the square, but Massie was smashing it. He hit nine fours and made 55. Despite the start Massie gave them, the batsmen were still struggling. Murdoch was trying to hold them together, and coming in at number eight was young Sammy Jones. Jones was a handy all-rounder. He and Murdoch moved the total to 114. Then Murdoch hit one into the leg side. They easily completed the single as the keeper threw the ball at the stumps. WG Grace went to pick the ball up. Jones, according to some, looked at him and nodded. Then walked down the wicket and attended to the pitch, paying no attention to what Grace did behind him.

While Jones tapped the pitch, God whipped off the bails. God then turned to the square-leg umpire and appealed; the umpire gave it. God claimed it. Murdoch was furious and complained to God. Even other English players complained. But God and the umpires did not change their minds. Under the laws of cricket, Jones was out. Half a century would pass, but Sammy Jones would not forgive Grace.

In the famed game when Grace refused to leave the field after being given out LBW, he went on to score 400 not out. When he left the field, the scorebook said 399, but Grace told the scorer to round it up. Grace had spent his entire career bullying people, pushing the term gentleman as far as it would go, laughing it up as a shamateur claiming huge expenses and getting his own way. He would have seen no difference between changing a score in a club match and running out the naive Sammy Jones.

But this was not a Grimsby XXII, it was a national sporting contest. These cricket matches now meant something more. You weren't playing for a team or region, you were playing for something bigger. On that day, that one slight stirred the beast within the Australians. And especially one man.

As Sammy Jones left the field, the next batsman in was the Demon.

Spofforth, a man of anger and fury on a good day, was precisely the wrong man to walk into that situation. Grace would have said something, or smirked, or just been smug, and Spofforth would have raged. Spofforth made a duck. And any noise made by any English player would have just made it all the worse.

Australia had a lead of 85. At the change of innings Spofforth went into the English change-room and abused Grace. Grace probably saw this as a victory in itself. After much swearing, Spofforth left Grace with 'This will lose you the match,' before saying to his own players, 'I'm going to bowl at the old man. I'm going to frighten him out.' And then a cry that Australian bowlers have, one way or another, believed ever since: 'This thing can be done.'

George Bonner, Australia's big hitter, and the sort of guy who looked like he had just walked off a farm, approached Grace. He spoke to him, looking down from his height of 6 foot 6 inches: 'If we don't win the match, WG, after what you have done, I won't believe there is a God in heaven.'

Monkey Hornby, England's captain, put himself up the order, promoted from number 10 to opener. He would make nine, his highest Test score. Spofforth had Hornby and Barlow out with consecutive balls. England was only 15. But then there was a partnership, the sort of partnership that ends games when you are chasing only 85. Grace was at the wicket. With only two wickets down, England passed 50. The bookmakers had Australia 6/1. And then the Demon changed ends.

Something happened to Spofforth at the Vauxhall end. Neville Cardus described it like this: 'There was the sense of the inimical in his aspect now. He seemed taller than he was half an hour ago, the right arm more sinuous. There was no excitement in him. He was … cold-blooded.' People often say that Spofforth went on a rage-fuelled rampage. But actually, what he did was far more sinister. The rage got to him. Then he focused it.

On the boat over, Spofforth had dressed as Mephistopheles. At the Oval, he became Mephistopheles.

Spofforth didn't explode the stumps of Grace's batting partner, he merely removed him. God was spooked at the other end. Maybe he saw the look in the Demon's eye, but he was out to Boyle only two runs later. When a team has someone with the gravitational pull of Grace, his dismissal leaves a gaping black hole. They only needed 32 runs with six wickets still in hand when Grace left.

A good bowler smells blood. You can often hear it from their scream at getting the breakthrough wicket. Other times it's in their eyes. You could see it with Shane Warne when he took the wicket of Herschelle Gibbs in the '99 World Cup. Curtly Ambrose and Fred Trueman had it for their entire career. It's the ability to take one wicket, and turn that wound into a corpse.

Who better for Australia. Who worse for England. The Demon.

Maiden. Maiden. Maiden. Maiden. Maiden. Maiden. Maiden. Maiden. Maiden. Maiden. Maiden. Maiden.

That was the 12 successive maidens bowled after Grace went out. Eventually, it was too much, and Spofforth just bowled Alfred Lyttelton. At five wickets down, with England losing blood, Hornby fiddled with the batting order more. Spofforth would have known that.

When Allan Steel came out ahead of Charles Studd, Spofforth's evil genius senses would have felt it. Steel could bat, but Studd had made three hundreds against Australia that summer. Charles was the more majestic of the majestic Studd brothers. And he was being moved down the order, even after it was his hundred that gave Australia its only first-class loss on tour.

Spofforth went through Steel like butter. Then Read. Then Lucas. Still no Studd.

There is a story that it became so tense at this point that one man expired. Another, that others viewed through an umbrella. Poor Charles Studd looked like a ghost as he walked out.

Studd started at the non-striker's end as Boyle took the wicket of Barnes. Then Ted Peate came in, took one look at Studd, decided that he was in no state to get the runs. Peate was an old left-arm spinner. He never passed 13 in a Test. England only needed nine. Peate had a friendly moustache, the sort a genial school bus driver would have. Spofforth's moustache wouldn't spit on a moustache like that. Peate wasn't physically equipped to play Spofforth on a normal day, and Studd looked even less likely. So Peate swung at Boyle. One he missed. Two he hit. Three he missed. Boyle hit instead.

The colonials had beaten the best of the empire. The Demon had defeated God.

Three days later the *Sporting Times* reported:

In Affectionate Remembrance
of
ENGLISH CRICKET,
which died at the Oval
on
29 August 1882,
Deeply lamented by a large circle of sorrowing
friends and acquaintances
R.I.P.
N.B.—The body will be cremated and the
ashes taken to Australia.

That was it; the Ashes now existed. As a word at least. Ivo Bligh, England's next captain, would travel to Australia to 'beard the kangaroo in his den and try and recover those ashes'. He would reclaim the ashes, find a wife, and also be given an urn.

There are many stories about Ivo's tour, and the urn. And they are all worth reading, or even travelling to Melbourne's satellite city of Sunbury where, just beyond the franchise fast food outlets and shopping centre, there is a place called Rupertswood Manor that has all the history.

But the Ashes were not yet a term or an urn. The term took 20 years to become a big deal. The urn took longer. The rivalry, this incestuous colonial versus empire never-ending fight that England won the first eight times, was built by two men.

Grace built the sport. Spofforth built the Ashes.

Chapter 7

SOUTH AFRICA AND THE BOSIE

I N SOUTH AFRICA, or Cape Colony as it was then, there were ads in the *Cape Town Gazette* and *Africa Advertiser* as early as 1808 promoting cricket matches. By 1843, Port Elizabeth had a cricket club. In the mid-1800s there were reports of various tribes playing cricket. But cricket was kept as exclusively white as possible. By 1889 they had a first-class set up, the Currie Cup, and were playing Test Cricket.

On 11 October 1899, the second Boer War broke out. It too was kept as white as possible: no one wanted the natives armed. International sport was still only new, but sport and politics were clashing already. All three Test nations – England, Australia and South Africa – would have soldiers in the war that finished on 31 May 1902, when the Boers surrendered to the English forces.

Since the decline of underarm, fast bowling had been taking over, but now spin fought back, thanks to a development in South Africa that would remain with the game forever more.

The philosopher Bernard Bosanquet believed 'what is finite is not real'. His nephew, also Bernard Bosanquet, knew this all too well.

Bosanquet invented a ball known by many different names. Wrong'un, googly, bosie. They all mean the same thing. It's a ball that looks like it is going to spin from leg to off, but actually spins from off to leg. It deceives the batsman. Bosanquet's contribution to history outlasted his philosopher uncle's.

The bosie won South Africa their first-ever Test series. It is also a term used for someone who is a bit dodgy, someone deceptive.

Bosanquet didn't finish his degree at Oxford. He just sort of floated in the posh world with that brilliant alliterative name. He was a batsman, who bowled a bit of medium pace. He was quite the sportsman, but his batting alone would never make a huge name for him.

Bosanquet's creation of the wrong'un is more remarkable because he made it while playing a game on a table tennis table called Twisti-Twosti. The object was to spin the ball away from a person on the other side, who was trying to catch it. Somewhere in the gladiatorial battle that is Twisti-Twosti, a wrong'un came out.

Not that Bosanquet went from Twisti-Twosti to Trent Bridge. It was a ball he would often bowl in the nets, and it took him years to perfect. When he did perfect it, he told his Middlesex teammates to keep quiet about it, and would still pretend it was a mistake. He had the perfect cover for this; most of his early wrong'uns were utter shite. The first one purposefully bowled by Bosanquet bounced four times and the batsman was either stumped or bowled, probably while laughing. But Bosanquet knew he had something special.

In 1901 Bosanquet took 36 wickets. The following season he took 40, with three five-wicket hauls and two of 10. By 1904 he was reeling them in: 132 wickets, 14 five-wicket hauls and four 10-wicket hauls.

Bosanquet only ever played seven Tests. As a player, despite being a *Wisden* Cricketer of the Year, he made no real impact. It was his invention that mattered.

•

South African cricket was still on matting at this time. Matting wickets are perfect for spin. The ball has something to grip against every time you land it, and it spins sharply. Reggie Schwarz had been a Middlesex player in the early 1900s, but had moved to Transvaal. He knew Bosie quite well, so when in 1904, representing South Africa, he saw Bosie destroy his team, he asked about this new ball. Within only a couple of weeks, Schwarz had conquered the wrong'un. The first time he bowled it, his teammates laughed, but he took 5/27. By the end of the 1904 tour Schwarz was South Africa's leading wicket-taker, with 96 at 14.

Knowing that this ball could be even better back on South African matting, Schwarz trained three Transvaal players, Gordon White, Aubrey Faulkner and Ernie Vogler. White was South Africa's best batsman at the time, Faulkner was a strong batsman and keen learner, and Vogler was an all-rounder. They all bowled differently. Schwarz only bowled wrong'uns. Faulkner bowled slow and deliberate while mixing between leg-spin and wrong'uns. Vogler bowled every single ball that cricket had invented: leg-spinners, wrong'uns, fast, swing, whatever. White bowled more like Faulkner, but wasn't as consistent, although his wrong'un was almost unpickable. These lessons meant South Africa batted deep and had six bowlers when England arrived for the 1905/06 tour.

Plum Warner led an average England team, missing some of its better players. South Africa started with eight wickets from their leg-spinners. England made it to 184. South Africa replied with 91. South Africa's leg-spinners took six wickets in the second innings, and England made 190.

South Africa's target was 284. It was almost a hundred higher than any innings in the match. When Aubrey Faulkner was run out, they were 6/105. They were chasing the third highest total in Test cricket's short history. In 17 years of Test Cricket, South Africa had never won a Test.

When captain Percy Sherwell came to the crease at No.11, in his first Test, South Africa needed 45 more.

The English lost their nerve. The South African fans had no real reason to believe in their side, but they forgot that. The chase excited them. They roared like winners at every run. England's bowling got more and more ragged. Plum Warner had been changing the bowlers around all day. Now Sherwell was hitting boundaries, legendary batsman Dave Nourse was defending like the side of Table Mountain. The cheering got louder and louder.

They had scored 44 of the runs, tying the scores. For three balls Sherwell defended. Then Albert Relf dropped one short and Sherwell smashed it. Before it even got to the boundary, South Africa had won a Test match.

A 17-year losing streak was ended by that long hop.

South Africa's leading wicket-taker in that series was Tip Snooke, a quick bowler. But their legion of leg-spinners took 43 wickets in five Tests, thanks largely to Bosanquet's innovation.

Having won, South Africa kept winning and finished the series 4-1.

If Bosie's uncle was right, the wrong'un was real, and therefore infinite.

Chapter 8

BOWLERS OF RENOWN

I n 1864 JOHN WISDEN, a fine bowler himself, began the publication that bears his name. *Wisden* waded in on the big issues of the day. Laid out almost every important scorecard they could find. And became a part of the game. It is known as 'the Bible of cricket'. In 1963 it decided to announce its greats of the game.

Wisden was, and still is, very much an English book about cricket. So when Neville Cardus sat down to compile his list of the six greats of the game, the players chosen were, much like the *Wisden* Cricketer of the Year award, judged as much on their county careers as their Test careers. He selected five players who played in the Golden Era, plus Don Bradman. Those five were WG Grace, Vic Trumper, Tom Richardson, Jack Hobbs and Sydney Barnes.

Tom Richardson only averaged 25 with the ball in Tests during an era when England's George Lohmann and Barnes averaged only one more between them. So we can assume that Richardson was picked largely for his 2104 first-class wickets. Richardson was a bowling machine: he bowled quicker than Barnes or Lohmann; he landed on a length; and he stayed at off stump all day. Richardson was the template for what modern bowlers would become.

Lohmann was an anomaly, taking 112 wickets in his 18 Test at 10.75. And Barnes was something else again.

Barnes is the bowler of the Golden Era. Barnes averaged 16 – 9 against South Africa, and although South Africa was ordinary, they were not quite the bumbling mess that Lohmann feasted on. In Barnes' time South Africa beat England twice. In Lohmann's they couldn't score in a brothel. Barnes averaged 21 against Australia.

Barnes played in the era when batting and pitches were as good as they ever had been. He took more wickets per Test than anyone, even Lohmann.

Statistician Kartikeya Date compares all bowlers to Barnes, calling it the Barnes standard. 'The most successful bowler takes the most wickets, most cheaply and most frequently. Using such a rule, we get a Barnes standard measure: wickets taken divided by the product of bowling average and strike rate. Barnes' measure is 0.276 over the length of his career.'

Barnes was one of the few bowlers in the history of the game to be a successful quick spinner. Barnes could get the ball to lift, he could bowl off-spin, he could bowl leg-spin, he could swing the ball and he was actually quick. He could succeed on any pitch. He was the Frankenstein's monster of bowlers. It was as if someone had created the perfect bowling machine: taller than six feet, wide shoulders, barrel chest, fast bowler's backside, long arms, muscular legs, and an endless tank. He was also aggressive. He worked out tactics for each batsman.

Barnes might have played on uncovered pitches, but the science of groundsmen was improving, and by the early 1900s wickets were becoming true. Barnes didn't mind. He bowled fast unplayable leg-breaks and then yorkers. Even 70 years after he was at his best, people still referred to him as the greatest bowler who ever lived.

Barnes was no gentleman either. He was a proper professional, even shunning county cricket because the Lancashire Leagues paid him more. He did flirt with Warwickshire early in his career, but they left him out of a game to fit an amateur in and Barnes left them for good. In Lancashire Barnes played for Rishton and Burnley.

Barnes was in the squad in 1901/02 when England sent their last private touring team to Australia. Archie MacLaren was Lancashire captain, and when George Hirst and Wilfred Rhodes were not available, he picked Barnes after just a handful of first-class games. Barnes was reluctant, as he liked the security he had at home. MacLaren persuaded him to go and many regarded the whole incident as 'the most daring experiment in the history of the game'. Australia won the series with ease, but Barnes was England's leading wicket-taker, despite getting injured after only three Tests.

He was obviously the best bowler in England, yet when Barnes got back to the UK he asked Lancashire, consistently for two years, for more money. His £3 a week in the summer and £1 a week in the winter was less than he made from one day of cricket a week in the league, and he wasn't killing himself.

In 1903, Lancashire dropped him from their team due to their disputes. Barnes never played county cricket again. This also meant that Barnes didn't play for England. He just disappeared back into league cricket: first Lancashire, then Staffordshire.

Eventually Barnes was brought back to Test cricket when the money was right and in 1907/08 he went back to Australia. England lost 4–1 again, but Barnes bowled well enough to continue to play for England, when he felt like it, and the money was right. During the 1912 Triangular tournament featuring the three nations he took 39 wickets at 10.

In 1913/14 England took a full strength team to South Africa. Gone were the days of handing the team to any old gentleman. South Africa could now play. Barnes was paid good money to make his way down south.

On the entire tour, Barnes took 104 wickets at 10.74. In four Tests, he took 49 wickets at 10.93 – one of the most amazing series by a bowler ever. Only Herbie Taylor could handle him, so much so that Barnes is supposed to have left the field once because he was so frustrated he couldn't take his wicket.

It was his first morning spell at the MCG on 30 December 1911 that saw Barnes at his best. The MCG pitch was as good as it could be. Australia had three legends of cricket in their top five. Barnes bowled 11 overs in 80 minutes. There were seven maidens. Six runs.

Warren Bardsley was out first ball; Charles Kelleway was lbw; Barnes bowled the mighty Clem Hill; then had Warwick Armstrong caught behind. At one stage Barnes had 4/1 from seven overs. Later Jack Hobbs caught Minnet to complete the set.

In Sydney, captain JWHT Douglas had taken the new ball, leaving Barnes fuming. In Melbourne, it took Barnes 80 minutes to get back at his captain and win England the Test.

The only batsman in the top five that Barnes didn't take was Victor Thomas Trumper.

Chapter 9

BLESS VICTOR TRUMPER

A LARGE MAN WALKED from his change-room to the Australian change-room. He summoned someone who'd earlier made a great hundred. 'Bring me your bat. Sign it.' He took the bat from the young man. Then the large man handed over his own bat, which was also signed.

'From the present champion to the future champion.'

Jack Fingleton, the Australian Test batsman, journalist and press secretary to former prime minister Billy Hughes, once wrote about an incident at a girl's boarding school. The prayers were said out loud. The last girl prayed for her parents, and then said, 'And, please God, bless Victor Trumper.'

And in the Lord's dressing-room, as WG Grace formalised things through a ceremonial exchanging of bats, that is exactly what the God of cricket did.

•

Victor Trumper and WG Grace helped form what people now refer to as cricket's Golden Era, which lasted from 1890 until the outbreak of World War I in 1914.

Victor Trumper was cricket's first ethereal beauty.

Many have tried to reconcile how Trumper could still be thought of as the greatest batsman ever to play, as others simply made more runs than him. Several batsmen of his era had better averages. Ranjitsinhji,

Stanley Jackson and Warren Bardsley all had him covered. Clem Hill made more runs than him. And Jack Hobbs averaged 18 more in the same period.

But as Harry Altham would write, Trumper was qualitative, not quantitative. Trumper made you feel better about life having just watched him. You were seeing an artist, a magician, a statesman – and as we will see, a genuinely great bloke – who played an attacking brand of cricket not seen again for 100 years.

THE DON COMPARES

Don Bradman was forever haunted by that beautiful ghost. While Trumper was a man who would throw his wicket away once he'd done enough, Bradman would bat until the opposition had been ground away by his boot. Bradman believed in beauty, and he loved talking about pretty batsmen, as long as everyone knew he was the best. When someone strayed from that, he wanted to correct them.

In *Farewell to Cricket*, Bradman wrote: 'I don't want to get into a discussion on Trumper, but in fairness to myself I may say this. If the argument is used that big scores were responsible for my average, then surely scores of only up to a hundred would not come into that. In that regard Trumper's record in England disclosed 19 centuries in 193 innings, mine was 41 in 120 innings. On a percentage basis, Trumper got one century for every 9.8 innings, where I obtained one for every 3.4 innings.'

Asking Bradman to understand why people rated Trumper above him is like asking a calculator to understand a painting.

EHD Sewell, the English first-class cricketer and author, said there was no good length against Trumper, just Trumper length. From that length he would hit the ball anywhere. Third man. Point. Cover. Mid-off. Straight. Mid-on. Midwicket. Square-leg. Where the ball ended up was mostly to do with his mood, not dependent on the delivery or the deliverer.

The same people who frowned when Ranji played the glance howled their discontent at Trumper's leg-side play. There is a picture of him in CB Fry's magazine that shows his front foot down the pitch, just outside off stump, but his bat face is closed. The ball is going to the leg side; its line and full length have little to say about it.

Batting for Paddington against Redfern, in Sydney Grade Cricket, Trumper once made 335 in a couple of hours. This despite the opposition having all nine fielders on the boundary – and in those days a six was actually only a five, which resulted in you losing strike. The square-leg umpire was on the boundary as well, for safety.

Today Trumper would be a player who hits the ball on the up. On a flat track that's possible. On the pitches Trumper played on, which included many sticky wickets, it's craziness. Your chance of surviving can't be better than 50 per cent. Trumper did it all the time.

The phrase 'sticky wicket' is so well known in the English language that it was used as the title of an episode of *M*A*S*H*. It has been uttered by US President Barack Obama. The great Vincent Price once used the break in films he presented on TV to explain the origins of the term. The best usage is probably by Barney in *The Flintstones*: 'Steady Fred, steady, I bat a Sticky Wicket.' It's a bad situation.

In the early days of cricket, it generally meant a wet pitch that got a bit dry and behaved like Glenn Close in *Fatal Attraction*. A normal everyday bowler on a sticky wicket can be turned into a Fred Spofforth. A ball off a good length still jumps up at your throat. Batsmen hate sticky wickets. Not Trumper.

He went completely the other way, and was often at his best the worse the pitch was. He played like he had no fear on a good wicket; the same on a bad wicket. When he was just making his name he asked the SCG groundsmen to prepare some practice sticky wickets for him. They made very wet pitches on a very hot day, then Trumper went out and practised on them. And by practise, you can assume he just got hit a lot.

In 1904 Wilfred Rhodes took 15 wickets on an MCG pitch that went beyond normal sticky, and was actually referred to as a sticky dog, which is a sticky, sticky wicket. Trumper was so good that England and Rhodes gave up trying to bowl him out, instead just bowling wide outside off stump and working over everyone at the other end. Trumper still made 74 out of 122. It didn't matter if it was a sticky pitch, a sticky dog, or a sticky Godzilla; Trumper could bat on it.

There is a photo of Trumper. He is in motion. His back foot is off the ground. His weight is pushing forward. His bat is cocked. His arm muscles are defined. His eyes are focused. A crowd behind him waits for the carnage. The detail is stunning. The photo captures the moment before the kill. It's black and white and beautiful. It is the image of Victor Trumper. It is the image of the golden age of cricket.

It is beautiful, but fake. It is Trumper. But not Trumper in action. It's Trumper in a photoshoot.

Trumper's character was as beautiful as his batting.

In Yorkshire once he was smashing the locals everywhere when a young bowler came on and Trumper shut up shop. It turned out that Trumper knew this guy was not long in the team, and that one bad performance would send him back to the coal mine. Another time he faced a young professional Australian playing in Lancashire who had been struggling. Somehow this guy clean-bowled Trumper for six. There are many stories of friendlier matches where Trumper gets to 100, finds the best bowler of the day, and hits the next ball from him straight up in the air.

Jack Fingleton talks about how even on a match day Trumper would play in the streets with the local kids, giving them his wicket so they could boast about it later.

Trumper's generosity even included money. He just gave away money and cricket gear (he had a sports shop). His testimonial money was kept by the organisers and sent straight to his wife, as they believed he would simply gift it to anyone who asked.

When fellow Test player Arthur Mailey once took the wicket of his hero, he said: 'I felt like a boy who had killed a dove.'

On the 1899 Ashes tour that gave Trumper to the world, he wasn't supposed to play, and was only added to the squad as an assistant to the manager to help with laundry and organise autographs. He was to receive expenses only.

He made a 50 in his last Test, in 1912. Two years later the world descended into war. Cricket paused as men, and many cricketers, were shot at for reasons few understood.

With the world in turmoil, 25,000 people go to a funeral in June 1915 in Sydney, which had never seen anything like it before. The men in their best hats walk in spooky procession with their heads down. Spectators line the procession, looking solemn. At the back of the procession are two horse-drawn carriages. The carriages are almost completely covered in flowers. So many flowers. Had they used all the flowers of Sydney, Australia, or even the entire cricket world, it would not have been enough. Not for him. Not for Trumper. Not for cricket's golden dove.

Victor Trumper was dead at 37, struck down by Bright's disease, his kidneys destroyed. He hadn't even beaten his average of 39.

The death of God.

Four months later, on 23 October 1915, WG Grace passed on from a cerebral haemorrhage. He was 67. He had cheated many times, but telling death that 'it is very windy today' while putting the bails back on just doesn't work.

Grace had been cricket's father, Trumper its son. They have been combined ever since as a holy spirit.

Chapter 10

CRICKET'S MIDSUMMER NIGHT'S DREAM

H E WAS A special player. He had to be, just to get in the door. An Indian, playing cricket for England, in the 1800s and into the golden age. Amazing.

He was known as Ranji, or Ranjitsinhji, but his formal title was Colonel HH Shri Sir Ranjitsinhji Vibhaji, Jam Sahib of Nawanagar, GCSI, GBE. His name apparently means 'the lion who conquers in battle'.

Ranji was once Chancellor of the Indian Chamber of Princes and represented India at the League of Nations. Ranji also went to the Rajkumar College for princes.

Ranji was adopted to ensure there would be a son to take over the Vibhaji throne on the Nawanagar region of India. As it turned out, an actual heir was created, leaving Ranji in limbo. His adoptive parents gave him an education fit for a prince, and he ended up at Trinity College in Cambridge.

Understanding almost immediately how the English worked, he started calling himself Prince Ranjitsinhji, even though he wasn't one.

After flirting with tennis, he took cricket seriously and found himself a cricket coach to improve his technique.

First, there was one problem to conquer. Ranji was afraid of the ball. He backed away, trying not to get hit. His coach, Dan Hayward, found a novel solution. He trained Ranji by tying his back leg to the ground. This one coaching technique changed cricket forever.

Before Ranji, no one had purposefully hit the ball to fine leg, which was like a forbidden zone. The better bowling and captaincy had become, the more fielders were put on the off side, so the leg side didn't have to be defended at all. Batsmen were expected to play on the off side like a gentleman. Maybe kids in the park and the street had hit the ball to fine leg before, but now cricket had a gentleman of delicate wrists doing so. And it was that combination that changed cricket. The leg glance had entered the game. Now batsmen could hit the ball to all parts of the field, except over the keeper's head – that innovation was 120 years in the future and would belong to Sri Lanka's Tillakaratne Dilshan.

It is part of cricket folklore that Indian batsmen have special, even magical wrists. It's like cricket's version of phrenology. This fetish of Asian cricket wrists starts with Ranji.

In Simon Wilde's book *The Strange Genius of Ranjitsinhji* he writes: the most disdainful flick of the wrists, and he could exasperate some of England's finest bowlers; the most rapid sweep of the arms, and the ball was charmed to any part of the field he chose, as though he had in his hands not a bat but a wizard's wand.

The Daily News' Alfred Gardiner said:

The typical batsman performs a series of intricate evolutions in playing the ball; the Jam Sahib flicks his wrist and the ball bounds to the ropes. It is not jugglery, or magic; it is simply the perfect economy of a means to an end.

Play wristy for me, cooed the old journalists.

Neville Cardus called him 'the midsummer night's dream of cricket'.

Ranji couldn't hit the ball hard, but by using the pace of the bowler and hitting to an empty field, he instantly became a quick scoring batsman. JN Pentelow quoted a farmer who said, 'Whoy, he only tooch it and it go to th' boundary!'

This shot actually made Ranji a freak, not a legend, at first. Like so many innovations – round-arm bowling, overarm, reverse sweeps, wrong'un, and later, the doosra – it was at first seen as wrong, cheating even.

He struggled to get into Cambridge's side, but in 1895 Ranji was recruited to Sussex by Billy Murdoch and CB Fry. It was that year he made his maiden first-class hundred. And from that moment onwards, Ranji became a legend. By mid-summer bigger crowds turned up to watch him. The local authorities advertised him as often as they could. He made 1775 runs at an average of 49 that year.

It was clear that Ranji should be picked for England. At that time the ground hosting the game selected the team. The first Test in 1896 was at Lord's, and Lord Harris was the selector. He didn't select Ranji.

Anthony Bateman writes in *Cricket, Literature and Culture* that 'the high-minded imperialist Lord Harris, who had just returned from a spell of colonial duty in India, opposed his qualification for England on the grounds of race'. Instead Lord Harris referred to Ranji, and players like him, as 'birds of passage'. Yet Billy Murdoch, Albert Trott, JJ Ferris and Sammy Woods were all born in Australia, played for Australia, and then played for England. They seemed to be as birdy in their passages as Ranji.

The Times, on the wrong side of history, wrote: 'There was some feeling about K. S. Ranjitsinhji's absence, but although the Indian Prince has learnt all his cricket in England he could scarcely, if the title of the match were to be adhered to, have been included in the English eleven.'

The journalist Home Gordon praised Ranjitsinhji within earshot of an MCC Member, who wanted Gordon to lose his membership for 'having the disgusting degeneracy to praise a dirty black'. Gordon also claimed to hear other MCC members complaining about 'a nigger showing us how to play the game of cricket'.

Three weeks later in Old Trafford a whole new selection committee sat down and Ranji was picked for the second Test. The Old Trafford selectors may have thought he was good enough, or English enough, or would just guarantee better gate receipts. Ranji asked if the Australians had a problem with him playing. They didn't, so he was in the team.

Ranji made a decent but slow 62 in the first innings, but England had to follow on. In the second, Ranji really got going. It took him only three hours to make 154; the rest of England added another 150. He had scored more than half the runs. The Australians said it was one of the great innings. It was only the second hundred on debut for an Englishman, the other belonging WG Grace.

Ranji made a record 10 centuries and 2780 first-class runs in 1896, equalling and beating WG Grace's previous records.

In 1898 on the way back from a tour of Australia, where he averaged 60 and did not enjoy some of the barracking of the crowds, he took a year out of cricket to pursue what he still believed to be his rightful throne. Over the years, he would often go back to India and miss key parts of the summer. It was partly for financial reasons, but it was more about claiming what he thought was his rightful position as Maharaja Jam Sahib of Nawanagar.

The summer of 1899 he averaged 46 against the Australians without making a hundred, but it was his last great Test series. By 1902 Ranji was in financial trouble again. He loved living the life of a gentleman prince, but lacked the means. The runs dried up. His career ended.

Ranji was a rainbow. He and his esoteric joints only played 15 Tests, but even though he only gave us a glance, it was a lasting one.

Chapter 11

A TARNISHED GOLDEN AGE

THEY CALLED IT the Golden Era of cricket. But cricket was more white than golden.

The fastest bowler in South Africa in 1892 was Armien 'Krom' Hendricks. He arrived from nowhere, and nothing was really known about him. He scared the touring English. England's Walter Read, the 1893 *Wisden* player of the year, said, 'If you send a team [to England], send Hendricks; he will be a drawcard and is to my mind the Spofforth of South Africa.' But they didn't. Krom was a Malay. His skin was the problem.

Cecil Rhodes, the Prime Minister of Cape Colony, remembered today for the scholarship he founded, suggested to Sir William Milton, an English rugby player and South African head of selection, that the South Africans leave Hendricks out of the touring team because of his race. The official decision was because it was 'impolitic to include him in the team'. As Bernard Tancred, a member of the squad, said: 'To take him as an equal would, from a South African point of view, be impolite, not to say intolerable.'

Instead Hendricks was offered a role carrying the players' luggage. He declined.

Krom Hendricks continued to play, when allowed, but by 1897, he was barred from all cricket. He disappeared into the same mist he had come from.

Indigenous cricketers didn't fare much better in Australia. Jack Marsh was, according to Plum Warner, the best bowler in the world in 1903. He was also the Australian record-holder over 100 yards.

Being fast and indigenous was always going to be a bad mix in those days. Cricket may not have had the class problem in Australia that it did elsewhere, but it would have been an embarrassment to be hit, or bowled, by a 'blackfella'. Marsh was also unlucky enough to be accused of throwing. Even Warner thought he was a 'shier'.

Marsh was first called for chucking in Sydney grade cricket. To prove it was a false claim, he had put splints on his arm, so they couldn't bend. He then went out and bowled. He took 6/125 from 33 overs 'bowling as fast as ever'.

Marsh never played a Test. He played only six first-class games. Warren Bardsley, an Australian captain, thought Marsh was as good as Syd Barnes. They both bowled leg-spin, off-spin and quick. Bardsley wrote that the reason why Marsh was 'kept … out of big cricket was his colour'.

Marsh left the sport that didn't want him. He would be killed outside a pub. The two men who were charged would be acquitted.

Cricket was not golden for everyone.

Chapter 12

THE ORIGINAL AUSSIE BASTARD

NORTHLAND IS A shopping centre in Melbourne, popular among the local youth as a place to hang out and kill time. In the 1990s, once they had picked up a few CDs from JB Hi-Fi, they would walk through the car park, cross Murray Road and settle in at McDonald's for a burger, a Coke and a chat with friends.

Above these kids talking about Eminem, Rage Against the Machine, Banamarama and Indecent Obsession were unusual photos. Framed pictures of the winning Australian Ashes team of 1921. The 'new Trumper', Charlie Macartney. The quiet hands of Bert Oldfield. Curly Bardsley. Nip Pellow. Hunter Hendry. Medal worthy Jack Ryder. And the boy who killed the dove, Arthur Mailey.

To most, these were just dead men on a wall. But what men. What facial hair. What stances. What actions. They were Ashes winners, and legends. From another time, another country, another universe. They didn't belong in a McDonalds. They belonged in cricket's Valhalla.

Of all the men, none stood out more than Warwick Armstrong. He looked like a conquering emperor from some far off land, who had returned with the spoils of war. He was larger than life, even 70 years after his greatest triumph. The Big Ship, as he was known.

When Warwick Armstrong walked down the pavilion steps, the pavilion knew about it. He was, at his heaviest, 140 kilograms. Every single gram of it was cricketer.

Australia was a country in its own right before Armstrong walked onto the field, but he added to the culture. Straightforward. Brash. Arrogant. He was harsh, but fair, as they say. Armstrong was a perfect combination of all this. Just your normal, passive-aggressive, funny Aussie bastard. He played in the Golden Era. But he was no dove. He had no beauty, no grace, no ethereal loveliness. He was just Armstrong, in name and in play. There are no odes to his batsmanship. His bowling was compared to that of a fat aunty. He was just a big son-of-a-bitch batsman who didn't get out, and a bowler who waited for you to make a mistake.

In 19 years of Test cricket he only made six centuries. There were times, like when he scored more than half Australia's total against South Africa and a revered 90 on a tricky pitch in Melbourne, where his batting shone. In the UK he averaged barely over 20, but he was certainly a player worth of inclusion through most of those years. His bowling made up for his lack of hundreds, and his batting average of 38 was not poor for the era. But he was just a man doing a job.

Warwick Armstrong didn't believe in walking. Warwick Armstong didn't believe the laws should apply to him. Warwick Armstrong would do anything to win. Warwick Armstrong was a proper bastard. Warwick Armstrong was Australian cricket as we now know it. Before that, it was the English who were the bastards.

There is a strong line of hard-as-nails Australian captains. Allan Border was made of the collected spittle of Australian disappointment. Ian Chappell was aggressive in every aspect of his being. Don Bradman didn't play to win, he played to annihilate. But before them, The Big Ship really showed them how.

Armstrong was ground zero for Australian arseholishness, as Frank Woolley once found out. Woolley played Test cricket for 25 years, but he never forgot his debut. Armstrong was the bowler. He bowled warm-ups for 15 minutes, testing the nerves of the debutant.

That was Warwick Armstrong. The man who birthed Australia's brutality.

When he was finally made captain, the good times continued. He was now over 40. His team loved him, and would follow him into fire. In 1920/21, Armstrong scored three of his six Test hundreds. He also won the series 5-0. Before he batted in Sydney he was padded up in the members, drinking whisky.

Armstrong took two proper fast bowlers, Jack Gregory and Ted McDonald, to England for the return series, which was unusual at the time. They won the first Test in two days.

At Old Trafford for the fourth Test, the weather was terrible and the first day of the match was rained out. Late on the second day, just after an Armstrong over, England thought they had enough to declare with. They informed the umpires of their decision and started making their way off. Australia's keeper Sammy Carter told Armstrong that in a two-day game, which this now was, you couldn't actually declare, as *Wisden* put it, 'later than an hour and forty minutes before Time'.

England was forced back onto the field, and Armstrong bowled the first over after the resumption. In the space of two overs, Armstrong had used the laws to win an argument and ensure his team wouldn't lose a Test, and then completely broke them by being the first and only man in Test history to bowl two consecutive overs in one innings.

In the fifth Test, Armstrong suggested to his bowlers not to dismiss the obdurate Phil Mead, as he was helping Australia draw the match. Late on the second and final day of the Test, Armstrong stopped setting the fields, used all his part-timers, and at one point picked up a newspaper and started reading it.

Under Armstrong, Australia's record was 8-0. They humiliated England, and Armstrong did everything he could to rub it in.

Chapter 13

AUBREY FAULKNER: GOOGLIES AND GOOD LOOKS

A UBREY FAULKNER WAS the sort of man that makes racists believe their own rhetoric. He was tall, broad-shouldered and looked like he was from some sort of superior sect that could, if it wanted, enslave us all.

To run away from a drunken, abusive father, Faulkner joined the Imperial Light Horse brigade and fought against the English in the Boer War. After the war he joined Transvaal as a batsman, and did quite well. But it was when Reggie Schwarz taught him the magic of the wrong'un that Faulkner took over cricket.

In 25 Tests he managed a double Test ton and a 6/17. Both away from home. Batting average 40. Bowling average 26. The only man in the history of Test cricket to average more than 40 with the bat and less than 30 with the ball. Calling him a genuine all-rounder seems like an understatement. Hell, his fielding was so good he could have got selected for that alone. They say he was so good looking that women just came to watch him. He was every damn thing. Googlies and good looks is what he should have called his autobiography.

Faulkner was the sort of all-rounder that South Africa seems to produce while the rest of the world is hoping for one. Aubrey Faulkner was Mike Procter, Clive Rice and Jacques Kallis, before any of them existed.

Faulkner was South Africa's first player to make 1000 runs and 100 wickets in Tests. He dismissed Jack Hobbs four times. Victor Trumper twice. They name stadiums after players this good.

In 1911, he moved to England to live. He became a cricket coach. He still played; he even scored a hundred in the Triangular Test series of 1912, but he stopped playing Tests in South Africa, and essentially retired from international cricket. He didn't play much first-class cricket either, other than a few gentlemen and players matches.

That was in 1913. By 1914, he had enlisted in the war.

In the Royal Field Artillery, Faulkner was active on the Western Front, fought in Macedonia and eventually landed in Palestine where, as an acting major, he helped reclaim Jerusalem. He was awarded for distinguished service and the given the Order of the Nile. The war also gave him malaria. It was this Faulkner, a broken-down war hero who hadn't played Test cricket in nine years, who faced up to Armstrong's marauding Aussies.

Australia made 174. Faulkner took four of their wickets, and the most likely result was an Australian innings win. The Australians hadn't been beaten in their previous 34 games on tour, and it didn't look like Archie MacLaren's mouth or side was going to change that.

In the second innings, still 71 runs behind and four wickets down, Faulkner came out to bat.

In his day job, Faulkner wasn't just a coach. He was the coach. He created what many call the first cricket school in England. His students over the years captained England, selected future England teams, and represented South Africa. The Faulkner School of Cricket was an academy of cricket before the term even existed. And he also wrote *Cricket: Can It Be Taught?*

This old broken-down coach who hadn't played a Test in years wasn't the sort of player a brutal Australian side would fear. His technique had deteriorated and his feet had stopped moving. And he constantly talked to himself through his innings.

He made a chanceless 153 against a bowling attack that boasted Arthur Mailey, Jack Gregory, Warwick Armstrong and Ted McDonald. It was a brilliant attack, and it was humiliated by an old man.

When Faulkner was out, caught Mailey, bowled Armstrong, the lead was 195.

Faulkner took two wickets. One of them was Armstrong, who put his lips together like he was about to whistle, but no noise came out.

Faulkner had silenced the bully. Archie MacLaren hadn't found a side to beat Australia. He'd found one man.

Faulkner retired from all cricket at the end of that year, as 40-year-olds tend to do.

Three years later, in 1924, when they made their way back to England, South Africa selected George Parker, who was playing cricket in the Bradford League for Eccleshill. He'd never played a first-class game.

In that first innings Parker took 6/152, yet he was a laughing stock. He bowled fast, but his actual overs took an unconscionable time to deliver. *The Guardian* said he was grotesquely erratic and described him this way:

> He is immensely deliberate as he walks to his bowling place; his eyes are cast on the earth, and he walks slowly and solemnly as though pondering mighty problems. The wildness of his bowling made a quite sensational contrast to his solid deportment.

Frank Woolley was shocked when Parker asked him if he thought his field was set right. No wonder, considering Woolley was facing Parker at the time.

At one stage Parker bowled for three straight hours. Then he took his jumper, and left the field without telling anyone, or answering any questions. When South African captain Herbie Taylor finally found him, Parker had told him that he'd had enough and just wanted to get off the ground. It was an innings defeat.

For the next Test, South Africa was desperate. So desperate that the now-42 retired cricket coach was brought back.

South Africa's attack managed two wickets, somehow both to Parker. Hendren made a fifty. Woolley a hundred. Sutcliffe a hundred. And Hobbs managed a double hundred. Had they not declared, they would still be batting. Another innings defeat.

Parker played three first-class matches and in them dismissed Herb Sutcliffe, Patsy Hendren, Frank Woolley and Jack Hobbs: all great batsmen. Then he just disappeared back to normal life and was never seen again.

For Faulkner, the embarrassment was much worse. He had been a legend. A drop-dead gorgeous, world-leading all-rounder. Now he was a man with no real balance, who had not even a hint of natural athleticism and seemed to hit the ball by accident. One of the greatest players ever would leave his last Test embarrassed.

Faulkner continued to coach, but despite coaching world-class players and many of the sons of gentlemen, he never quite made enough money from coaching.

There is a dark history in cricket. There is something about the game that chews people up like no other sport. It's the Woody Allen of sports, permanently on the couch, analysing itself. Its players do the same.

There is too much cricket – it takes up so much of your time, and yet gives you so many quiet times. Then there is the travel. You are away from home for months at a time. Away from life.

Perhaps the rate of cricketers suffering depression is overblown. But it's never quite felt like that. Cricket has the ability to lift someone above the ground, or put them in it.

In Test cricket, Aubrey Faulkner dismissed batsmen 82 times. He ended by dismissing himself. It was 1930. He wrote to the secretary of his cricket academy: 'Dear Mackenzie, I am off to another sphere via the small bat-drying room. Better call in a policeman to do investigating.'

Chapter 14

NEW BOYS JOIN THE CLUB

T HE IMPERIAL CRICKET Conference opened its doors in 1926, and they decided to let in more Test nations. The West Indies, India and New Zealand entered Test cricket. Considering the time, the history of these countries, and the racial implications, it was quite a bold move.

The West Indies wasn't a country, but the countries that formed it were part of the Commonwealth. That was enough. The authorities decided cricket was for Commonwealth nations.

The first reference to cricket in the West Indies was in 1806: a mention in the *Barbados Mercury* of a dinner after a game at St Anne's cricket club in Barbados. The so-called West Indies Campaign, part of the Napoleonic War, was raging there at the time.

Despite there being few black players selected, the black community followed cricket. Proper England teams toured, not for Tests, but for exhibitions. Pelham Warner played for a Lord Hawke XI that lost, according to Warner, because of two professional bowlers named Wood and Cumberbatch, both black. Warner thought that not picking black players was holding back the quality and spread of cricket in the region.

Barbados refused to play Trinidad if they picked black players. Despite this, Spartan, an all-black side, won the Barbados challenge cup. In 1900 the first West Indies team toured England, and it included five black players. Leburn Constantine was one. *Wisden* called it an experiment; it wasn't even first-class. Yet they still beat Surrey by an innings. Six years later they took six black players, and beat Yorkshire.

CRICKET'S MISSING NATION

Cricket could have, and probably should have, opened itself up even further, and any team with a regular touring team, or a decent level of cricket at home, brought in as well. Ceylon. Ireland. Scotland. Perhaps the US. Even Argentina would have fit this bill.

Argentina was a quality cricket nation from 1900 until 1939, even if their cricketers were largely British expats. Their first-class cricket of this time was so good some thought it was superior to that of South Africa and New Zealand. The MCC toured Argentina twice, in 1912 and in 1926, both times Argentina beat them in one match, while losing tough series 2-1.

Argentina had already fallen for another English import, football. So there was no reason why cricket couldn't have been cultivated there. But Argentina was not given Test status because the Imperial Cricket Conference decided that only Commonwealth countries should be Test playing nations. When World War II happened, the Brits left Argentina, and so did cricket.

The ICC eventually gave Argentina membership, as an associate, in 1974. They are currently in the sixth division of the world cricket league, which in 2014 was won by Jersey.

The second over the West Indies ever delivered in Test cricket was by a man who would end up as Baron Constantine of Maraval in Trinidad and Nelson in the County Palatine of Lancaster. At the time, they called him Learie.

Learie Constantine was the son of Leburn Constantine. Learie averaged 20 with the bat, and 30 with the ball. He was also a great fielder.

Constantine was born into the black lower-middle classes. He was an average student; he became a solicitor's clerk. His father banned him from playing cricket for a few years so he could concentrate on his studies. He came back to the sport just before he was 20, and was so talented soon he was playing first-class cricket. His first game was played with his uncle in the team. His second game had his father in it. He was a child of cricket.

That allowed him to travel to England and represent the West Indies in first-class cricket. His style of cricket was not the English way; it was a style that would be a gift to cricket for years to come. He attacked; he was reckless; he was beautiful; he was athletic; he was the West Indies. Jack Hobbs, Warner and pretty much everyone else who saw him just loved him. He made his maiden first-class 50, he took his maiden first-class five-wicket haul while in England. They called him the world's greatest fielder.

Cricket was more to him than just a game; he saw cricket as a way to improve his life. England might have still been racist, but being a good cricketer meant something. It meant he could transcend his background, his skin colour.

Learie left that tour with a mission to improve his game. His dream was to be a professional in the UK. So he added pace to his bowling, worked on playing slightly less crazy shots, and even trained himself as a slip fielder. He wasn't looking for Test glory; he was looking for a job.

Even before the Test, Constantine had been a success. He'd won a match in seven hits against Derbyshire. He'd made his maiden first-class hundred at Essex. But it was at Middlesex that Constantine left the biggest impact.

The crowds came to Lord's to see him. In the West Indies first innings he entered the wicket well behind the follow-on target, so he smashed his 50 in 18 minutes. A few minutes after that he was 86 and the follow-on had been avoided.

He took the new ball in the second innings. Middlesex were bowled out for 136. Constantine ended with 7/57.

The West Indies had to chase over 250. At seven in, he walked. They still needed more than half the total. Constantine batted for exactly 60 minutes. He made 103. He broke a bowler's hand in that magic hour, that epic hour. It was one of the great hours in cricket history: the hour of Learie Constantine.

The West Indies beat Middlesex by three wickets.

Five years later Denis Compton started playing for Middlesex. According to him the players were still talking about Learie's match.

The West Indies lost all three of their Tests to England on that tour, all by an innings. Constantine took the first Test wicket for the West Indies. Hobbs said it was one of the fastest spells he'd ever faced. At the end of the tour Constantine had made the most runs, taken the most wickets and held the most catches of any of the West Indians.

Nelson Cricket Club in the Lancashire leagues contacted Constantine and offered him a professional contract. Constantine had done it; he had earned himself a career.

Constantine played for Nelson as a well-paid professional, a black man, playing the whites' sport, in their country, and being well paid for his magical abilities.

CLR James, one of the greatest cricket writers of all time, and a close friend of Constantine, wrote: 'He had revolted against the revolting contrast between his first-class status as a cricketer and his third-class status as a man.' So he moved to Lancashire to make a career on and off the field for himself, and as James put it, 'honour [and] a little profit'.

When Constantine took 5/87 on 30 February 1930 at Georgetown, British Guiana, in the third Test of the return series, he led the West Indies to their first victory over their colonial masters.

Strangely, on the exact same day as the first Test England played in the West Indies, 11 January, 1930, New Zealand too played their first-ever Test, also against England.

Charles Darwin went to New Zealand in 1835, and mentioned cricket was evolving there. Cricket was big in Wellington in the Te Aro flat, which is where the Basin Reserve now stands. Cricket progressed slowly there. The Maoris were allowed to play. But even teams of 22 New Zealanders were beaten easily by English touring teams.

It was thought that New Zealand cricket would always struggle to compete against the bigger countries, but by 1894 they had a domestic league, and in 1906 their own first-class competition, the Plunkett Shield.

When England arrived in 1930, it was essentially an England A side. It included the great KS Duleepsinhji, a pretty run machine, and the 42-year-old Frank Woolley, by then a ghost of himself. The squad that travelled to the West Indies was better, as the common thought was that the West Indies was a quality side.

New Zealand lost a rain-affected match within two days. They improved as the series went on, and thanks to rain and some quality batting, drew the remaining three Tests. New Zealand did not win a Test before World War II. Their best result was 0-0. Australia didn't play them at all. England kept sending second-grade teams, and played them in shorter Tests than against the other teams. And South Africa beat them easily in two Tests.

New Zealand was in Test Cricket, but it had made no mark, left no impact, and only played five series before the war.

Some thought New Zealand too small. Others thought India – the sixth Test nation – was too big.

British sailors were reported to have played cricket in India as early as 1721 in India. In 1780 there is a mention of a Calcutta Cricket Club, which was for 'the manly exercise of cricket'. That would make it older than the MCC. It's clear that from 1792, there definitely was a club of that name playing where Eden Gardens is now. These were not locals, but the English forming their own fun.

In 1848, the Parsees of India formed a club, which is still active as the Young Zoroastrians Cricket Club, funded by the early beginnings of the now billion dollar Tata Group. It seems like Parsee children were playing cricket from almost the first time they saw it. An English journalist once remarked it looked like they wore pyjamas while playing, which is exactly what the coloured clothing of Kerry Packer's World Series was called a hundred-odd years later. When they played an army side, the army regiment asked for that match to be called 'Officers with umbrellas vs natives with bats'.

The Bombay Gymkhana ('ball house' in Hindi) was formed in 1875 for whites only. Here was cricket at its most exclusive sense. Rich men sitting in a tent with food and drink in the foreign land they had taken over, as the locals served them while gently fanning them in their colonial uniforms.

When the locals did play, cricket was separated by religion or race.

The Europeans, Parsees, Hindus and Muslims all had teams in the quadrangular tournament. Later it would become a pentangular tournament when the Rest were brought in, made up of Jews and Christians. This tournament in Bombay, and then others like it, would start to spread cricket around India, including Bangladesh and Pakistan, which were still part of India at the time.

India had demanded their entry through the quality of their cricket, largely because of Colonel Cottari Kanakaiya Nayudu. The MCC took over a team in 1926/27. In a match at Bombay, Nayudu smashed 153, with 11 sixes while playing for the Hindus.

It was fitting that he was India's first captain, although it only happened because the Maharaja of Porbandar, the official captain of the team, stood down. In Ramachandra Guha's *A Corner of a Foreign Field* the Maharaja is referred to as having more Rolls-Royces than runs. So Nayudu was a far better choice.

England won the toss and batted at Lord's in 1932. Here they ran into Mohammad Nissar. He was more bull than man, and he was really quick. In his opening spell in Test cricket he bowled to Herb Sutcliffe and Percy Holmes. Two weeks earlier Sutcliffe and Holmes had opened for Yorkshire and made an opening partnership of 555. Nissar bowled both of them in a few minutes. When Woolley was run out, England was on the verge of an embarrassing collapse.

Then Douglas Jardine came in, and steadied them enough so that they ended up over 200, making himself a handy 79. The odd fact is that Jardine was Bombay-born, and there was a thought within the newly formed Board of Control for Cricket in India (BCCI) that they needed a noble-born captain from England, and it was Jardine's name that came up.

Instead twice in that Test Jardine made runs that mattered. It was a low scoring match that England won by 158 runs. With Jardine making 79 and 85 not out, he pretty much won the game on his own.

The unit Nissar took five wickets, CK Nayudu would make a fighting 40 despite the fact he injured his hand while fielding. India were also missing Iftikhar Ali Khan Pataudi, or as most know him, the Nawab of Pataudi senior. He would play Test cricket soon after – for England.

A year later at the Bombay Gymkhana, roughly 50,000 people turned up to see India's first Test at home. At the ground they put up temporary tents and shamianas. Most of Bombay would have come, had the ground been big enough. This time, to be safe, England brought a full strength team; India were a team too good to take lightly. England won 2-0.

But it was the next tour to England where India went wrong. Very wrong. England had given them cricket, but also given them a class system. On their first Test tour they had narrowly avoided picking Maharajah of Vizianagram, or Vizzy, as he was unaffectionately known.

Vizzy was a rich man, and he loved cricket. He had a cricket ground in his palace, and he paid great cricketers to come and play there. He was a throwback to the rich English men of a century before. And like many of them, Vizzy thought he could play. He was wrong. He was given the title of deputy vice captain of their first tour, but pulled out as he wasn't made captain. In 1936, he was.

HISTORY REPEATS

The most recent version of Vizzy was in the 1996 World Cup, when the United Arab Emirates fielded a team. The UAE captain was Sultan Zarawani. Zarawani was rich, and Emirati, so that qualified him to be captain. South African quick Allan Donald was pretty much at the peak of his pace at this time. He was so smooth in his run-up, like an angry killing machine. Everything was perfectly in order, and then what came out of his hand was pure fire. Lightning. White lightning.

Sultan Zarawani came out to bat at number eight; his leg-spin had been smashed as Gary Kirsten had made 188 not out, and South Africa well over 300. Now he was about to face Allan Donald, and he walked out in a floppy hat. Not even a cap, but a floppy. Richie Richardson played in that World Cup; now that was a man who could bat in a floppy. Almost no one else could. Zarawani was basically saying he had no idea. Pat Symcox, the mouthy South African off-spinner walked up to Donald and said, 'Al, this guy's asking for it', so Donald bounced him.

Donald said, 'When I struck him, I thought I had killed him. The ball made just the most horrible thud when it hit him. I was just so shocked by his response. He just put his floppy back on and continued batting.' He batted for seven more balls before making a duck and being taken to hospital.

After the World Cup Zarawani never played for the UAE again.

The Maharaja of Porbandar was a man who could play a bit of cricket, but also knew it would be ridiculous for him to captain India. Vizzy thought nothing of it. India had a few decent players in their squad, probably none better than Lala Amarnath, an all-rounder who could bat in the top order and bowl decent medium pace. An ideal player for English conditions really. Vizzy sent him home before the first Test.

Vizzy had no idea how to field. He didn't actually understand the fielding placements. He misused every bowler he had. The batting order changed without rhyme or reason. Players were picked based on who they abused at the breakfast table, and the rumour has it that he offered gold jewellery to one player to run out Vijay Merchant. In the warm-up games he would offer money and gifts to the opposition hosts in order to get helpful bowling come his way.

In his three Tests, batting at nine, he averaged 8.25. And that flattered him. Nine was probably too high. Well, being in the team was too high. He was probably a decent number nine in your local club team, but you wouldn't pick him, unless he paid for your clubrooms. Which is sort of what Vizzy did. He bankrolled the tour. And the tour before.

Vizzy was not the only person picked because of his class. England had to have a gentleman captain, never a professional. South Africa had enforced their white-only policy. The West Indies were only to be captained by whites. Australia and New Zealand had still not yet chosen any native players to represent their nations. And there wasn't even a Women's Test match played until 1934/35.

Vizzy was booted out of cricket after his horrendous tour of England, and for years he had nothing to do with the game, until he became a commentator late in life. His commentary was so bad even his captaincy and batting looked good in comparison. India lost that series 2-0 as well, their only three series before World War II.

Vizzy was knighted during that tour, because that's what happened to men like him.

Chapter 15

DON'T SMOKE, DRINK OR BE SEEN WITH MEN

T HE ENGLISH WOMEN who toured Australia in 1934/35 were all single. Married women were simply not allowed to be away from their families. These single women had to pay £80 per head for the honour of representing their country. They were also told not to smoke, drink or gamble or 'be accompanied by a man'.

Betty Archdale was their captain, a daughter of a famous suffragette, and a strong bat. She led from the front in the low-scoring series that England won 2-0. England also beat New Zealand in their first Test of that period.

In the follow-up, Australia and England played one of the great women's series. Australia held on in the first Test, even after they were bowled out for 102 in the second innings.

In the second match, Australia had a lead of 80 runs after the first innings, but when they had to chase 152, they batted much like their men often did in small totals, and ended short. The great Molly Hide, who averaged 35 with the bat and 15 with the ball in women's Tests, took 5/20.

In the third and deciding Test, Betty Snowball made 99, and the Test was drawn with England needing a further 115 to win, while stumbling at 3/9.

Cricket authorities made no effort at all to help the women in any way. They weren't involved in the organisation of women's cricket at all. It was as if you could play Test cricket only if you were from the Commonwealth and had a penis.

Chapter 16

THE TIGER AND THE FOX

Batsmen were now dominating the game. Pace bowling had been troubled by improving pitches and improving batsmen. Cutter bowlers got less movement; pace bowlers didn't get the inconsistency of earlier years. Spin began to take over; not the cutting fast spin of Syd Barnes, but the spin we now know – slow and deliberate, an art of deception.

Australia had two great spinners. The Tiger and The Fox.

These days an attack by aliens is more likely than two leg-spinners in the same attack, but in the 1930s Australia played Tiger Bill O'Reilly and Clarrie Grimmett in the same attack all the time. You don't worry about two leggies when the two leggies in question would end with Test bowling averages of 22 and 24, despite the fact they bowled against some of the best batsmen who ever lived.

Tiger was a fast bowler in every way except his wrist. His wrong'un jumped up at batsmen. His leg-spinner was medium-paced, started on leg and ended on off, almost every ball, like a metronome. He once bowled a bad ball, but no one can remember when or where. They say no batsmen ever dominated him. He simply wouldn't allow it. He was a warrior with an iron wrist.

Clarrie was every bit a spin bowler. He was an artist. His action looked rubbish, and he bowled in a cap. He bowled slow, and loved deceiving batsmen through the air as much as off the pitch. He didn't worry about the wrong'un much – but he invented the flipper. To bowl it you have to click your fingers while the ball is in your hand, before it pitches on a good length and then skids low, usually onto the pad of the surprised batsman. In the almost 100 years since, only a handful of men have ever perfected the flipper as a weapon.

Together they were music: sweaty, groovy, funky music. Grimmett was actually born in Dunedin on Christmas Day 1891. O'Reilly said he 'must have been the best Christmas present Australia ever received from that country'.

Grimmett made his first-class debut at 17 for Wellington, but during World War I moved to Sydney. Because of the war, there was no first-class Cricket. After that, Grimmett moved to Victoria, and never really got a chance there, except in one game against South Australia where he took 8/86. It was as many wickets as he'd taken in the previous 10 years he'd been in Australia. The next year, after having made his move to South Australia, at 33, he would make his Test debut.

Clarrie took a long hard road to Test cricket, but when he got there, he averaged six wickets a Test. Was the first player to make his debut after 30 and take a hundred wickets. And is still the quickest bowler to 200 wickets.

Even with all that, people say O'Reilly was better. When O'Reilly died in 1992, *Wisden* called him the greatest spin bowler of all time. He died the same year Shane Warne made his Test debut – as if he was waiting for him.

England had Headley Verity. Verity was a professional cricketer in the Lancashire leagues before he made it to County cricket. He wasn't a superstar. He bowled medium pace, batted a bit, and was ok. But after a discussion with Yorkshire, the 24-year-old moved himself to spin in the hopes that he could replace Wilfred Rhodes if he ever retired.

Verity was magic. His quick pace and accuracy made the batsmen take risks, and his bounce was hard to handle. Verity believed the batsmen would make a mistake, and on flat pitches he would wait as long as he had to for that mistake to come.

On sticky wickets, playing Verity was like playing an angry tiger snake with a PhD in astrophysics and a magical sword. Once he took ten 10-10.

Yep, 10-10. In an innings. There is a whole book on it. *10 for 10: Hedley Verity and the Story of Cricket's Greatest Bowling Feat* by Chris Waters.

Verity's record in first-class cricket was 1956 wickets at 14.87. In one day at Lord's, Verity took 14 wickets.

Even South Africa, a team so weak they didn't win a series in the 1920s, had the great Cyril Vincent, a left-arm finger-spinner who was their greatest bowler of this era. Part of South Africa's problem was that while other countries played regular first-class cricket competitions, South Africa did not. The Currie Cup was only played nine times between the wars. In Vincent's entire career, he played only two Currie Cup matches. Money was tight. South African improvement was slow.

Chapter 17

JACK HOBBS, HUNDREDS AND HUNDREDS

JACK HOBBS GREW up a few Albert Trott hits from Fenners, the Cambridge cricket ground. But Hobbs wasn't punting on the river with a jumper knotted around his neck, talking about summering in the south of France. Hobbs' Cambridge was a dark virtual squalor. It had crime and dirty streets, and his dad was neither a lord, nor a gentleman, but a groundsman and an umpire. Good, honest, underpaid work.

Hobbs grew up like most cricket fans the world over: playing with a tennis ball. He was no child prodigy, received no real coaching, and never made a hundred until he was 18.

When his father passed, they played a benefit game to raise money for his mother, and at that game he was brought to the attention of his hero, Tom Hayward. Hayward was a very fine Test player. Hayward was the second man after Grace to score 100 first-class 100s; he conquered Australia, opened for England for more than a decade, and managed to achieve all that as a professional. In first-class cricket, Hayward made 43,551 runs.

Hobbs had found his idol, and with the two of them together, batsmen had found some hidden code that turned great batsmen into run machines.

Hobbs started before the war, and while the world might have been fawning over Victor Trumper's elegant savagery, Hobbs just made runs. More runs. Quieter runs. Life-changing runs.

When Armstrong's fast bowling army of 1921 had invaded, Hobbs managed only one Test. And it almost killed him. Despite stomach pains,

Hobbs still tried to play, but it turned out he had acute appendicitis. His doctor said that Hobbs may have not seen out the day without an emergency operation. Hobbs didn't play again that year.

The reason Hobbs played despite the fact he was almost dead was that if he didn't play, he didn't get paid.

Hobbs was a gentleman, not by birth, but by conduct. He was pragmatic, dour, consistent, businesslike, a craftsman, and as Matthew Engel once wrote, 'not an artist'. Hobbs may not have been an artist, but footage from the time shows he wasn't ugly. Old pathe videos show an older Hobbs coming down the wicket, not getting to the pitch of the ball and continuing to hit it on the up, with an angled bat as his back leg gracefully dangles.

Gideon Haigh wrote:

Hampshire's Alex Kennedy once recalled bowling the first ball of a match to Hobbs at The Oval. It was a late out-swinger on off stump; Hobbs dispatched it through square leg for four. Hobbs smilingly apologised: 'I shouldn't have done that, should I? I was a bit lucky.'

That's a humblebrag right there.

That is kind of what Hobbs had to do his whole career. Apologise for being better than his betters. According to Plum Warner, Hobbs was a professional who batted like an amateur. We tend to worry more about race, sex, and religion than we do about class. But there were very real effects of class in Hobbs' life. Hobbs couldn't stay in the same change-room or hotel as players that weren't good enough to share a field with him. And he had to call them mister.

The world that Hobbs lived in was summed up by Martin Williamson:

Professionals were often treated much as servants would be and were expected to be as deferential to amateurs and committeemen as a butler would be to the master of the house. They had separate hotels when they travelled, separate changing rooms and food at the grounds, referred to by their surnames only, and at most counties could never aspire to captaincy. Even scorecards made a small but marked distinction – amateurs were given full initials, professionals surname only.

It went even deeper than that. There were many bowlers who were professional, because bowling is tough. Bowlers keep having to front up for hours, days, weeks, months and years on end. What gentleman would want to do that? But batting, well that's fun. A couple of lucky inside edges, a play and miss while winking at the sweaty monster coming down at you. Perhaps get a 50, and then throw it away with your 17th unsuccessful attempt at the perfect cover drive that day. That was the 'job' of an amateur batsman.

What the run machines did was bat like professional bowlers had. Like their lunch, their livelihoods, depended on it. Like they'd be fired if they failed.

Hobbs wasn't a class warrior with a bat. Hobbs was part of a movement that existed well before him, and still lives: he was a batsman who loved the crease. Their moment, their life, is all about the next ball. He wanted to inhabit the crease. It went beyond wanting to win a sporting event, it was all about the next moment facing up. These creatures that just want to inhabit the crease, forever, if possible. It's a state of mind that turned men into legends, icons and gods.

Hobbs had his father's work ethic, his mother's fire and Hayward's blueprint. What came next was a batsman so good even Grace and Trumper had to take a back seat.

We don't even know how many first-class hundreds Hobbs made. *Wisden* says 197. The Association of Cricket Statisticians says 199. All in all, he made 61,760 runs in first-class level. Sachin Tendulkar, combining all three formats of the game, in domestic and international cricket, made 50,192.

World War I took years out of his cricket. According to Leo McKinstry in *Jack Hobbs: England's Greatest Ever Cricketer*, Hobbs was at cover point in a game for Surrey at the Oval, when Ferdinand was shot dead on 28 June 1914, in Sarajevo.

After the appendicitis operation, Hobbs was never the same. He would now often get out when he made a hundred largely due to his health. Although, as Hayward once remarked after making 315 not out and only receiving £5, 'Well, it's no use me getting 300 again.' Hobbs kept making hundreds, because that's what he did.

The other problem for Hobbs was that by the time he retired, batting machines had taken over world cricket. He was the greatest batsman who had ever lived for most of his career, but by the 1930s batsmen were clocking cricket like it was some flawed 1980s video game. Hobbs was just the first master of the machine.

Chapter 18

'WHY HIM DON'T LIKE TO BAT?'

GEORGE ALPHONSO HEADLEY. Headley was a strange cricketer: a young black man who was born in Panama while his Jamaican mother and Barbadian father helped build the famous canal. After that, he lived in Cuba before his mother took him back to Jamaica. When he made his first-class debut, he was actually waiting for his visa so he could study dentistry in the US. The visa was delayed, and so he played for Jamaica against a visiting team led by Lord Tennyson.

Headley made 211 in his second first-class match. It was the highest score against a touring team from England. At one point he scored exclusively in boundaries, hitting 13 straight without a single, two or three. Tennyson said Headley reminded him of Trumper. Headley gave up dentistry.

Even with that innings, Headley still wasn't picked for the West Indies first Test tour.

When Test cricket arrived in the West Indies for the next tour, Headley was at three. It was in Barbados, and Headley was seen as a Jamaican, despite the fact he had a parent from each country. When he came out to bat the crowd had a go at him. Headley made 22 in the first innings. In the second, he made 176. He wasn't booed again.

The second Test was played on matting in Trinidad. Headley was not used to it and failed twice. But in the first innings at Guyana, or British Guiana as it was then, Headley made a hundred while Clifford Roach made his double hundred. In the second innings, Headley added another. England tried to bore him out as well, to frustrate his attacking instincts as they hoped for a draw. Headley wouldn't do that either. He was going to make a hundred, a stylish hundred, his way.

Headley went by many nicknames, one that included his race, but the one that should have stuck was Atlas. He carried a nation – actually, several nations. When he played, Headley made over a quarter of the West Indies' runs before World War II. He scored two-thirds of his team's hundreds as well. He was a run machine. In his first series, Headley would make 703 runs. Had the second Test not been on matting, he might have broken 1000.

Headley, like the other run machines, was a different kind of man. He simply couldn't understand why others would play stupid shots, why others would get tired, why others would give away a start. When he saw a player give away his wicket, he would often say, 'Why him don't like to bat?'

As he could hit the ball where he wanted and his placement was so precise, he'd hit the ball as much as he could to where the bowlers were fielding, tiring them out in between spells. When the spinner came on, he'd smash the first ball back at them to try to injure their hands. Supervillain batting.

When World War II began, Headley was averaging 66 in Test cricket.

That final Test of the 1930 series, a timeless Test, England set the West Indies a chase of 836 after Andy Sandham made the first-ever Test triple century – and a third of his career runs. On day five, England declared.

On the evening of day seven, George Headley went out to bat. The score was 4/398. He got to 223. The rain set in after that and the match was drawn on day nine by agreement, as England had a boat to catch.

Had Headley still been in, the boat might have waited.

Chapter 19

BRADMAN, THE BATTING MENTALIST

52. 6996. 29. 99.94

People all over the world recognise these numbers.

52 Tests.

6996 Test runs.

29 Test centuries.

99.94 Test batting average.

They are Bradman's numbers. Bradman was a run machine like no other.

This machine had been developed in Bowral. Streamlined in Sydney. And unleashed on the universe. It was an independent industry. A global franchise. There were days when all it did was tick over digits. If it failed, it made headlines. Its biggest malfunction was still a success by any other measure. It converted. Built. Shaped. Constructed. Sold. Amassed.

People questioned whether it was human. Even the most famous number, 99.94, seems to be a glitch of software. A cricket number that almost repeats. But can never be repeated.

We know Bradman was once a boy; we know he honed his craft by hitting a golf ball with a wicket at a water tank. But it is hard to believe Bradman was ever actually a boy. Bradman had an eye like a gimlet and wrists like quicksilver. He probably counted his sultanas, and found a way to trade seven of them for three ham and cheese sandwiches. While other kids strove hard for perfect handwriting he might have flogged himself with a stick until he mastered it. And when it came to maths, his teachers probably asked for his advice.

Bradman's first superpower was to read the bowler as he ran in. All batsmen do this, but only Bradman could tell what ball the bowler was going to deliver before it had left the hand. And he did it for 20 years.

We now know that it is harder to face a delivery at 140 km/h from a bowling machine than 150 km/h from a human. Bowling machines don't have tells. They don't betray their intention. They have no wrists. There is nothing to read at all. Bradman could read a bowler's intentions.

Did he know before the bowler turned at the top of his mark? Did he know several balls in advance? Did he know the morning of the game every ball that would be delivered? Bradman raised these questions because he was a batting mentalist who seemed to know what bowlers would bowl, even when the bowler didn't know.

If that was his only super power, it would be something, but Bradman had more. Bradman was hungrier than normal people. He was meaner than normal people. He was smarter than normal people. He was quicker than normal people. He was mentally stronger than normal people. He was more patient than normal people. He worked harder than normal people. He wasn't normal. Not really in any way.

That's how you become Bradman.

In Malcolm Knox's *Bradman's War* he writes:

He never forgot how the New South Wales selectors snubbed him when, as a boy, he had travelled from the country to trials at the Sydney Cricket Ground. He never forgot how, when he took his first interstate tours, the senior men teased him as a bumpkin. He never forgot the merciless batting of the great England team of 1928–29, when, as 12th man – he never forgot that either – he spent days in the sun picking Wally Hammond's cover drives out of the gutter. He never forgot the teasing from England's spin bowler Jack White, who chided Maurice Tate for dismissing Bradman in his first Test: 'Hey, you got my bunny!'

It's all part of what made him. You couldn't remake him now, even as an experiment. It was a fluke, a one-off, an anomaly.

When Bradman went to England in 1930 he scored 2960 first-class runs, 974 of those in five Tests, 300 in one day. You know, it made a dent. Not just in England, but in cricket.

Something had to be done to stop him. That something was one of the great sporting tactics of all time. A cricketing act of beautiful bastardry.

Bodyline.

As good as most players are, the laws aren't changed for them. Bodyline changed the way the sport was played, for one man. It eventually changed the laws of the game as well.

Bradman made 334 at Leeds in 1930, scoring 300 in a day. In the same Test were Jack Hobbs, Herb Sutcliffe, Stan McCabe and Walter Hammond. They were all playing for second place from then on in. After that innings Plum Warner wrote, 'England must develop a new type of bowler and fresh ideas and strange tactics to curb his almost uncanny skill.' Warner would be manager on the 1932/33 tour. After being humiliated by Bradman at the Oval, the Surrey captain, Percy Fender, said, 'I feel sure something new will have to be introduced to curb Bradman.'

England had been beaten by peak Bradman. Had they bowled the same way to him again, they would lose again.

It is generally believed that bowlers set the agenda by delivering the ball, and batsmen just react to it. But once a bowler works out a new way of doing something, batsmen evolve with him.

They called the next innovation fast leg theory. Or Bodyline.

England needed to change how Bradman batted. Change him from god from the machine to a man who could bleed.

Bodyline was new, but there were precedents.

There was an Australian bowler called Jack Scott who had tried this fast leg theory in a shield game. The fast bowler would start by bowling around the wicket at a right hander. There would be between two and four catchers close on the leg side. Behind them are men on the fence as well. It was like the whole game is being played slightly behind your back when you bat.

Scott's NSW captain Herbie Collins didn't like it, so he stopped it. Scott bowled it again only when he moved to South Australia and played under Vic Richardson, Ian Chappell's guru and grandfather.

There had been stories that Nobby Clark, a left-arm quick, had bowled some leg theory in an English trial game that Jardine, the Bodyline captain, had led. Harold Larwood, Bodyline's front-line weapon, had also used it once or twice in a Test match before. And Learie Constantine had used it against the English in that first West Indies home series.

It just hadn't been done well. Or consistently. Or been well practised. It was just a tactic that on occasion the odd bowler and captain would try to see what happened.

Bradman's 974 runs had completely obliterated England. Before that series, they had seven wins, one loss and two draws in their previous 10 series. They were the best team in the world. The previous Ashes they had won 4-1. They were used to winning, and some of them were willing to do whatever was necessary to win again.

England had also seen what short fast bowling could do to a man.

At the Oval in 1930, Bradman made 232. But Percy Fender saw something. The pitch had briefly been a bit sticky after some rain. Bradman had received a short quick one at him, and he had stepped out of the line of the ball. Like all good bowlers, Harold Larwood noticed, and so did Fender. But still, it was just a one-off, and he had made 232 despite it.

Another man had seen something too – a man who, decades later, would die at Goodna Hospital for the Insane. This man knew that Bradman didn't like the short quick one. He saw it in six balls. He saw the flaw in the machine in the god from the machine.

Eddie Gilbert was his name. He was fast. Many say the quickest of his time. He never played a Test. He played only 23 first-class matches over six years. Eddie Gilbert had made the unwise career move of being born Indigenous, which in Australia at that time meant he was not human, but part of the flora and fauna.

Queensland was still haunted by Bradman's last visit, when he made 452, for many years the highest score in first-class cricket. And he was not out. So they picked their quickest bowler, despite his skin colour.

When Eddie Gilbert took a wicket first ball, the crowd cheered with delight. Not so much for the wicket, but because Bradman would be coming in next.

Bradman was carried to the wicket by the applause of the opposition supporters. There might still have been great interstate rivalry at the time, but Bradman belonged to everyone.

The first ball Gilbert bowled, Bradman handled. The second one knocked him over as he tried to get out of the way. A couple of balls later Bradman tried to hook the ball and ended up with the bat leaving his hand. Then Bradman tried to hook again, this time edging behind. Gilbert had knocked him over, knocked the bat out of his hand and got him out for a duck.

According to Bradman, it was the six quickest balls that he ever faced. They might have been the first six balls of Bodyline.

Gilbert was good enough to sit a national hero, an icon, a legend, on his arse, and take his wicket, but he wasn't good enough to overcome his skin colour. Like Jack Marsh, and many others before him, he was suspected of chucking. In Victoria he was called 13 times. Bradman also wrote later that he thought Gilbert was a chucker.

There is no doubt he had a weird bowling action. It was a catapult fling at the crease after a short run-up by a short man. Alan McGilvray, the voice of Australian cricket, said it was hard to even tell if he was chucking, as his arm moved so quickly.

Gilbert found it very tough to play shield cricket. Much of the time he was injured. And those running the settlement would take most of his playing wage, which made it hard for him to afford equipment and travel. Not to mention he had to get permission to leave the settlement in the first place.

After 23 matches, 87 wickets, 28 average, 56 strike rate, Gilbert was back on his settlement. He struggled with drink and gambling, and in 1950 ended up in the hospital for the insane. They tried shock treatment to fix him, but he had Alzheimer's, so it was just useless torture. Gilbert spent his next 28 years in that hospital.

At nights he would often be found wandering around a cricket ground next to the asylum. That ground is now the Eddie Gilbert Memorial Oval.

Gilbert once said, 'It's all right to be a hero on the field, but a black man can be lonely when he is not accepted after the game.'

When Gilbert dropped Bradman, it made so much noise it was heard back in the UK.

WORLD'S BEST – FOR A LITTLE WHILE

After Jack Hobbs retired, England replaced him with two more batting machines: his opening partner Sutcliffe and, as if Sutcliffe wasn't good enough in '28/29 as Bradman was making his debut, a bloke called Wally Hammond, who scored 905 runs in that series. Hammond was the world's best batsman from that time until Bradman made 334 at Leeds barely 18 months later. Shortly after that, Hammond went two runs past 334, with a 336 against New Zealand, but there was no real wrestling away that crown.

Hammond was a man who batted big. He was bigger than a lot of the other run machines. He had bowling shoulders that just happened to make beautiful cover drives. Drives that provided more than 30 first-class double hundreds. Hammond was better than Bradman on sticky wickets, and was an overseas warrior, averaging more away than he did at home. Hammond was so brilliant that he was appointed the first professional captain of England. Although, in a weird twist of fate, and much like when South Africa allowed black men to play in South Africa as honorary whites, Hammond was made an amateur after being a professional. He was so good, England literally let him climb up the social ladder and lead a team that included some of his 'betters'.

But Hammond, as good as he was, wasn't perfect. Hammond's biggest weakness was against fast bowling. The West Indies saw it. Herman Griffith, Manny Martindale, Leslie Hylton, Vincent Valentine and Learie Constantine dominated Hammond with quick bowling.

Vincent Valentine only ever took one Test wicket and that was Hammond. Leslie Hylton is better known for being the only Test cricketer who was executed. He killed his wife.

There were also letters Fender received from friends in Australia that suggested Australian batsmen would often get inside the line of the short ball when playing it on the leg side. Losing control of it in order to make sure they weren't hit. Fender showed Jardine these letters: they chatted about their theories.

Letters and stories were nice, but Jardine was completely won over by something he could see.

Jardine watched all the footage of the 1930 Ashes tour. He was looking for something. Harold Larwood, Percy Fender and Eddie Gilbert had already seen it. When Jardine saw it, he let out cricket's most famous backroom cry, 'I've got it, he's yellow.' The footage he had in front of him at the time was Larwood making Bradman flinch at the Oval in that 232.

Jardine rounded up Bill Voce and Harold Larwood and talked to them about his theory. His leg theory. They liked it. They went about preparing to bowl to such fields and worked on exactly how it would work. Jardine and Warner discussed it.

In Larwood, Jardine had the perfect bowler. Larwood was fast. Larwood was accurate. Larwood was tireless. He'd worked in the mines, so bowling his guts out in the Australian sun bouncing a few Aussies was nothing. Tiger Bill O'Reilly described facing Larwood:

He came steaming in, and I moved right across behind my bat, held perfectly straight in defence of my middle stump. Just before he delivered the ball, something hit the middle of my bat with such force as to almost dash it from my hands. It was the ball.

And then there was Jardine himself. As a young man, Jardine had made 96 not out against Warwick Armstrong's touring team. The story goes that Armstrong used some of his lovely gamesmanship to delay the game, denying Jardine his hundred. That would explain the sort of man Jardine became.

Hollywood has long known that the best villains are posh English people. They have a natural coldness and the perfect elocution that make them seem even more devious. When they were making the Bodyline miniseries, they cast Hugo Weaving as Douglas Jardine. In his film career Weaving has also played the evil Agent Smith, the evil Red Skull and the evil Megatron.

Jardine was at his most cold when discussing his tactics. He never said bouncer or bumper. He didn't even say short ball. No, he called it fast long hops. Which makes it sound like a Warner Bros character. And he never said Bodyline. It was always leg theory. Despite the fact that leg theory was more common for when you actually bowled outside someone's leg stump with spin or medium pace. Sometimes they added fast to leg theory. Larwood and Voce weren't aiming at the legs.

When Jardine arrived in Australia, he used the tactic sparingly. Enough to let batsmen know it was coming. When Bradman missed the first Test after struggling in a tour match against it, Jardine privately thought he had pulled out through fear.

But Bodyline didn't start with Australia surrendering; it started with Stan McCabe running straight into the attack armed with a hook and a cut. As the bombs went off around him, Larwood and Voce taking nine wickets, McCabe stood fast. In four hours of cricket, as England tried to destroy Australian batsman, McCabe took them for an undefeated 187. They said he batted for 'death or glory'. McCabe found glory.

McCabe was never a batting machine. He was more Ranji and Trumper than Hobbs and Bradman. His batting was for fun, not annihilation or accumulation. Against England he played an innings of 232 that was so good Bradman wished he had made it.

At times, Bradman would wonder out loud why McCabe didn't do that all the time. Only Bradman could look down on a batsman who made three of the greatest innings in Test history as an under-achiever.

McCabe's cutting and hooking delighted Australia during that Sydney Test, but Australia didn't survive. Larwood still took 10 wickets. England still won.

The next Test was a slow wicket at the MCG. Bradman made a golden duck in the first innings. Some say Jardine did a war dance. In the second innings Bradman made a hundred, and over half Australia's score. Larwood was hobbled from his heavy workload – 49 overs at Sydney – and an injury picked up in a tour match. Australia took full advantage from the break in hostilities to fight back. After two Tests, the series was 1-1.

When a new marine enters into a horrible war zone, their fellow marines greet them with, 'Welcome to the suck'. The third Test was in Adelaide. Adelaide was the suck.

Jardine could have gone back to normal methods after Melbourne. He had been spooked by the loss. But with a fit Larwood, and the series level, he went all in on fast leg theory. Death or glory.

There were dissenters within the English team, those who thought this was too brutal, 'not cricket' and wanted the barbarity to stop. Gubby Allen refused to bowl around the wicket short at the body, but still ended with 21 wickets, and still bowled short. He would bowl short, but like the gentleman he was born as, not like a mine-working brute. Hammond and Les Ames were also against it. The Nawab of Pataudi snr, who made a hundred at Sydney, told Jardine he wouldn't field in a leg theory position, Jardine said, 'Ah, I see his highness is a conscientious objector.' War is hell.

That is what almost broke out in Adelaide.

A record crowd turned up for day two of the Test. On the way to the ground England batsman Eddie Paynter had been knocked to the ground, it was assumed, by an irate Australian fan.

The bomb went off when Bill Woodfull was hit. The field had been normal. Fingleton was attacked outside off stump by Allen. The field was set normally for Woodfull. It was just a great short fast accurate ball. He was bent over in pain, clutching at his heart, Jardine simply said, 'Well bowled, Harold.' Other than Laurence Olivier's 'Is it safe?', few lines have ever been so seemingly innocuous, but actually chilling. After Woodfull had finally got his breath back, Larwood was about to come in when the field changed. Arthur Mailey said, 'Just with a nod of his head Jardine signalled his men, and they came across to the leg side like a swarm of hungry sharks.'

When the crowd started booing the field change, the police started planning for a riot. This faux war was now turning dangerous.

Woodfull lost his bat at one stage, then finally his wicket. The crowd booed it all.

On day three, the carnage kept coming. Bill Ponsford, good enough to have a stand named after him at the MCG and a Test average of 48, decided to just turn his back on the ball and let it hit him. Hoping to tire out the English bowlers. In almost four hours of bruises, he put 83 runs on the board. Bert Oldfield, Australia's wicketkeeper, top-edged a ball and fractured his skull.

Woodfull ran out on the ground. How the rest of Adelaide didn't follow him is a mystery.

Australia was very upset at what happened. England was very conflicted. When Warner went into the change-rooms to speak to Woodfull on the close of day two, Woodfull said, 'I don't want to see you, Mr Warner. There are two teams out there; one is trying to play cricket and the other is not. The matter is in your hands, Mr Warner, and I have nothing further to say to you. Good afternoon.'

Woodfull never really considered retaliating, even when diplomatic relations were being worried about. At the time that made him a hero. Someone who stood above the barbarity. He had three bowlers he could have brought in.

Right after someone had shouted, 'Get stuck into this ****** Pommie, Gilbert. It was his ******* mob that took all the land from your ******* mob,' Eddie Gilbert smashed a ball into Douglas Jardine in a tour game, giving him a deep purple bruise. Then there was Laurie Nash, one of the few bowlers to throw on purpose, known as a wild thug who was just too mad for the Australian selectors to ever take a gamble on. And Tim Wall, who before the fourth Test took 10 wickets in an innings against New South Wales. In that line-up was Bradman, Fingleton and McCabe. Wall took them all for 36 runs.

Instead, when Jardine set Australia 532 to win, Woodfull carried his bat as the rest of Australia was beaten up. Woodfull had his meaningless, and courageous, moral victory. England won the Test, and the series, 4-1.

It wasn't that Australia had poor bowlers: they had Grimmett and O'Reilly. O'Reilly only took a few less wickets than Larwood in the series. But he couldn't strike psychological blows like Larwood could.

Australia lost. But Bradman still survived. Bradman was still the top scorer, and managed to average 56. Nothing for him, but still more than anyone else, and a successful average in any other batsman's life.

Bradman scored quickly; he took more gambles than usual. He backed away and scored on the off side. His innings weren't precision perfect; they were jittery and fraught with danger. But he took runs from England, and made them worry about his scoring rate. They still got him quicker than ever before, but he took them down as best he could. He was half a Bradman, just your normal run-of-the-mill everyday run machine. England halved him.

The fact that English media went with Jardine's terminology, leg theory, while the Australian press went with Bodyline, meant that back at Lord's, the MCC had no idea what was really happening. As the tactic had never been practised on this scale no one could really imagine what it was like without having seen it. When they did see it, back at home, the MCC knew cricket had gone too far towards batsmen. The laws were changed to help bowlers, to ensure brutality like this wouldn't happen again.

Larwood was injured for 1933, and Jardine continued to captain England. But it was Australia's tour in 1934 that opened up the wounds. The MCC asked Larwood to apologise to Australia; Larwood said, 'I've nothing to apologise for.' He believed Bodyline was a good tactic, and he was only doing what Jardine had asked him to do. And, most importantly, he had won his nation an Ashes.

His last Test was the last Test of Bodyline. He was never selected again. Eventually he would find more love by moving to Australia. A country that once compared his bowling to being publicly stoned embraced Larwood as a legend.

Jardine continued as captain, and even faced the West Indians using Bodyline against him. Some say no one played Bodyline better than Jardine. But the longer he stayed in charge of the side, the more problems it made for the MCC. The MCC was split. Jardine took the gentlemanly option of just stepping down.

The working class man was ignored; the gentleman was politely dealt with. All was right with cricket again.

Bradman had helped Australia through the Depression, and he survived Bodyline. England didn't survive Bradman. They wouldn't ever beat a team with him in it again.

Chapter 20

OFF TO WAR

Towards the end of World War I Adolf Hitler, then a Lance Corporal, bullied a bunch of British prisoners of war to teach him about cricket. It turned out that, like writing, governing, and growing a moustache, Adolf was not much chop when it came to cricket. Hitler thought the sport was soft and too English. He called the pads unmanly and un-German. He wanted a bigger and harder ball, as well as a new motto, 'Ohne Hast, ohne Rast': Unhasting, Unresting. Unfortunately, he never faced Larwood.

The Gentlemen of Worcestershire went on a cricket tour of Germany in 1937. They won all their games and played in the Berlin Olympic stadium that Jesse Owens had used to humiliate Hitler the year before.

In 1935 the West Indies won their first-ever Test series, by defeating England at home. Headley and Constantine made 90 each, and Constantine added five wickets to win the second Test. In the fourth and deciding Test, Headley made 273 out of 535. Constantine slogged some at the end of that innings, and took three wickets in each innings.

It was Learie who took the last wicket to clinch the win.

Four years later those two teams played in the last pre-war Test. They finished the Tests before the war stopped play. Headley made two hundreds at Lord's, and England won the series 1-0. The last batsman out before the war was the great run machine Wally Hammond.

In that last Test Constantine took a five-wicket haul.

Constantine continued to play cricket during the war. As part of his role as a UK government welfare officer, he played in fund-raising matches. Before one game, he went to a hotel he had booked in London, the Imperial. When he arrived they made a fuss about him being black, and offered him only one night, and not the four he had booked. His boss heard and came over, and that's when the manager and manageress started saying, 'We won't have niggers in this hotel.' They eventually backed down and let him stay in a hotel they also owned around the corner.

But Learie wouldn't let it go. He took it to the courts; it made the parliament as well, and made England start confronting its racist atti-tudes. During this time he also worked with West Indian migrants to help them with their work conditions and employment. After the war he coached, commentated and wrote about cricket while he studied law. He went back to Trinidad, ran for parliament and became the Minister for Communication of Trinidad. Constantine became Trinidad's High Commissioner to London. In 1962, he was knighted. Constantine lost his post as High Commissioner after speaking out about a Bristol bus company that would not employ black people.

The House of Lords made him a peer in 1971, the first black man to receive that title. He passed away that year. He was awarded the Trinity Cross, Trinidad's highest honour, and a state funeral. At Westminster Abbey they had a memorial for him.

Think about that: Westminster Abbey had a memorial for a black man who got his chance because he was quick in the covers. The man who felt he was treated as third-class while he played Test cricket. That man helped change a foreign society, and move his country towards independence, spoke out for what he believed in, bowled as quick as the wind, could make a hundred in an hour and was unpassable in the covers. Cricket has had a lot of great men in the covers, but it can only claim one Learie.

When war was about to put a halt to play, one of cricket's final acts was a glorious back-foot straight six into the Vauxhall stand at the Oval. The crowd cheered Learie as they always had.

On 3 September 1939, Britain declared war on Germany. On 1 September the last county match was completed. Sussex were bowled out for 33 in the second innings against Yorkshire. One bowler took seven wickets: Hedley Verity, who had played in Bodyline, and had taken the magical 10/10.

In Catania, Sicily, 1943, shrapnel hit Hedley Verity in the chest. His men stopped to be with him. He gave them one last order: 'Keep going.'

Verity died. Test cricket kept going. Past faux wars. Past real wars.

Chapter 21

DASHING HERO
WAR BUDDIES

URING THE WAR two men, one an Englishman, the other Australian, met in a game of cricket in India. One was playing for East Zone, the other for the Australian services team. One had already played Test cricket and association football. The other had already played first-class cricket and Australian rules football.

It was a friendship that helped England. In post-war Britain, cricket had to step up. It had a role to play. It had to fill the newspapers with something better than the current life, of rubble and rationing. England was once the head of an empire. England was once the heart and darkened lungs of the Industrial Revolution. England had been great.

England now was a shadow of its former self. Its raping of other lands was coming to a close. Its importance as a superpower was gone. The countries it once ruled were taking over for themselves. It was a fading empire. A battered land.

It needed heroes. It needed inspiration. Enter Denis Compton and Keith Miller.

Neville Cardus got as close to explaining this as anyone.

Never have I been so deeply touched on a cricket ground as in this heavenly summer, when I went to Lord's to see a pale-faced crowd, existing on rations, the rocket-bomb still in the ears of most, and see the strain of anxiety and affliction passed from all hearts and shoulders at the sight of Compton in full sail ... each stroke a flick of delight, a propulsion of happy, sane, healthy life. There were no rations in an innings by Compton.

England loved Denis Compton.

English cricket, and England the nation, needed a showman. It needed a sense of humour; it needed a saviour. Compton was all of that. The sort who would take a catch at slip, and then turn around to pretend he'd missed it. He referred to his bowling as a party trick, never mind 622 first-class wickets. That was the man. He scored the opening goal for Arsenal in his first game. He was the man that Brylcreem first gave a hair product contract to. The man.

Years later when composer Tim Rice accepted his Oscar for best song, he thanked Denis Compton in his speech. That's some cricketer.

Compton used to wear long sleeves, but roll them up at the elbows. He batted without a hat. There probably wasn't a kid born in the '40s or '50s who picked up a bat in England and didn't imitate that look. That's not a cricketer, that's an icon.

England loved Keith Miller, too.

Miller was just a boy from rough-and-ready Sunshine in Melbourne. He was going to be a jockey until he grew. Then he became a footballer of note, playing for Victoria. Then he became a cricketer as well.

Miller was everything Bradman wasn't. Fun, flamboyant, devil-may-care, rugged, handsome and easy-going. Bradman thought of cricket as war; Miller fought in the war.

Bradman kept the ball on the ground, and his foot on the throat. Miller hit the ball in the air, and one foot in the air. He was lucky to survive as a fighter pilot during the war. He flew night missions over Germany; bombs landed on cricket fields as he played; and once he had a tank with napalm loaded in it get stuck to his wing, but it didn't explode. Miller loved life. He lived life to the max. He didn't accumulate awards. He gallivanted with royals.

It also didn't hurt that Miller was, by some distance, the greatest all-rounder Australia had ever produced. His bowling was fast, and clever. His batting was aggressive and worry-free, yet he still made almost 3000 runs and seven centuries. Miller could bat top order and take the new ball. And had he cared for stats, he would have averaged lower than

22 with the ball, and higher than 36 with the bat. But he didn't, and that was part of his legend.

This was a movie star, playing a bit of cricket. He was all chin and hair. It was practically illegal to write about him and not say 'dashing'. The man could not take a bad picture. There is one of him in full slog sweep mode, the bat wrapped around him as he watched the ball. It's just perfect. And when he bowled it's almost like he was posing for the camera.

The MCG put up a statue of Keith Miller. It doesn't feel like a statue of a cricketer; it feels like a statue of a superhero.

Miller was the representation of an Australian man of that time. Chiselled, Strapping. Funny. Easy-going. He connected with the English every bit as much, if not more, as he did with Australia. Other than Trumper, Australia has always had a complicated relationship with its greatest cricketers.

Compton and Miller helped heal nations with their deeds, but more importantly with the way they played. They might not have changed the world or righted wrongs, but Miller and Compton were exactly what sport is at its best: not war minus the shooting, but glorious escapism from normal life.

Chapter 22

THE INVINCIBLES

THIS AUSTRALIAN SIDE included the best new-ball duo that had ever lived: Ray Lindwall and Keith Miller. Their opening batsmen were Sid Barnes, who missed his best years during the war, and still averaged 63, and Arthur Morris, who spent a decade as one of the best batsmen in the world. The back-up bowlers were two cunning left-arm quicks, Bill Johnston and Ernie Toshack. They also had the swing of Sam Loxton and his happy hooking. There was also Lindsay Hassett, Neil Harvey's feet and Neil Harvey's hands. And, as he would be at the end of the tour, Sir Donald Bradman.

This was a team.

English cricket, just like English life, was on rations after the war. Surrey had in all probability accidentally given Major Nigel Bennett the captaincy, mistaking him for Major Leo Bennett. They thought it right to keep their original Bennett, despite his lack of cricket skill. But it wasn't like the English team was a bunch of Major Bennetts. Denis Compton. Bill Edrich. Cyril Washbrook. Alec Bedser. Jim Laker. And Len Hutton. They were all there.

But they were individuals against a united Australian team. That team would play 31 matches. They would draw eight. They would lose none. Fifteen of those matches were won by an innings; two were by 10 wickets, another by more than 400 runs. Essex bowled them out in a day. That day Australia made 721. Australia had all five of the *Wisden* Cricketers of the Year. England had five-day Tests for the first time.

There was also a new ball every 55 overs. There was nowhere to hide from this invincible team.

The Invincibles.

Australia won the series 4-0, making their total post war record 7-0, one less than Armstrong's 8-0. They went through a whole tour unbeaten. That was the magic. On the fifth day at Headingley they chased 404 for victory, all on that day. They got there three wickets down. Even with Bedser and Laker bowling 50 overs between them.

Cricket writer Peter English tells a story of Bill Brown walking through the Gabba one day almost 50 years later. Brown only played two Tests in that series, and didn't even make a 50. But fans rushed over to him, just to get a handshake as he walked around. 'A man wearing a straw XXXX sombrero asked his mate why this old guy was getting such special treatment. He quickly understood the three-word reply. "He's an Invincible."'

Despite all that, the single most remembered moment from the whole series was an Australian failure.

The Oval was damp for the last Test. England batted first; England batted badly. They made 52. And then the Australians coasted past their score. A total and complete day of utter humiliation for the team that batted first. A few minutes before stumps, Eric Hollies, the English leg-spinner, took Sid Barnes' wicket. Arthur Morris expected a night-watchman to come in. Instead it was Bradman.

Bradman was 173 not out when the winning runs were hit at Headingley in the Test before. He was in form, even if he wasn't quite the batsman he had been before. But this was different. This was, with Australia already well in the lead with nine wickets in hand, very likely to be the last innings he ever played. England captain Norman Yardley walked up and shook Bradman's hand. That was different. Yardley then told his team to give Bradman three cheers, also different. Then Yardley turned to Hollies and said, 'That's all we'll give him – then bowl him out.' That was the same.

Since that day Bradman has said he had no idea that he needed four runs for an average of 100. Which is a surprise, as he played his entire career as if he counted every single run.

Bradman claims he was anxious when he faced the first ball. Hollies was around the wicket, and he had a slingy action. Bradman went back and across, middling the first ball. Bradman claimed he didn't see it. The crowd cheered.

The second ball is a bit wider of the stumps, and fuller. This time Bradman steps forward. It's not a clean step, it's not precise, it's not very Bradman. He flings his hands through the line; it's a drive, of sorts, but he's short of the ball. The bat flings wildly without any certainty of purpose as Bradman loses his balance. A man desperately trying to keep his balance, his back foot anchored, his front foot dancing accidentally. The stumps have been hit. That front foot takes three hops before Bradman turns around. His back foot is still in the crease. Bradman's first step as a normal person, not a Test batsman, is awkward.

Bradman looks to the sky, tucks the bat under his arm. The gloves come off and he walks from the field as if he were a baker playing in a club side. Almost oblivious to the world standing to give him an ovation.

Arthur Morris made 196 at the other end, and was ignored. Eric Hollies said to his teammates, 'Best fucking ball I've bowled all season, and they're clapping him!'

They've been clapping him ever since.

After 1948, as England the country got back on its feet, England had their best era in modern cricket. Perhaps because cricket from the '50s was so boring, England never got the credit for how good they were. New Zealand had Sutcliffe and Reid. Australia had Miller, Davidson, Harvey, Benaud and Lindwall. South Africa had Adcock and Tayfield. The West Indies had Worrell, Hall, Weekes, Walcott and Sobers. And England dominated cricket.

England? Well, they had Fred Trueman. Jim Laker. Denis Compton. Alec Bedser. Ken Barrington. And Len Hutton.

From 1950/51 against New Zealand until 1960 against South Africa, England played 19 series. They lost one. They drew four. This might have been a dour period in cricket, but England ruled the dour world. They out-doured them all.

Every one of those players above has a bunch of books written about them. Most of them have stands, or grounds, named after them. Trueman was the first bowler past 300 wickets; some still claim he was the greatest bowler who ever lived. Hutton had the world record for the highest total, and some said he was as good as Hobbs. Jim Laker once took 19 wickets in a Test Match, and averaged 21 with the ball.

Alec Bedser bowled 106,118 first-class balls, and only left the field once, to vomit, and then came back on. Denis Compton has a stand named after him at Lord's, and a batting average of 56. And Ken Barrington averaged more than Hutton or Compton.

This was the last time anyone could claim that England was the undisputed champion of the world. It had spread this game throughout its empire in its own awkward and pompous way. But the game was no longer England's. Cricket was now a game of its own.

It had a language, a culture and could exist without England.

England will always be the father of cricket. But after World War II, children grew up, new ones were born, and England was just another part of the game.

Chapter 23

LITTLE BROTHER WANTS TO PLAY

NEW ZEALAND WAS still very much the little brother of Test nations. It never felt that more than when it played Australia for the first time.

'We failed and that is all there is to be said,' is how Walter Hadlee put it.

The Basin pitch was wet. The original pitch was so wet it was abandoned. Hadlee – whose son Richard would be a star – decided New Zealand would bat first in this one-off Test in 1946, thinking it was such a slow wicket that Australia's new pace sensations Ray Lindwall and Keith Miller would be of no use. On the verge of lunch, the Kiwis even got themselves to 37 for the loss of only two wickets.

After lunch, Australia used the wet wicket to drown them. 3/37. 4/37. 5/37. 6/37. 7/37. Then, a fight back, of sorts. 8/39. 9/40. 10/42.

New Zealand's lower order was in near binary mode. 1, 0, 0, 0, 1, 2, 1*.

Australia batted a lot better, but they were also caught out on the wet pitch at the start of day two. They declared their innings at 8/199 after Jack Cowie, probably New Zealand's first top class bowler, took 6/40. This allowed New Zealand to make amends. To get some pride in their Tasman derby. They didn't. Yet again they only had two batsmen make double figures. They made it to 54. The match didn't last the full two days.

In his last-ever Test, Tiger Bill O'Reilly took 8/33, and celebrated by throwing his boots out of the change-room window.

Australia did much the same to New Zealand when they played their second Test – 27 years, 8 months and 29 days later. One bad Test and New Zealand had to wait 10,136 days for a rematch.

Much like England and Ireland today, Australia did little to encourage their closest cricketing neighbour. In that time, New Zealand played series in and against every other Test-playing nation. It would take them 40 years to win their first Test series.

It was only years later that this first match against Australia became an actual Test. The Australian team did not wear official blazers; the Australian Cricket Board did everything they could to ensure that no one thought they and New Zealand were in any way equals.

New Zealand cricket got better than it was at the Basin against Australia, but not much better. For 20 years they struggled. Not one of their bowlers would take a 10-wicket haul. Only one would take a hundred wickets, the seamer Dick Motz, who retired with exactly 100 wickets. They never scored more than 500 in a first innings. They barely ever scored more than 400 in a first innings, but they scored less than a hundred in seven first innings.

Their dashing all-rounder John Reid, who could play, once said:

I told a lot of lies. We'd gather as a team and naturally I'd try to be as positive as possible … I'd try to encourage our fellows, to explain that everyone is human, that they all got nervous, had failures. But in the back of your mind there was this knowledge that, all things being equal, we were in for a rough time.

They were rubbish as a team.

While Australia ignored them, England sent second-rate sides, and the rest of the world played them rarely, New Zealand produced someone that people could not ignore.

In 1949 New Zealand went to England and they drew all four Tests. At this time, England didn't deem them worthy of five-day Tests. They saw the Kiwis as a charity case. One man changed that.

In six innings he scored 32, 82, 57, 9, 101, 88 and 54. Not exactly a mountain of runs, but New Zealand didn't lose that series, and on three occasions, this man stonewalled England. His name was Bert Sutcliffe: he was a legend, a champion, and for many years, he was New Zealand cricket.

Sutcliffe was classical, a master of all shots, especially the off drive. It was as if New Zealand cricket had invented a fictional Norse god to come in and save them. No New Zealand cricketer had ever made a mark on Test cricket. The entire country had yet to make a mark. And after 12 Tests, Sutcliffe already had. New Zealand had a player.

The 13th Test was the problem.

Neil Adcock was fast. He was patient zero for South African quick bowling. Adcock had this flock of hair that would stand on end as he hurled the ball in. It was cute. It was the only thing cute about him; the rest of him was terrifying. He bruised everyone he played against. Australia's Colin McDonald once said, 'Tell this bastard I've got a family to go home to.'

This day in Johannesburg, 26 December 1953, Adcock was bowling length balls, at pace, that according to Sutcliffe were going 'almost vertical'. Both New Zealand's openers were hit before they were out. People at the ground talked about the sound the ball made on Sutcliffe's head for years afterwards. Sutcliffe slumped to the ground unconscious.

He got up, and even walked off the ground. As Sutcliffe got to hospital, Lawrie Miller was hit right on the heart, and started spitting blood. Two other players were hit as well. At the hospital, Sutcliffe lost consciousness again.

The image of Sutcliffe going back out to bat at Ellis Park looks more like a war photo than a cricket one. His head is covered in a bandage. There is a huge lump on the back of his neck. According to Richard Boock's *The Last Everyday Hero*, captain Geoff Rabone 'and a couple of first-aid men raced into the middle to readjust the Kiwi's bandages, which had been weeping blood during the exchanges. They eventually decided to tape a white towel around his head.'

Sutcliffe should not have been out on the ground. He was bleeding, had a serious head injury and could have died if he was hit again.

Instead, Sutcliffe hit back. He took on Adcock. He smashed the great Hugh Tayfield. His team wasn't safe, and now neither was any South African bowler. It was a bloody counter-attack. Sutcliffe went past the follow-on with a six.

When the ninth wicket fell, Sutcliffe was left alone, and he and the South Africans started walking off the ground. No one believed New Zealand's number 11 would walk out.

The previous day, Christmas Day, was a rest day. Nothing of note happened in South Africa. Back home in New Zealand there was a massive mud slide at Tangiwai. It took out a bridge. Before anyone could be alerted a train tried to cross the bridge and slammed into Whangaehu River.

The death toll was 151. One of those was Nerissa Love, who was the fiancée of New Zealand seamer Bob Blair. It was Blair who was due to come in at 11. That was the reason that Sutcliffe, and everyone at the ground, assumed the innings was over.

But there was a number 11 batsman. Blair came out while the flags behind him were at half-mast. The ground went silent as he walked on. Sutcliffe put his arm around him.

On the worst day of his life, Blair hit a six. Sutcliffe hit a few more. They put on 33 runs. It is one of the greatest moments in cricket history, and all that happened is a number 11 walked out to bat.

New Zealand still lost the match, but they won something in that Test. Their cricket was finally something more than just turning up and being smashed. It had an identity. Blair, Sutcliffe and many of the others who were injured stood up, even when they had every reason not to. New Zealand may not have been winners, but they weren't losers.

Sutcliffe was never the same again. He never made another hundred against teams with fast bowlers. His average dipped from 50 down to 40. Teams around the world knew that peppering with fast short balls would get to him.

Bert Sutcliffe played 42 Tests. Not one against Australia.

Chapter 24

PAKISTAN EMERGES, AS DOES SOBERS

Pakistan really believed they should have been a Test nation from the time they were a country. It would have made sense. After partition, Gul Mohammad, Abdul Hafeez Kardar and Amir Elahi were ready-made Test players, originally from India. Yet cricket refused them entry.

Pakistan had held their own against the West Indians in 1948. They thought this proved their claim. Not for the first time in cricket, Pakistan misunderstood the pace of the track they were playing on. In 1949 they were rejected by the ICC because they didn't pay a membership fee or have competitive domestic cricket.

MKR Collector, the secretary of the Board of Cricket Control for Pakistan, believed a grave error had been made. When Pakistan beat an MCC team by chasing 288 in the last innings with a 64 from Hanif Mohammad, they won the series 1-0. Collector went to London to plead his case. This time the ICC agreed.

Their first Test was to be against India. Lala Amarnath was India's captain, but he was born in Lahore, now in Pakistan. Cricket now had two intense rivalries, and both started very incestuously.

Pakistan's captain was the Oxford-educated Abdul Kardar. In his younger days Kardar was a dasher. And of course in his younger days, he was an Indian player. According to Osman Samuiddin's *The Unquiet Ones: A History of Pakistan Cricket*, his batting was once described as 'Eastern mistake'. Which was itself a mistake, misheard by the person on the news desk – it should have been 'Eastern mystic'. He was an attacking batsman, and his habit was to run down the wicket and try to smash the first ball of spin for six. So he probably made a few mistakes. As captain of Pakistan he was a tyrant.

India won the toss and batted. Vinoo Mankad failed at the top of the innings, but Vijay Hazare did not. Vijay was another whose best days were eaten up by the war. He played 30 Tests, averaging 47, but his first-class average of 58 and the fact he scored two hundreds in the one Test against the side that was about to be called the Invincibles tells you of his class. But that first innings: that was more important. This was India versus Pakistan, the origin story. And India was 4/76. The men out were heroes of Indian cricket: Mankad, Roy and Amarnath. Vijay just stayed put. By the time he was out, India was almost at 200; he'd only made 76. The tail wagged as they approached 400. Vijay's 76 turned out to be half of what Pakistan would make.

TO BE A VERB

'Vinoo Mankad' started as a proper noun. 'Mankad' became a noun. And a verb. He may have averaged 32 from his left-arm finger-spinners, made Test centuries in England and Australia, and even been a *Wisden* Cricketer of the Year, but this is not why Mankad is known today.

He is known for mankading Australia's Brown. Australians are very carefully taught to hold the bat in your left hand, drag it behind you and then take off for a few steps when the bowler releases. Some batsmen go early. It's easily done. Mankad noticed Brown doing it. In a tour match, he warned Brown, as was the cricketer's protocol, that he was out of his crease. Then Brown did it again. And Mankad mankaded him. Or as the Urban Dictionary defines it: 'A specific run-out dismissal in the game of cricket. When the batsman at the non-striker's is run out by the bowler before the ball is bowled, due to excessive backing up, he is said to have been mankaded.'

Mankad did it again to Brown, on the same tour, in a Test match. The Australian press tried to demonise him. But the Australian players took it for what it was: a mistake by Brown that Mankad capitalised on. And Brown had been warned, again.

That is because of Vinoo Mankad. This is what he should be famous for, not a legal run-out, or even a freakish partnership. He should be famous for this. Not the first wicket; that was a run-out. Not the last wicket – someone else got that – but the other eight. They were all his. Including Hanif Mohammad, who made a third of Pakistan's total. All in all Mankad bowled 47 overs out of the 104.5 overs. In all of those he gave away 52 runs. In the second innings, he added 24.2 overs out of 58.2 overs. And another five wickets. That's 13 for the match. Pakistan made 152, exactly double Vijay's score.

Pakistan would win the next Test, by an innings. The supercool Fazal Mahmood took 12 wickets in the match and Nazar Mohammad made a hundred. But it was the team of Mankad, five wickets, and Vijay, 146 not out, that got the 2-1 lead that India kept. *Wisden* gave the series 508 words. These days, *Wisden* has a whole Indian edition.

Mankad is better than a verb. In India's history, there have been very few all-rounders better than him.

Pakistan progressed quickly. They won their fourth series, and their fifth.

In Bridgetown, they had a harder time. Their honeymoon was long gone. Everton Weekes and Conrad Hunte helped the Windies to 579 runs. In response, Pakistan made 106.

The main destroyer was Roy Gilchrist. Gilchrist was a shocking human being. He was one of the fastest bowlers in the world, and just as aggressive. Gilchrist would bowl off 18 yards if he was getting annoyed. If he was really annoyed, he'd bowl beamers as well, at the batsman's head, especially on flat Indian wickets. In a Test at Nagpur, Indian bats-man AG Kripal Singh smacked three straight boundaries and then had a go at Gilchrist. The next ball Gilchrist intentionally overstepped by metres and delivered a bouncer which hit the batsman on the head and dislodged his turban. Later in life, Gilchrist would attack a player in a Lancashire league with a stump, and also be found guilty of brutal domestic abuse.

Pakistan followed on almost 500 runs behind. At stumps on day three of a six-day match, Pakistan was 1/160. Hanif Mohammad was 61 not out. He expected his captain, still the regal Abdul Kardar, to have a chat to him. He never did. But as he got into bed there was a note from Kardar, which read, 'You are our only hope.'

A day later he was 161 not out. That night, the note said, 'You can do it.'

A day later he was 270 not out. That night, the note said, 'If you can bat until tea tomorrow, the match will be saved.'

A day later, the match was drawn. Hanif had batted for 907 minutes, for 337 runs, more than half of Pakistan's 657. He even won over the West Indian crowd. At first they were as hostile as Gilchrist; by the end they were telling him what ball Gilchrist would bowl next. Gilchrist was made to bowl 41 overs, probably angrier in every spell he bowled.

Hanif would make an even more remarkable score not long after: run out, for 499. According to Hanif, he 'played only one lofted shot in the innings, a straight drive for four'. Bradman had the first-class record at the time, 452; Hanif went past it with an on-drive. Hanif looked at the scoreboard and he was 496, and there were two balls left in the day. He hit the ball to point and there was a misfield, so he went for the second to get himself back on strike. Instead he was run out. But as he left the field, it said he was on 499.

Funny thing is, Hanif's 337 was not the highest score of the series. That belonged to a man who had not yet scored a test ton.

Gary Sobers was in his 17th Test. His highest score was 80. His batting average was 34. And he was 21 years old.

Gary Sobers' next score was 365 not out. Sobers had gone past Len Hutton's Test record.

Wisden described it this way:

Hutton's record score did not survive the tour either, for Garfield Sobers, the 21-year-old West Indies left-hander, making his first Test century in the third Test at Kingston, hit 365 not out in 10 hours eight minutes, three hours twelve minutes less than Hutton took in his innings against Australia at The Oval nearly twenty years previously. Although Pakistan was handicapped by injuries to bowlers, Sobers nevertheless played a brilliant innings.

Sobers' career was well documented, helped along by playing a lot in England, after TV had arrived. His six sixes in an over against Glamorgan's Malcolm Nash is on video; his 254 at the MCG has been much written about. But that 365 not out, a world record that lasted for 36 years, has barely been covered.

Sobers was also the first globetrotting professional cricketer. His job was playing cricket on whatever continent he was needed. He once played in Rhodesia, and said he would have played in South Africa, except for the grief he would have got. On one occasion he had to be convinced to play for his country, as the fee would be less than what he got in English League cricket.

The cricket writer Ray Robinson called Sobers 'evolution's ultimate specimen in cricketers'. Which is ironic, because at birth he had two extra fingers, which he claimed to take off himself. Sobers was raised by his mum in a shack in Bridgetown's Bay Land. It was formerly an area where slaves lived, and was now for the local plantation workers. The local cricket club was for whites only.

As he proved with the 365, and his Test average of 58, the man could bat. And his batting wasn't a bunch of pushing or prodding. The most amazing thing about his batting was that after he smashed the ball he didn't fall over from all the effort he put into the swing. Barry Richards called him cricket's first 360 degree cricketer, not for where he scored, but because his bat would end up after the shot where it began before it: behind his shoulders.

His batting might have been amazing, but Sobers wasn't a batsman. He wasn't even an all-rounder; he was everything. Other than wicket-keeping, Sobers fielded everywhere. In every single position he was great. Old West Indian fans still argue about where he was best in the field. There is a legendary story of him playing league cricket in England where a batsman hit him back over his head, and he called 'leave it to me' and went and caught it. Just in front of the sightscreen.

Then there was the bowling. Sobers could seam and swing it at good pace. And Sobers could spin it. He could spin it with finger-spin, or with wrist-spin. He only ever took six five-wicket hauls, but still ended with 235 wickets.

Sobers could do it all; Sobers did do it all. Sobers was 'a West Indian cricketer, not merely a cricketer from the West Indies', as CLR James once said.

Chapter 25

THE 'W'S

S OBERS WASN'T THE only one. West Indies cricket of that time was something special. Everton Weekes would finish with an average of 56. Clyde Walcott an average of 58. And Frank Worrell, well he averaged 48 and could bowl a bit.

All three of the Ws are greats. All three were born within a mile of each other. All three within 18 months. All three delivered by the same midwife.

Of all the midwives who have helped deliver cricketers, she surely had the softest hands. Her catch of Worrell is one of the most important moments in cricket.

In 1960, black people could not immigrate to Australia. The Maoris of New Zealand were still seven years from having the *Maori Affairs Amendment Act*. Enoch Powell was still working on his racist 'Rivers of Blood' speech back in the UK. The Indo-Pakistani War of 1965 was around the corner. The Caribbean was still a long way from racial equality. And South Africa was firmly in the apartheid era.

The Test-playing world wasn't really in a good place. On top of all that, the West Indies was still picking white captains based largely on their whiteness.

In the 1950s, CLR James and Learie Constantine used their eloquent voices to push for a black captain. These were now two important men, the writer of the Caribbean and the champion turned politician. People were listening. But the most important thing was they had Frank Worrell.

Worrell was black. But he wasn't poor, not in the Garfield Sobers sense of the word. He was well brought up. He was educated at the University of Manchester. He was a smart, distinguished man of the world. A natural diplomat. Plus, he could bat. Neville Cardus wrote 'he never made a crude or an ungrammatical stroke'.

In the cricket world as it was then, Worrell would have been the perfect captain for any nation, had he the right kind of pigment in his skin.

By 1960, the noise had become loud enough, and the time was right. After 12 years in the team, Worrell was named captain for the 1960/61 tour of Australia.

Test Cricket by this point was dull. Really dull. Batsmen batted not to lose their wicket. Bowlers bowled not to give up runs. Captains seemed to push for draws. Cricket was stuck in a rut.

The West Indies were known as a team with a bunch of good players, but not as a good team. They were often accused of playing Calypso cricket. It meant an exciting brand of cricket, but it also meant they were there for good times, not hard graft.

It was this sort of attitude that Worrell was trying to get rid of. He wanted them to play entertaining cricket, but as a team, and for a whole match, without ever giving up. Almost every Test cricket team in the world is divided by class, religion, geography or race, but only the Windies are divided by country as well. Worrell had to bring them together.

Richie Benaud was another natural captain. A leg-spinning all-rounder, and in his own right, a fantastic cricketer. He made 23 first-class hundreds. He took 248 Test wickets at 27. He was one of the greatest all-rounders ever to play for Australia.

Benaud is these days better remembered as the voice of cricket on TV, but he did many other great things for cricket. And if explaining cricket to the world was the best thing he ever did, 60/61 was the second best.

It started when two captains made a pact to play attacking cricket. Richie Benaud said, 'Let's have a good series.' 'Yeah, it should be a lot of fun,' responded Frank Worrell. Stumps on day one at the Gabba, the Windies score was 7/359. Sobers made a hundred. Alan Davidson said, 'If you could get a set-square and cut the gap between the fieldsmen in half – he just kept putting it through the gaps; the centre of the gaps. It was a wonderful innings.' The Windies made 453. Norm O'Neil made 181 for Australia, who ended up with a 52-run lead.

Here the West Indies ran into Alan Davidson. Davidson was a left-arm swing bowler. Until Wasim Akram existed, no one was better with their left arm than Davidson. The ball seemed to act unnaturally out of his hand; it curved around like a video game. His standard ball to a right-hander seemed to leave his hand over the wicket, end up outside off stump, before curling back into the stumps.

In the West Indies second innings, Davidson was swinging it. The West Indies batsmen kept getting in; Davidson kept getting them out. He took six wickets, 11 for the match. Worrell and the gem Rohan Kanhai both made 50s.

Australia was set 233. Soon it was 6/92. At tea on day five, the team still needed the best part of 124 runs. By this point Don Bradman was a selector. He wandered into the change-room to have a cup of tea.

'What's it going to be?'

'Well, we're going for a win,' replied Benaud.

'I'm very pleased to hear it.'

Most teams in world cricket wouldn't take on a challenge like that now, in a far more exciting era. But back then, a side with four wickets and more than a hundred runs needed for the final session, they would have pressed snooze. Instead Benaud and Davidson attacked. The wicket had just started to fall apart. Davidson knew he needed to make a mark, so he smacked the off-spinner Sonny Ramadhin as hard as he could to put the pressure back on the Windies.

The cricket that Benaud and Davidson played would be familiar to anyone who lived through ODI cricket in the '90s. They hit controlled boundaries, dropped the ball at their feet and ran, tried to hit wide of boundary fielders for twos and kept the bowlers honest by rotating the strike. Bob Simpson played in that game, and it was he who coached the Australian team of the '90s that changed how ODIs were played. Benaud and Davidson were 30 years ahead of the game. It was measured slog, run, run, run and repeat.

It was one of those runs that ended Davidson. He wanted to face Wes Hall, as he thought one more hook and 'we'll be home'. Benaud just wanted them in singles. He dropped one out to mid-wicket and took off.

Davidson was slow; Joe Solomon was quick. Run-out. Benaud faced the last of Sobers' over, but couldn't get the strike back. Australia needed six runs off the last over, an eight-ball over. They had Benaud at the crease, and three wickets in hand. Wes Hall was bowling. Wes Hall had been bowling non-stop for what felt like all day.

Wes Hall had perhaps the most intimidating action of all time. His run-up was long. He started with his head down, like he was summoning up some spirit to help him. There was no pace; he was loping. His left shoulder would stay dipping down, as if he was expecting to have to force his way to the wicket. It was an angry run. His right arm would repeatedly cock back, like he had an old revolver in his hand. Each step was quicker and more purposeful than the last. By now he was sprinting, not running. He was about to take off. A leap. Leap is the wrong term. Ballet dancers leap. This was an aerial thrust. He was a fighter jet breaking the sound barrier. He was in mid-air.

Hall's now well above the ground, and he's looking at you, straight at you, with his eyes peering down from this great height, over his strong front arm. His right arm jams out sideways, like it is about to punch someone; an umpire in the wrong position would be decapitated. At the crease all that uncoils instantaneously as he lands in 'maximum pace position'. He hasn't even delivered the ball yet, and he's already beaten you.

They say Wes Hall was only six feet two. No one who ever faced him would say that. Hall was a giant.

It was 5.56pm; this was the last over. Six required off eight balls. Three wickets in hand.

Hall already had four wickets when the last over started. Now he is bowling to Wally Grout, Australia's safe hands behind the stumps, but no great hands when batting. Grout is so nervous he can't find his gloves at one stage; turns out they are in the roll of his pad. Hall hits him. Some say thigh, some say in the chest; what is clear is that Benaud is going to run for anything, and Grout is happy to be off strike.

Five off seven required. Three wickets in hand.

With Benaud on strike, Australia has maintained their control. Worrell had told Hall to cool it on the short balls. But now Hall sees his chance: Benaud is a compulsive hooker; Hall would give him one more chance. Benaud swings hard. There is method but far more madness in his shot. He gets some glove on it and Gerry Alexander takes the catch.

Five off six required. Two wickets in hand.

Ian Meckiff is now on strike. Hall goes full and straight; Meckiff makes contact but Hall almost stops it, and mid-off picks it up. No run.

Five off five required. Two wickets in hand.

Hall slips one down the leg side. Alexander takes it well, but Grout is off for a run. Alexander ignores Grout and throws to Hall, who is standing mid-pitch in front of the stumps. He takes the ball, turns around and throws hard from two metres away, missing the stumps by a metre. At the stumps is a frustrated Worrell, who could have taken the ball easily had Hall got the ball anywhere near him. Worrell just keeps looking from Hall to where the ball went, trying to work out how it had happened.

Four off four required. Two wickets in hand.

Grout gets a straight full ball; he tries to shovel it away. Instead it goes straight up in the air. It is a truly horrible cricket shot worthy of no run. It's up there for so long that Hall can get over to it. Only, so does Kanhai. In the confusion Hall looks like he is going to annihilate Kanhai; instead he just touches him on the head. Hall gets his hands to the ball, but drops it – actually it cannons off him and Grout almost gets a second run. The West Indies have given up two wickets in two balls. 'The Good Lord's gone and left us,' Hall told the square leg umpire Col Hoy.

Three required off three. Two wickets in hand.

Meckiff had looked unlike scoring off his first two balls. Hall goes quick and short. Meckiff now plays the shot Benaud should have played, a controlled pull shot. It should have been four, but Conrad Hunte saves it just inside the fence and sends the ball back as hard as he can. Grout has completed two, but sees a chance to steal the third run. Steal the Test. Alexander loses the throw in the sun, but finds it again. He takes the ball before it gets to the stumps and takes the bails off. Well, the entire middle stump actually. Grout dives. Grout stays down for a while. He slowly gets himself up by doing an exaggerated push-up. He never looks at the umpire. The West Indies are celebrating.

The scores are level. There are two balls remaining. One wicket left.

Lindsay Kline had been very nervous before coming in. During the Sobers' over before this, he had turned to Colin McDonald and asked, 'I won't have to go in, will I?' McDonald assured him, 'No, I don't think so.' Now he is nervously entering the field. He is not only going out there; he is facing the most important ball, or balls, of the match. Frank Worrell says to Wes Hall: 'You know if you bowl a no-ball you'll never be let back into Barbados.' Hall delivers a length ball; Kline defends it on the leg side. He's not sure what to do; Meckiff just runs. Joe Solomon picks up the ball just in front of square leg. He has one stump to hit.

In the words of Joe Solomon:

> The secret is balance, to be four-square steady as I took aim. You see, I was an East Indian country boy from Berbice, in the sticks, and before we could walk we'd be pitching marbles; later we'd steal ripe mangoes by downing them with sharp little flat stones, not aiming at the fruit, of course, but at their stalks.

The rest is in the photo. Tie. The first tie.

The series kept going with great cricket. Australia won the second Test, the West Indies the third.

The fourth was almost as good as the first. Kanhai made a hundred in each innings to give Australia a chase of 460. They never got close. Worrell, Sobers and Hall all took wickets. At 3.39pm, poor Lindsay Kline had to come in again. This time, he had far more than two balls to face. Kline was a handy left-arm wrist-spinner. But in 101 first-class matches he'd never made a 50. He wasn't a ferret, but he wasn't much better than a bunny.

Somehow against the pace of Hall, the skill of Worrell, the endless persistence of Gibbs, the whipping spin of Valentine and Sobers' wrist spin, finger spin, and fast swing, Kline remained. In his whole career he'd only ever passed 10 once before. He was a solid number 11, but a number 11 all the same.

Kline had 101 minutes to face a champion bowling attack. The West Indies ran through their overs; they bowled 905 balls in the day, where modern teams manage 540, with extra time. There were ten straight maidens at one stage. Everything was tried.

Kline ended 15 not out. It was his career-high score. But being not out meant more.

The last over was Wes Hall bowling to Ken 'Slasher' Mackay. Mackay was a son-of-a-bitch player. While this might have been an entertaining series, Slasher was a bloke who played for draws. He could bat a bit, bowl ok, but was mostly there to be a hard bastard. He was there to chew gum, kick ass and take names. Well, chew gum, and stand there. This was a perfect situation for him. He had no back lift, liked to leave the ball and only had two shots, a guide on the off side and a shovel shot to midwicket.

Hall's over took nine minutes. The last ball had Hall aborting his run-up and a spectator coming out on the ground. Then a no-ball that tricked the crowd into thinking the game was over. Then several minutes of trying to get the crowd off the field. Then finally a short ball from Hall that just hit Slasher on the chest. They say Slasher just let it hit him and never stopped chewing his gum.

Australia won the last Test by two wickets. Slasher was again at the crease; he made three from 51 balls.

It was during that tour that Wes Hall had a conversation with Australia's longest serving Prime Minister, Robert Menzies.

Hall told Menzies he wasn't a good guy. That he drank, smoked, like the ladies and yet here he was talking to the Prime Minister of Australia. While Hall had a brother who was a good man. A happily married family man, a doctor, who never missed church. Yet, the black fast bowler told the white politician, he can't come into Australia because of the colour of his skin.

Before Australia had won the series, both boards decided that all Test series between Australia and the West Indies would be for the Frank Worrell Trophy. Worrell hadn't even finished his first-ever tour as captain. In four Tests he had shown what a man he was. Even as they lost that last Test, the Australian crowds cheered them. They laughed when he presented the Frank Worrell trophy to Richie Benaud – after he first wiped it with his blazer. He and his team received a standing ovation as they walked off the MCG.

But Melbourne kept giving. They had a street parade for the West Indian team. Half a million people were reported to be on those streets as the West Indians were brought through them – one-quarter of the population. It would be a further six years before Australia would count its own Indigenous people on a census. Yet the city stopped and applauded this team. They applauded that series. They applauded Frank Worrell.

Worrell retired soon after. He would run a university. He would be a Jamaican senator. But at 42, the world lost him. It was one of the few times he never made it to 50.

Worrell had changed the way his team played. He had changed the way his team was lead. He had changed the sport itself. And changed the country he played against.

Chapter 26

THE SAD STORY OF
SOUTH AFRICA

I n 1961, the Commonwealth status of South Africa was revoked.
Under ICC regulations, they should not have been able to play in Test
Cricket. But teams went on playing them. Well, New Zealand, Australia
and England played them home and away. They were part of the club.
But South Africa would not play India, Pakistan or the West Indies.

In 1964 South Africa was banned from the Olympics. Then in 1966,
banned from the Football World Cup. An All Blacks Rugby Union team
was supposed to tour there that same year. When the South African government asked that they send an all-white team, the All Blacks cancelled
the tour.

But the Australian cricket team visited in 1966/67. The South
Africans considered Australia world champion, which was arguable.
South Africa won 3-1. Their first-ever series victory over Australia. Three
years later Australia would be back there. South Africa did not play a
series in between.

The three main South African bowlers – Trevor Goddard, Mike
Procter and Eddie Barlow – averaged 16, 17 and 21. The fourth bowler
was Peter Pollock. Pollock once said, 'When you are above a certain pace,
every batsman is a bit wary of you. People get out of the line.' Pollock
was above that pace. His brother Graeme also played ok in that series.

The other match-winner was wicketkeeper Denis Lindsay. In his first
innings he came in at 5/41, and made a 50. In the second, with South

Africa only 140 in front, he put on 182, the lead went over 400 and the Test was won. In the second Test he came in after the follow-on, with South Africa 4/64, and made an 81 that scared the Australians a bit in their only victory. In the third, he was in again at 4/83 and made 137 out of 300. In the fourth, he made 131 in 101 minutes. Australia never went past 150 in either innings and was saved by the rain. It was only the fifth where he failed; Australia still lost.

Lindsay played the sort of carefree innings you can when your career isn't completely dependent on batting, much as Australia's Adam Gilchrist later did. In his career up until that point he had scored 415 runs; in that series alone he managed 606. It's still a world record for keepers.

Australia was still the team to beat when they arrived in 1969. They came straight from India and looked ghostly upon arrival. Graham McKenzie, who many thought the best bowler in the world, was struggling with a virus he picked up in India. Procter called them the 'unofficial world champions'. Ian Chappell was thought to be the best batsman in the world. Chappell had scored well against England, smashed the West Indies and in India he'd done very well. All the time he was arrogant and aggressive, the perfect Australian number three.

South Africa still had the same bowling line-up. They still had Lindsay. They still had Graeme Pollock. But they added to it. They added a Barry Richards, a Lee Irvine and a Colin Bland.

Bland would end his career with an average of 49. That would be the thing that most people would refer to when you retire, but not for Bland. Lindsay might have been the prototype keeper batsman; Bland was the prototype cover fielder.

In an era not known for its fielding, Bland was worth between 20 to 30 runs at cover. He was like the Flash: all you saw was a blur, but that meant stand your ground. When fans would watch the team train, Bland would put on a stump-hitting clinic to entertain them.

Other than spin, you could pretty much take a skill and South Africa had the master of it.

In Barlow, Goddard and Procter, they had three of best all-rounders in the world. Barlow averaged 45 with the bat, 34 with the ball. Goddard 34 and 26. And Procter? Well, Procter was 25 with the bat, and 15 with the ball. He only played seven Tests.

Procter bowled chest front on, holding the ball in both hands, and then a windmill action. It was like he bowled the ball twice, and off the wrong foot both times. Even if he did bowl two balls, you still wouldn't have hit either of them. Procter wasn't tall; he was shoulders, neck and talent. Procter was faster than most bowlers, more talented than most bowlers and he had an action that freaked people out. He would bowl right arm around the wicket and swing the ball back in to right handers. Because he was Mike Procter.

Then there was Peter Pollock. He was the quickest bowler in the world by this point. Pure pace, height and an out-swinger. Pollock took his wickets at 17. Which, compared to Procter's 13, looked expensive.

This was a great attack. Ian Chappell averaged only 11 in the series.

The only time South Africa was not in control was brief, when John Gleeson was bowling. As with most mystery bowlers, they are generally only ever good when you don't know what they are doing.

Part of the problem is that batsmen read bowlers for a living. They will find the weakness. With Gleeson, it is said that the English had a huge problem picking him, but Basil D'Oliviera worked him out, and happily went down to tell Geoff Boycott what he learned. 'I worked it out in the second Test,' Boycott replied. 'But don't tell those buggers in the dressing-room.' Boycott denies that story; he also denies ever truly picking Gleeson. As the story plays into the reputation of both men, it continues to be spread.

In the first Test the South Africans simply didn't know which way he was spinning it. Ali Bacher gave up and just slogged him. But that wasn't going to last forever. One batsman, in his first Test, had only faced him for a few balls, but he'd worked him out. As Bacher tells it, 'That night at the team meeting, Barry told us that if Gleeson had a lot of fingers over the ball, it was the leg-break, and if you only saw thumb and index finger, it was the off-break. That just showed the genius of Barry.'

The genius of Barry Richards was something else.

At Kingsmead the world would see it. Bacher played a trick on Bill Lawry, asking him to go out early for the toss. Lawry did so, won the toss, took one look at the grassy pitch, and decided to bowl. Lawry was excited, until he saw the South Africans mowing the pitch.

Richards went about smashing the Australians everywhere. Everything went to the boundary, no matter where it came from, or from whom.

Richards is tall and elegant at the crease. His feet close together, his front elbow pointing at the bowler. His hands seem to work on a level that no one else's ever could.

In this knock, Australia were so worried they started stalling before lunch. Lawry, sensing that Richards might make his hundred, dropped down to take a very long time sorting out his shoelaces. Richards was 94 at lunch. South Africa were 2/126.

After lunch Richards was joined by Graeme Pollock. Graeme Pollock's Twitter profile reads thus: 'I am the South African Cricket Legend of the Century and I retired as the second most successful Test batsman ever with an average exceeding 60 runs.' The Australians didn't need that introduction; they had seen Pollock on the tour before. In one innings he'd made 209 out of 353.

Now he was batting with Richards. Australian Paul Sheehan, one of the few fielders almost as good as Bland, said that when Pollock came in that day he seemed to say, 'You have seen the apprentice. Now look at the master.' Bacher saw it too: 'Graeme had watched Barry bat supremely. He saw the centre stage was taken. Being a great batsman he would never say it, but I could sense him thinking aloud to himself, "That is great batting. I could do the same if not better."'

In the hour after lunch at Kingsmead, the fans in the ground – the whites, who were supporting South Africa, and everyone else, who was supporting Australia – saw perhaps the best hour of batting in Test match history. Pollock and Richards put on 103, in an hour. This tired, under-manned, poor Australian bowling attack was fodder, nothing more. The quick hands of Richards and the heavy strokes of Pollock built a batting monument in the middle of the ground.

Richards made 140, out of the 229. Barlow went in next: 'After the Lord Mayor's show, there was no room for me out there. I was embarrassed. Those two have made a mockery of batting.' Pollock stayed in.

Ian Chappell sensed this could get ugly. 'We've got a problem here, mate,' he told his skipper Lawry. He pointed to Pollock. 'This bastard is going to see how many Barry gets and then he is going to double it.' Lawry tried four men in the covers; Pollock went through them. He tried 7-2 fields; Pollock ignored them. Sheehan was in the ring. 'There were four fieldsmen on the off side, trying desperately to stop drives that were splitting the gaps and racing away to the fence. I don't think I am imagining this, but some of those drives hit the pickets so quickly and bounced back almost to where you were fielding, so you did not need to run too far to get the damn thing.'

Pollock went past the South African record; he broke a partnership record with Tiger Lance as well. But 274 was not enough. He was still disappointed he didn't get the three hundred. Pollock would end that series with a Test average of 60. Of those who played more than 20 Tests, he is second. He played his last Test before his 26th birthday.

Don Bradman said Pollock was the best left-hander he ever saw. Others said no one ever counted out an over better than Pollock. A four, a two, and then a single off the last one. Milk the bowling, keep the strike. He might have been the best batsman other than Bradman, or that might have been Richards. But we'll never know.

•

Newlands Cricket Ground is in the shadow of Table Mountain. On the other side of the mountain is the city of Cape Town, the beach and the South Atlantic ocean. Ten kilometres away is Robben Island, where Nelson Mandela was held.

When England toured in 1956/57, a man walked seven miles to get to Newlands to watch his country play. He walked through a city that was set up to keep him down. He walked, because people like him had to walk. When he arrived at the ground, he stood in the segregated part of the ground. The area that was for people of his colour.

We don't know when this man was born, but we know that in '56/57 he would have been in his prime. We've heard rumours, stories and fables. But we were not allowed to see him, and he was not allowed to play. Because this man was standing where he was because of *swart gevaar*. The black threat.

South Africa was a place where people rushed to find gold and diamonds. In that stand, under the sign for coloureds, watching a team that didn't represent his country, was one of the many precious commodities that South Africa ignored.

Basil D'Oliveira. Dolly.

As *Wisden* said, 'The man himself was not a secular saint or a political campaigner: he was, above all else, a cricketer.'

Learning to play on the streets and then moving into his father's cricket side made D'Oliveira like thousands of players before and after him. But he was different. He was a cricket champion wrapped in the wrong skin. Instead of smashing first-class runs, he dominated the non-white cricket leagues.

D'Oliveira could really hit the ball. He didn't make runs; he dominated teams. He was the captain of non-white South Africa, the best of the ignored. The West Indies was supposed to tour with Frank Worrell to play against the non-white team. The tour was cancelled. It was then that D'Oliveira almost gave up cricket.

There was no reason to keep playing. There was nothing left for him to do. He couldn't make a living from it. He couldn't represent his country.

Luckily a letter that he had sent to John Arlott, the English writer and broadcaster, about playing professionally was passed on to the right people. Lancashire journalist John Kay heard that Middleton in the Lancashire Leagues was desperate for a player. The money was £450 for a year; £200 of that would go on his fare out there. D'Oliveira had a wife and a young kid, but like Learie Constantine before him, cricket was his hope of a better life.

He failed in his first five innings, barely spoke the language and the weather didn't warm him up. Then he found runs. Soon he was producing at such a level that he was making more than Sobers. He had a career.

Cyril Washbrook, then running Lancashire, wrote him off as 'a Saturday afternoon slogger', but season after season the slogger made runs. D'Oliveira spent a year qualifying in Worcestershire and then played his first season for them and made 1691 runs that summer. Not bad for a slogger. The next year he was in England's team to play the West Indies.

D'Oliveira did all this while lying about his age. He was born in either 1935, 33, 31 or even 27. This unwanted liar started his career well. After 10 Tests D'Oliveira was averaging 50. Age did not weary him, whatever his age was.

England toured the West Indies in 1968. D'Oliveira had his first real slump. Charlie Griffith and Wes Hall were there, but it wasn't the express pace that worried him; he failed against all the bowlers. Only one fifty on the whole tour. D'Oliveira struggled with the pressure at this point; he took to drinking and partying, and some in the West Indies called him a sell-out for playing in a white team.

On top of all that, at the end of the next summer, there was supposed to be an English tour to South Africa.

The South African government were very worried about D'Oliveira. They even had a secret dossier made on him, and he was watched closely at all times. They knew that they couldn't allow a coloured player to come back to South Africa and play in another team. To humiliate them, to spite them.

The South Africans also didn't want anyone to know that they didn't want him to tour. They hatched a plan to bribe D'Oliveira. Or secretly get to the MCC selectors and convince them not to pick him if they wanted the tour to go ahead. By South African government, we're not talking some lowly clerk: this was all BJ Vorster, the South African Prime Minister.

Think of this. In early 1968, with all that was going on the world – Vietnam war, the events in Paris, black power Olympians, the Martin Luther King assassination, the USSR invading the Czech Republic – and the leader of a country that was in turmoil amid trade sanctions was getting county cricket scores for political reasons.

Those reports were probably that D'Oliveira was working hard on his batting. He knew he hadn't performed in the West Indies, and he worked hard to ensure his batting was back in top form. He did enough to keep his spot in the first Test. In that match he took two wickets, and scored an undefeated 87 against Australia.

On the morning of the second Test D'Oliveira was dropped.

Two men, one being journalist EW Swanton, came to D'Oliveira and suggested he pull out of the tour to South Africa. He dismissed both men and went about his duty as 12th man before heading back to county cricket. D'Oliveira lost all form and averaged 12 in this period as the stress got to him. England managed to draw the second, third and fourth Tests.

The MCC contacted the top 30 cricketers in the country to see if they were available for the South African tour. D'Oliveira was not contacted. That must have been the worst 87 in Test cricket history to get him dropped out of the best 30 players in the country.

Then D'Oliveira was offered a £4000 coaching contract through a South African tobacco company. It was massive money for a man in his position who was out of the team. He talked about it with his agent, the legendary newsman Reg Hayter, and they decided that he was so close to the squad that he would be silly to make a decision beforehand.

An injury to a teammate earned him a call-up for the fifth Test. At 4/238, he entered the match. It was just before stumps. A huge Oval crowd was watching. The MCC was watching. The South African PM was waiting. Everyone wanted to see what would happen next.

D'Oliveira hooked. And made it to stumps 23 not out.

The next day, he was dropped on 31. But his partner, John Edrich, and the umpire Charlie Elliott both encouraged him. As he made his 50, Elliott whispered to him, 'Well played – my God you're going to cause some problems.' Once set, he did what he had always done – played aggressively – and made 158.

The message was passed to the MCC from South Africa immediately: 'Today's centurion is picked, the tour will be off.'

England won the Test; D'Oliveira broke a tricky sixth-wicket partnership as well. Doug Insole, the MCC chairman of selectors, asked D'Oliveira if he was available to tour South Africa. Cowdrey made it clear he wanted him in his team. It now looked like he would have to be picked to play against his old country.

There were up to 10 people in the selection meeting. No one showed support for D'Oliveira's selection. His Test batting average was 48. His bowling was handy. But he was not picked.

In Peter Oborne's book *Basil D'Oliveira: Cricket and Controversy*, he writes that if you judge this as a cricket decision it was 'not an outrage'. Certain newspapers even backed the decision. Not, oddly, EW Swanton, and not, obviously, Learie Constantine. Oborne is right. But it was odd, and suspicious.

Then another player, Tim Cartwright, pulled out of the squad, possibly injured – and D'Oliveira was in. Oborne believes the MCC 'had had enough and were bowing to public opinion'.

BJ Vorster told a rally of fellow racists, 'We are and always have been prepared to play host to the MCC … [we] are not prepared to receive a team thrust upon us by people whose interests are not the game, but to gain certain political objectives which they do not even attempt to hide.'

The MCC cancelled the 1968/69 tour.

What should have happened after this was that all teams stopped playing South Africa. But as you now already know, Australia went there the following year.

South Africa weren't so much banned from cricket. Tours just dried up.

Basil D'Oliveira took 551 first-class wickets at 27. But we never saw the best of him. He once said of his time in South Africa, 'I was some player then. I was over the hill when I came to England.'

Racism stopped Jack Marsh from playing for Australia, George Headley leading his country and D'Oliveira representing his.

Racism also denied the rest of the world the opportunity to see how good the South African team of 1970 was. Mike Procter can see the silver lining though. 'If 44 million people's lives were improved by us not playing cricket for 22 years, then it was worth it.'

Chapter 27

ABORIGINAL CRICKET

Racism was not exclusively South African. Indigenous Australian cricketers had existed from the time cricket did in Australia. The first Australian tour of England in 1868 was by an Indigenous team. Tom Wills, the creator of Australian rules football, was to lead them, but got arrested in Sydney.

Englishman Charles Lawrence, who had been on England's first tour of Australia, took over the Australian Native XI team.

His teammates were Dick-a-Dick Jungunjinanuke, Peter Arrahmunijarrimun, Johnny Mullagh Unaarrimin, Cuzens Zellanach, Sundown Ballrinjarrimin, King Cole Brippokei, Tiger Bonmbarngeet, Red Cap Brimbunyah, Bullocky Bullchanach, Mosquito Grougarrong, Jim Crow Jallachmurrimin, Twopenny Murrumgunarriman and Charley Dumas Pripumuarraman. The most notable name was Dick-a-Dick. But the most stunning is Jim Crow Jallachmurrimin. At the time Jim Crow was a racial slur for black Americans from the South.

The best player was Johnny Mullagh Unaarrimin. A proper all-rounder, he made 1698 runs at 23.65 and took 245 wickets at 10. Unaarrimin was a real player, and he helped carry the team, along with Lawrence, through most matches.

People didn't just come to watch this team play cricket; they also wanted to see the entire Indigenous experience. A cricket match, and a tribal experience. During the breaks and after play, they received a lesson in Indigenous ways.

Unaarrimin smacked a crowd member in the face with a boomerang in Liverpool, 'injuring his brow'. Dick-a-Dick Jungunjinanuke was the true star of these pursuits. To entertain, and to collect a bit more coin, Jungunjinanuke would challenge people to piff balls at him, which he would deflect with a boomerang and shield from 10 paces. You would be rewarded if you hit him, which, according to legend, happened only once on the entire tour. But not, oddly, the time seven men threw at him in unison. At Lord's, ever the showman, he had 10 top hats thrown at him.

The players also threw spears, but were beaten by WG Grace in a cricket ball throwing contest. The team played in 47 matches throughout England during the six months they were there. Their record was 14 wins, 14 losses and 19 draws. Australia has had worse tours. With Unaarrimin being a genuine superstar, with one English player saying he'd never bowled to anyone better, and the 14 wins, you would assume that Indigenous cricket would grow and grow. That never happened.

This tour was either ignored, or just downplayed for years. It was largely due to the name and mouth of Ian Chappell, the writing of former Australian off-spinner Ashley Mallet and the book *Cricket Walkabout* by John Mulvaney and Rex Harcourt that these men eventually got their due. When Chappell originally made a call for them to be officially recognised as Australian cricketers, many laughed, and a few more thought it was a terrible call.

By the strict interpretation of Clarence Moody's now official Test matches, these men were not Australian cricketers. But they deserved some recognition, so more than 130 years after their tour, the members of the Australian Native XI were inducted into Australian Cricket's Hall of Fame.

Eddie Gilbert, as we learned, never played a test. Jason Gillespie is the only Australian Test player to be Indigenous.

Chapter 28

MULTILINGUAL COOL CAT CREATES SPIN SYMPHONY

THE NAWAB OF Pataudi had a son, Mansoor Ali Khan Pataudi. When the nawab died in a polo accident, his son became the nawab, at age 11. At age 21, the son became the captain of India.

Six months before Pataudi junior's Test debut, a shard of glass from a car accident rendered him a one-eyed batsman. Those who saw him bat say he was never truly the same afterwards. He would bat with his hat over the bad eye. It didn't stop him from making a Test double hundred. It also didn't stop him from coming out at the MCG on a green top in 1967, at 5/25, with a pulled hamstring that didn't allow him to play front-foot shots and hooking Australia for a 75 in the first innings and a 54 in the second.

Those innings were just part of the legend of Tiger Pataudi. As a young cricketer Frank Woolley coached him. Tiger studied at Oxford. He spoke French and Arabic. His wife was an actress. Perhaps the coolest photograph of a cricketer ever is one of Tiger standing on a balcony. It could be James Dean or Idris Elba looking out over the Brighton shore, but it's Tiger. Tiger was a movie star, even without the acting.

In 1967 England beat Tiger's India 3-0. India was used to losing to England. Unlike Australia, England might have played all the Test nations quite regularly, but they still looked down on them. *Wisden* certainly didn't take the smaller countries seriously, and that was certainly how many English fans felt.

India the country was still trying to find its way. England had owned it, separated it, and milked it, and now India was trying to make one nation out of hundreds of societies. This was still a fresh young country trying to live within the English rules by which they thought they had to abide, while trying to work out what India actually meant. People knew what it meant to be Tamil, Punjabi or Bengali, but what was it to be Indian?

The cricket team was much the same. They were playing the game the way England had played it. Their batsmen were defensive and their bowlers were mostly seamers or all-rounders. They were polite and resolute, more dour than dashing. Cricket was the national game, but it was still the game England gave them, not their own creation.

Australia, England and the West Indies all had fast bowling weapons of mass destruction. Tiger Pataudi did not.

What Pataudi did have was spin, more spin than most, and better spin than most. He had a swarm of spin. Compared to being bombed by pace bowlers, this was like being killed with art. Overwhelmed by beauty.

In the third Test at Edgbaston, India lost by 132 runs. India had played four spinners. EAS Prasanna, Srinivasaraghavan Venkataraghavan, BS Chandrasekhar and Bishan Singh Bedi. It would be the only time all four played in a Test match together. But they would be known as a quartet from then onwards. Or, The Quartet.

Most teams at this point would use the spinner as one of their four bowlers. Like having a plate of steak, sausage and chops, and then having a piece of broccoli in the corner. You know you need it, but no one really wanted it.

Except Tiger Pataudi.

He used spinners, whether home or away, like other teams used pace. The Tiger made Indian cricket. Instead of picking club-level seamers, he used Test-level spinners and just backed them. It couldn't always work – it didn't always work – but India had their first good run in Test cricket.

Prasanna was a planner, a schemer. After his early Tests he went off to study and get a degree. He was the brains of the operation. He moved batsmen where he wanted them: when they came down the wicket at him it was seemingly of their own will, but it was more because he had dragged them out. When they came down, or played the big shot, the ball they thought was there, wasn't. It had dropped or drifted. His arm ball seemingly had a mind of its own, wobbling off outside the batsman's grasp. He was an off-spinner by title, but he was more a fancy conman.

Chandrasekhar had polio when he was a kid, and this withered his right arm. But his arm certainly fought back, because as a leg-spinner he was quick, and most of that was his frenzied last-second whip. His hero was Richie Benaud. When he bowled a good delivery, it was unplayable, zipping off the surface. He only needed to beat you slightly at his pace and you were gone. In a quartet of spin, he was the only leggie. The others were more reliable; he was more exciting.

Venkat had an 18-year Test career. If one of The Quartet had to miss, it was generally him. Playing as a spinner, and coming in and out of the side, is one of the hardest skills to master. Venkat certainly did. It wasn't uncommon for him to only play one Test in a year. But he was a class act, and a quality bowler, the Ringo Starr of this group.

Bishen Bedi was a dream. He would gently amble up to the crease and cure the ball down to leg and straighten it to off. It was as if he floated to the crease and delivered whispers. It was so pure, you felt like you could drink it. It looked so easy, too. You would see a bunch of kids watching him and running back to the *maidan* or park to try it them-selves. Bedi would bowl all day, with only small changes in pace or flight. As a captain you just pressed play and watched him go.

India had beaten New Zealand and then travelled to the West Indies and won there. It was clear that this new way of playing was suiting them.

India had been playing Test cricket for 40 years, but they hadn't beaten England. Due to their constant struggles, they were only given a three-Test series when they arrived in 1971. England had just won the Ashes thanks to John Snow. They had also beaten Pakistan. They were a decent side.

It was a series that had Geoff Boycott and Sunil Gavaskar opening the batting. These two men would end up with 8114 and 10,122 runs in Test cricket respectively. Both men batted like nothing else mattered. These were two men who took little joy out of anything other than staying at the wicket. And considering the great bowling era they lived through, few in the history of the game did it better than them.

In the first Test, India had played well, and the biggest moment was when Snow clashed with Gavaskar. Snow was suspended. Gavaskar spent a career clashing with people. India was to chase 183 in the final innings. Gavaskar made 53, but no one else made runs, and they ended up limping to stumps on day five with two wickets in hand (one was Chandra, and he really couldn't bat), still needing 40 odd runs. England had the better of the second Test as well, and would have won it had it not rained on the last day.

This draw took India's record to six draws and 15 losses from 21 Tests against England.

At the Oval, England batted well in the first innings, and India struggled, but their tail did some damage and they ended up only 71 runs behind. Day two had been rained out. The crowds had been low and most people assumed there would be a third and final draw.

India was using the Venkat, Chandra and Bedi section of their quartet. Before lunch on day four, the English openers were batting fine when Brian Luckhurst smashed back a drive that Chandra accidentally knocked back onto the stumps, running out John Jameson. The score was 23. With the score on 24, Chandra bowled his quicker ball; John Edrich never got around to playing his shot before he was bowled. Next ball Keith Fletcher was out as well.

After lunch, India's captain Ajit Wadekar brought all the catchers around the bat. Leg slips, duelling short legs, short cover traps, deep slips for Chandra: he had them all. And England just couldn't handle it. They had struggled with the spin all series, but had just been better than the Indian batsmen. Now, when the pressure was on, with fielders around the bat, they all disappeared. England made 101. It was their lowest total against India.

On a pitch with no real spin, no freakish bounce, and no natural variation, the Indian Quartet had blasted out England, with guile. Chandra took 6/38 on his own. To Indian fans, to India, Chandra brought down an empire.

India needed 174, and they played like a side who was not playing against a Test opposition, but against a country that had enslaved and divided them. Their innings took more than 100 overs. They sat and waited, rather than dashed and took. Farokh Engineer, the stylish keeper and Brylcreem hair model slogged a few around, and S Abid Ali, one of their forgotten seamers, scored the winning run.

The ball never got to the boundary: the Indians in the crowd had surged onto the field. India had won the Test. India had won the series. They had beaten England. They had beaten their masters.

They were a country that looked after their own future. They were a cricket nation that played the game their way.

Tiger didn't even play in that series. But it was the team he created.

Chapter 29

JUST ANOTHER DAY IN CRICKET

Watching so and turning around
each moment's passing form
searching slow the mental loft,
looking for life's downy nape,
gently resting in safe harbour
after rounding storm-swept cape
– John Snow

Jenner is hit on the head. Jenner getting a short delivery outside the line of leg stump, he backed away towards square-leg, the ball followed him across and hit him on the head, just above the left ear, and I can see blood starting to come out of that wound.
– ABC Commentary

TERRY JENNER'S HEAD is bleeding on the SCG pitch. The ball has flown to cover. Cover. The crowd is booing. The umpire warns John Snow for short-pitched bowling. He takes his cap and walks towards the boundary as the crowd hoot and holler. Cans of beer, some empty, some full, are thrown in his direction. Snow sees some English fans and nods his head before taking up his spot on the boundary.

Trevor Guy is so incensed, angry, pissed off, belly-full of rage, that he reaches out and grabs Snow. Guy is an Australian fan. Just a bloke on the boundary, a few cans in. He swings at Snow with the sort of punch people pretending to be drunk in westerns threw. Three English fans drag him back. Snow leaves the boundary. England leaves the ground.

Umpire Lou Rowan says it is safe to continue. The sight-screen attendant is hit on the back of the head by a bottle and has to be taken to hospital. Just another bad decision by Rowan.

England would come back out. Jenner would come back out. England wins the Test. England wins the series. England would not get an LBW on the entire tour. Snow would get 31 wickets. Tailenders now got bounced. No one is safe.

Snow was a proper fast bowler; he had less trouble with batsmen than he did administrators. He once knocked over Sunil Gavaskar when trying to stop a run off his bowling. Another time he ripped Gavaskar's necklace off with a bouncer. He never met a captain he didn't argue with. He never met a batsman he didn't want to bounce. John Snow also wrote poetry.

As the tireless online historian at Cricketcountry.com, Arunabha Sengupta, once said, 'John Snow was the cricketing equivalent of those samurai swordsmen who easily exchanged weapons for the calligraphic brush. He was a fast-bowling poet, with two collections of poetry: *Contrasts*, published in 1971, and *Moments and Thoughts*, in 1973.' If he was a samurai, he would have thought deeply about his actions, right after he sliced you open.

Another book of Snow's was called *Cricket Rebel*, and he certainly lived up to that title. But Snow was no more scary to face than Neil Adcock, Wes Hall or Fiery Fred Trueman. It was just now that some of the niceties of cricket were passing. There was an unwritten code that fast leg theory would not be bowled again after Bodyline. That had long gone. Then there was a bowler's code that they wouldn't bounce each other. That was being eroded as well. Test cricket was no longer for gentlemen and professionals. It was now for survivors.

It was that same 1970/71 series that two other important things happened. The first one-day international was played. In 1962, Michael Turner, the secretary of Leicestershire, came up with an idea for a knockout tournament of cricket where both teams were limited to 65 overs a side. Cricket had often played one-day games, but no one had ever used a limit on the overs. The Midlands Knockout Competition was a success, and the next year England played a countywide competition, the Gillette Cup.

One-day cricket was not a worldwide success, but it did seem to be working. So when a Test match in Melbourne was ruined by rain, the two teams faced up in an ODI on 5 January 1971. The ball was red, the overs had eight balls and the kits were white.

Graham McKenzie bowled the first delivery to Geoff Boycott. Bill Lawry faced the first ball for Australia. One-day cricket didn't exactly start with a bang. Australia won with 6.2 overs in hand. *Wisden* did not carry a report of the game.

Lawry didn't last the summer as captain. He was the first Australian captain to be dumped mid-tour, after a draw in Adelaide. Lawry found out from fellow Victorian Keith Stackpole, who heard from an ex-player, who probably heard from some bloke at the pub. Australia was only 0-1, they held the Ashes, and a win in Sydney would save them. Lawry was also one of the best batsmen in the team, averaging 40 that series.

They called Lawry the Corpse with Pads, and in that series his runs were coming at 13 an hour.

The real reason that Lawry was gone went back to the dispute over play and conditions during the previous two tours to India and South Africa. The players stayed in horrible hotels in India. They had two long series scheduled back to back, and they were massively underpaid. Lawry and the team had refused to play in the fifth, and extra, Test against South Africa to make a stand.

'It was a grab for money,' Lawry said of the board. 'South Africa was leading 4-0. The board said, no you won't. It was typical of the board, unfortunately. We would probably have been beaten 5-0 but we were prepared to play if they were prepared to pay us a reasonable amount of money, which we weren't getting at the time.' The board was ice cold, and said: 'If you don't play for us, who will you play for?'

Chapter 30

THE WOMAN WHO CREATED THE WORLD CUP

MEN WEREN'T BEING paid enough. Women weren't paid at all. In fact, they paid to play. The latest ICC rights deal to televise cricket fetched a reported US$1.9 billion. But the first World Cup started after a conversation with an England captain over a glass of sherry. That captain was Rachael Heyhoe-Flint. In 1973, two years before the men, the women played in the first World Cup. Unshackled to a bunch of conservative men who merely wanted to keep traditions and good chairs in their various long rooms, women's cricket might have been broke and ignored, but it was also nimble. The teams were Australia, New Zealand, Jamaica, Trinidad and Tobago, England, Young England and an International XI. Women's cricket has had great players, and even of recent times, some great teams, but it has always lacked depth. At this stage, it lacked teams. And coverage.

Heyhoe-Flint and the other players went around town putting up banners. She also tried to drum up as much media attention as she could. It was tough. The first game was between New Zealand and Bermuda. It rained, and no one turned up to watch it.

In the 1973 final, England's Enid Bakewell smashed 118 and Australia never had a chance. Heyhoe-Flint bowled the last over. As she walked back to her mark all the fielders had moved back to the boundary as a joke. A few minutes later she would lift cricket's first ever World Cup, given to her by Princess Anne.

It would be two years until the West Indies men would lift the men's equivalent.

Heyhoe-Flint hit the first six in a women's Test. She batted for 521 minutes in making a world record 179 against Australia at The Oval to draw a Test. She averaged 45 in Tests. Made three hundreds. She was the cricketer of her time. Of all time.

But her legend is not just that of a player: it is that of the woman who brought women's cricket to the world. She made people talk about it. She stood on street corners taking donations. She found sponsors. She wrote about the game as a journalist, often writing match reports of matches she was in, just to make sure someone covered them. WG Grace wasn't out on street corners grabbing people's spare change or writing up a solid 150 words on matches he played in.

She captained the first women's team at Lord's. She was in the first group of women MCC members. She is a life member of the MCC. She is on the board of Wolverhampton Wanderers. She was one of the first-ever female sports commentators. The first woman inducted into the ICC's Hall of Fame and one of the two first women appointed to the board of the ECB. She became a House of Lords peer, a baroness. She was a remarkable woman, a tireless worker for women's cricket even now.

There will be better cricketers; there will be better administrators. There might even be better promoters in the women's game. But there will never be another Rachael Heyhoe-Flint. She promoted a game that no one wanted. She forced cricket into the newspapers. She came into a world where Len Hutton could say 'A woman playing cricket? That's just like a man trying to knit!'

And when Rachael Heyhoe-Flint played, the ICC had no interest in women's cricket. They didn't have an interest in this woman. This cricket pioneer. This one-woman cricket industry. This cricket hero.

The second woman into the ICC Hall of Fame was Australia's Belinda Clark. Women's cricket was left behind for years in Australia. There was an active club scene. But from an international standpoint it barely existed. Belinda Clark made it exist. At first she did so just by being better than everyone else. That is the surest way to win Australian fans. And she was so good.

A hundred on debut. Six more in her career. And the world's first double century in ODI cricket – for either sex. Test average 45. ODI average 47. There were also two World Cup wins, as captain. They would name the medal for best Australian women's player after her. She would then go on to guide the future women's players, before switching to the men's. She has commentated on cricket as well.

Then there was her team. Of her 101 games as captain, Australia won 84. She had the world's quickest bowler, Cathryn Fitzpatrick, and Karen Rolton, who was probably, possibly, an even better batsman than Clark. Not to mention Zoe Goss, who once dismissed Brian Lara: one of the best all-rounders in women's cricket.

And yet, like club cricketers, the women had to pay to play. Goss paid a levy from her debut in 1987 until 1997. 'I probably spent a good down-payment on a mortgage while I was playing, if you added up the player levies that we had to pay for state and international cricket,' she once said.

Chapter 31

NZ GETS A LEGEND, AUSTRALIA GETS HAIRY

IAN CHAPPELL WAS made captain. Chappell was born to be Australian captain. His grandfather Vic Richardson had captained Australia. Spiritually there was a bit of Don Bradman and Warwick Armstrong about Chappell. Australian mongrel.

His first real obstacle was a man called Glenn Turner. If Chappell was a spit-in-your face and a kick-you-in-the groin sort of bloke, then Turner was an overly officious manager at a fast food chain.

It took four years for Turner to make a first-class hundred. But once he made one, he made a lot – a hundred of them in fact. 103 to be precise.

It was cold and grey in Lancaster Park on 9 March 1974. For Christchurch, not a massive surprise. The wicket was green, so green that Turner told his teammates all about it. Australia was playing with a full-strength side. Barely two months earlier New Zealand had almost won a Test against Australia when the rain robbed them of their chance.

Australia took in two spinners. One of them, Kerry O'Keefe, didn't bowl a ball in the entire match. Bev Congdon sent Australia in, and only Ian Redpath handled the pitch. Australia struggled all the way to 255. New Zealand struggled as well. The pitch was not a minefield, but it was consistently helpful to the seamers.

Turner played and missed, left balls badly, scrapped and hoped. But Australia couldn't get him out, and at stumps on day two he was on 99 not out, for the second time in his career. The next morning it took him 35 balls and more than half an hour to get his hundred – and then he went out in the same over. His innings had been shaky, but because of it New Zealand took the lead.

It was that morning that Lancaster Park woke up. The crowd had come in to see Turner, but they liked the Australian top order collapse just as much. There were 15,000 there, and now New Zealand had a mob, and a chance. Ian Redpath stalled them again, as did a Doug Walters partnership with Kerry O'Keefe, but Australia could not work out the pitch. They set New Zealand 228 to win.

The Kiwi crowd got stuck into the Aussies. The Aussies got into the Kiwi players. Turner batted. This was already looking like the best Test match ever played in New Zealand. The Australians couldn't believe they might lose. At 3/62, they were on top, but when Brian Hastings joined Turner, they set in, and the Aussies didn't handle it well.

Turner wasn't an Australian-style cricketer, or even a New Zealand one. Even before his time playing county cricket in England, he was a very English-style player. He thought a lot about the game, studied it, worked hard for his runs, put a price on his wicket and was never in a hurry. He was an English professional, in job and outlook.

Turner wasn't about dominating; he was about scoring. You could see how the Australians would have been frustrated by him. Christopher Martin-Jenkins referred to him as 'almost frail-looking, pale-faced and serious-minded'. It's hardly tanned, arrogant and moustachioed. He was well travelled, nerdish, and his wife was Indian.

All of these things would have annoyed the Australians. But most of all, they were now working out that he might be the Kiwi to beat them in a Test match. This is an Australian team that was born in the era when Australia refused to play New Zealand, when New Zealand was afraid of Australia. The Australians looked down on New Zealand, when they thought of them at all.

Now this team had the upper hand. It was embarrassing. And as Turner batted better and better, the Australians got more and more pissed off. 'There was an unhappy incident late in the day which led to a request for Ian Chappell to apologise for allegedly foul and abusive language directed at Turner,' reported *The Cricketer* magazine. 'This was an unfortunate business, for otherwise the game was played in a proper spirit.'

In Turner's book, *My Way*, he suggests that Chappell said derogatory things about his wife's nationality. Since then he has said that Chappell threatened to fight him. Whatever Chappell did do, it was unsuccessful. Turner remained.

On the last day New Zealand needed only 51, with six wickets in hand. A crowd turned up. There was still fear that New Zealand might not do it. This was a new era, a new kind of cricket, but they had no history of success, just exclusion and loss. They had won four Tests in their entire history at this point, none against the first three Test nations. And this was Australia: the bully, the big brother. Had Turner gone out, Australia might have run over the top of them.

Turner didn't go out. He made his second hundred, and in the match he scored almost half his side's runs. When the winning runs were hit, he was at the non-striker's end.

There is a story that a man who was driving past the ground heard that New Zealand was about to win, stopped his car, left the motor running and ran into the crowd to see the final runs. That is what this Test meant to New Zealand. They won respect. They lost the next Test but drew the series.

In 41 Tests Turner averaged 44: more than Sutcliffe, more than any New Zealander before him – and most of them after him. In the West Indies he scored two Test double hundreds in one series.

In 1982 Turner played his last season of county cricket for Worcestershire, the county that gave him a career, and a straight bat. On the day he made his hundredth hundred, he kept going, all the way to 311. Not out. All of which were scored on that day. That was a great day. Turner had a lot of them.

That last morning at Lancaster Park, where for once it wasn't cold and grey, was glorious. Turner started as an English professional, but he ended as a New Zealand legend.

Chappell barked a good game, but all that anger and aggression needed the team to back it up. He already had Rod Marsh, a wicket-keeper unlike any before him.

Wicketkeepers had been hidden up at the stumps, huddled behind run machines and WG Grace's massive arse. Their job was not to make mistakes. They made wry observations. They had soft hands.

Marsh was Ian Chappell's wicketkeeper. Marsh was a diver. A show-man. A stuntman. A mouth. A slogger. A star. If wicketkeepers are drummers, he was Keith Moon.

When Marsh was paired with the fastest bowler in history, magic followed.

•

In comes a bouncer; the batsman gets under it. Marsh starts to go left, the ball goes right, he plucks it near his face one-handed like he's some ninja master, then he looks back at the bowler shocked.

The ball beats the batsman at belly height, but it just keeps going: it seems to pick up height and pace that will never end. Every single part of Marsh stretches out as he jumps in all his unatheletic glory and wills himself as high as he can get. The ball hits his hands and he quickly hits the ground, tossing the ball off to slip. Then he turns to have a moment alone, taking big breaths.

The ball goes down leg. It takes some glove. Marsh uses a couple of quick steps. These aren't the standard sidestep wicketkeepers employ; he is running, then he dives, taking the ball at leg slip. Marsh is buggered. It takes him three seconds to even throw the ball up and celebrate the wicket.

If you are the next batsman in, you know what is coming. You've seen Marsh dancing around the field. That's not how wicketkeepers usually act.

One of your teammates, probably the 12th man, jokes about whether it's possible to bowl six byes. You've seen all the batsmen fail to get for-ward and edging away. Another leaves the crease shaking his wounded hand, and when you pass the dismissed batsman, if he's looking up, you see his eyes. If he's looking up. If he can look.

With this bowler, you'd heard the whispers, stories, myths, legends, gossip and bullshit. 'You don't see it.' 'A blur.' 'There was blood every-where.' 'It follows you.' 'I don't remember what happened.' 'Just a shadow.' 'Wild as a meat axe.'

'Good luck.'

Marsh is 30 metres back. When you mark your guard you look back. He seems even further away. You see all the slips; it feels like they are leaning on the sightscreen. They look like the missing gang from *The*

Warriors. You can see their mouths move, but they are too far away for you to hear them. Not that you have to: you know they're abusing you; you know they're swearing. You just look back and see moving moustaches and unbuttoned shirts. They are the very definition of that hostile Aussie masculinity. When they do shut up, they chew gum. They passive-aggressively chew gum.

You have to win them over. If you flinch, if you moan, if you hesitate, 'you're weak as dog's piss, mate'. Harsh, but fair.

The crowd is making an odd noise. It's a low rumble. You've not heard it before. You see a lot of brown chests and big hair. You can smell their collective sweat. One of them seems to be holding the ball. He looks exactly like the guy you saw at the Tugun Surf club driving his Torana around doing donuts; smoke everywhere, the smell of burnt rubber, and a devious smile on his face. It's not the same guy, but it's the same sort of guy.

There is no look of impending violence on his face. It's just a face, just a standard Australian fresh look. Marsh and the slips look more violent, from what you can see of them. Someone at cover point, the only person in front of square, is clapping. 'C'mon, Thommo.'

Jeff Thomson's run-up is jaunty. Put it in shorts on a beach and you'd laugh at him. Well, you'd smirk. You don't smirk, because the run-up is too short and what will happen next won't give you time. At the crease it is awkward; it is like watching someone who doesn't quite know how to bowl. But he ends up side on; his right arm is low, his delivery stride massive. He's somehow turned from a jaunty kid on the beach who doesn't know what he's doing into a human catapult, all in one step.

To get to Test level you have done your 10,000 hours. You have batted on streets, backyards, *maidans*, driveways, nets, synthetic turf, sticky dogs, pancakes and trampolines. You have faced bowlers of all races, creeds and actions. You have faced old men with bags of tricks, young strapping men who bowl like the wind. You have done it all. That is how you got to be a batsman for your country. Now you are facing this.

You are wearing pads. They are there to protect your shins and knees. They are made from canvas, and have cotton stuffing and stitched-in cane wood strips. For the first time in your life, they feel inadequate. You have gloves as well. They look like little sausages; you think there is cotton in them. One of the thumbs has a plastic end to protect you.

You can feel your thumb sweating inside it. You have a towel around your front thigh. Anything to soften the impact. Then there is the protector, the one thing all cricketers own. The box. It is small and plastic, but the plastic isn't NASA grade, and if it is hit just right, it snaps open and, in the worst case scenario, snaps back closed with your manhood now on the outside.

You're fully dressed, have safety gear and are holding a club. But you feel naked. Alone.

That was what it was like facing Jeff Thomson from 1973 to Christmas Eve 1976. That is when fast bowling went from fast to apocalyptic. There was perhaps no one ever as quick as Thommo. Perhaps it was a trick of his action – perhaps others were quicker – but out there, without helmet, without adequate protection for the rest of your body, Thommo was the quickest, scariest motherfucker to ever bowl a cricket ball.

And in that period, Thommo had a partner.

There was a time when Dennis Lillee was a real quick. His idol was Wes Hall. Watch the footage of him from the 1972 Ashes and you can see it in the way his right hand cocks that imaginary revolver as he comes in. Lillee was wild then. Probably the world's best bowler, but almost out of control. In some ways, he still had the same last few steps as he would years later, still close to the umpire, still bolt upright, but everything felt dangerous. His elbows were wild. His legs were everywhere. And when he landed, you could sometimes see how close it was to all going wrong.

It was already wrong by that point; it was only later that Lillee found out his spine was fractured in three places. Lillee found out at a young age the real truth of sport – you're only important as long as you're necessary. Why would the Australian Cricket Board of that time worry about this broken guy? They'd just find another. Lillee worked in a bank, and got some money from a cleaning contract. The world's best bowler was worth more to a bank than to the Australian Cricket Board.

In his spare time, Lillee went off with his high school PE teacher, a doctor and sportsman by the name of Frank Pyke, and he rebuilt his body for bowling. Then, while he was there, he rebuilt his mind.

Lillee made his body perfect for fast bowling. He then bowled perfectly within that frame. But what he did to his mind was the real thing. Lillee started as a fast bowler with an out-swinger. He came back as a fast-bowling surgeon who could go up in pace, down in pace, bowl cutters, yorkers, understood bouncers and could hit any spot on the pitch he needed to.

When a pitch was made for batting, they say Lillee would just hit a perfect line just outside off stump for hours. Always from the same end. The story goes that he would do that to dent that area of the pitch. To make it uneven. To give him his own pitch that no other bowler knew about. And then in the second innings he would pounce on his spot.

You're not facing a bowler at that point; you're facing a supervillain.

Lillee, Lillee, Lillee. The crowd is chanting.

Lillee wasn't just a bowler, he was the bowler. Perhaps the greatest that lived. But to his country, he was more than just the man with all the tricks. He was free, smart, angry, driven, stylish, talented and Australian. He was what the entire country wanted to be. Now, he is what the country still wishes it was. If you go to any Australian cricket ground, from Test to park, there will be at least one bowler who appeals like Lillee.

Lillee, Lillee, Lillee.

The third thing Lillee added was swagger. His hair was like a lion mane. He had chains around his neck. He rocked a headband when no one else would. Seemingly the better he bowled the more unbuttoned his shirt. Puffs of chest hair poked out just to show how manly he was. His eyes were wild, and deep, like he could see into the batsman's soul, and wanted to dismiss that as well. His appeals weren't polite enquiries; they were angry revolutionary pleas. He staged a full-body appeal, his knees bent, his hands gesturing, his face demanding. The umpires were powerless to resist him.

Lillee, Lillee, Lillee.

Even his walk back was seemingly designed to instil fear into the batsman. His first book was called *Back to the Mark*. It was a walk that had the windscreen wiper finger to remove the sweat. As Gideon Haigh once described it: 'It went from the centre to his left, then back to the right'. He had the determination of a man who would not lose and the aura of someone that the earth rotated around. Any old clip of Lillee has the ball just seemingly arriving in his hand when he got to the top of his mark, without him looking or breaking stride. The ball knew where it belonged.

Lillee, Lillee, Lillee.

Lillee was from Perth. It's a four-day drive, if you're lucky, from Perth to Melbourne. It's the same country, but at times, only just. The MCG was legendary before Lillee's grandfather was born. But it was like the MCG with its whopping great heaving bosom was just waiting for Lillee to arrive to fulfil its destiny.

Lillee, Lillee, Lillee.

Lillee and the MCG were a perfect combination. No actor in a theatre, conductor at a podium, or orator on a soapbox could match the chemistry that Lillee and the MCG had. Lillee and the MCG made 82 wickets together, in 14 matches.

Lillee, Lillee, Lillee.

The chant would lift Lillee, and Lillee would lift the chanters. Starting as a hymn, ending in a scream. It would go on forever. Out there was a ferocious tall creature, and the ground was sweating and bowling with him. The more they chanted, the better he got.

Lillee, Lillee, Lillee.

Richard Hadlee took 431 Test wickets. On bad days he thought, 'WWLilleeD'.

Lillee, Lillee, Lillee.

The MCG when packed for a cricket game is like a large, sweaty, angry man with a beer belly, unhappy relationship and dead end job. When Lillee bowled it was transformed into a virile, seething beast.

Lillee, Lillee, Lillee.

Lillee and Thommo bowled together in 26 Tests. They took 119 and 98 wickets in those 26 Tests. A bomb at one end, a sniper at the other. From 1974 to 1976 Lillee and Thommo combined. One was the quickest there ever was and the other was the best there ever was.

They were called the Ugly Australians, but it was beautiful. Batsmen didn't dominate; they barely survived.

Against the West Indies, in 1975/76, Australia won 5-1. Only one West Indian was in the top five scorers. He saw a lot of Lillee and Thommo. He was Clive Lloyd.

Chapter 32

YES MR PACKER

ONE-DAY CRICKET WAS now getting noticed. Cricket was just beginning to have financial value. So it was a perfect time for a man by the name of Kerry Packer to say, 'Come on gentlemen, we're all whores. What's your price?'

Packer's offer to the Australian Cricket Board was rejected. Their sport could not be bought – or even paid what it was worth. While using an old carpet showroom as an office to save money, the ACB said no to a big man with a big voice and an even bigger chequebook.

The Australian Cricket Board in the late '70s was not entirely amateurish. It had a small staff, less than 10. It had some money, from TV deals, advertising and ticket receipts. When 1977's Centenary Test was being organised, they even sent an official to the US to see how sports marketing really worked. They were trying to move into the future. But cricket boards don't really move into the future; cricket drags them there.

The board was made up of old men and one such man, Donald Bradman, had more to say than most. But this was not a group looking to help cricketers pay their mortgages. And if the players complained, well, 'the players are not professional'. Or as one ACB employee put it: 'They are all invited to play and if they don't like the conditions there are 500,000 other cricketers in Australia who would love to take their place.'

The players already knew this. They saw from their hotel rooms, their lousy pay and the fact that they had to tend their own injuries that the board didn't care about them. A first-class hack cricketer in England was a professional, even if like Jim Foat he could average no more than 18 with the bat across his career; an Australian icon like Dennis Lillee, the best in the world, was a bank employee.

Other sports had started to move on. Aussie rules football, quickly growing into Australia's most watched sport, was paying its players better and better. They had to compete with the other clubs for the best players. Rod Marsh's brother, Graham, was a professional golfer who made more than the entire Australian team. Cricket in Australia, and in most of the world, was amateur. The ACB didn't even contact your employer on your behalf to get you some leave. You were on your own.

Cricket was worth something. It was worth even more if there was a new law passed stating more Australian-made programming had to be shown on your TV station. Cricket is one of the best sports for TV. There is a natural ad break every three to five minutes. It goes all day. It brings people back in with an ongoing narrative. While the story changes, you can miss some and still watch it without feeling like you missed the entire plot. And it goes for five days. That is covering a whole lot of your TV schedule.

The old men in cricket administration had bigger concerns, like that of the team blazers. Gideon Haigh wrote that the minutes from board meetings at that time 'can go for pages talking about the specifications of a blazer pocket'.

While old men worked on the perfect blazer pocket, there was an enormous shadow looming over their self-congratulatory Centenary Test. Australia won by 45 runs – the same margin as 100 years earlier. And like 100 years ago, a bunch of amateur cricketers had done it for Australia. In the first Test, Fred Spofforth had not played, but instead worked in a bank. In this match, bank employee Dennis Lillee took time off work and picked up 11 wickets.

The shadow though, he was more important. He was a married guy with a couple of kids who was involved in publishing a women's magazine and had taken over his dad's company. When the players were first contracted by this guy, they had no idea who he was.

'Who? Kerry Packer, never heard of him.'

The cricket officials knew who he was. They had been insulted when he suggested they were whores who might be bought. They had knocked back his advances when he tried to buy cricket for his stations in

Melbourne and Sydney. His offer was way above the Australian Broadcast Corporation's offer, but the ACB stayed with the national broadcaster.

If you can't buy the cricket board, what do you buy?

While England's board (the TCCB had finally replaced the MCC) and Australia's board celebrated a century of their own excellence, Kerry Packer, Austin Robertson, John Cornell, Ian Chappell and Tony Greig signed up the best cricketers in the world. Secretly. They were just a bloke with daddy's company, a player manager, a comedian and two cricketers, and yet somehow, without any cricket official knowing, they signed up the best cricketers in the world. The South Africans loved the idea, as their team wasn't about to be brought back. The Pakistanis signed up because their board was still very amateurish too. And virtually every single player in the West Indies signed up, because they were just becoming awesome, and they thought they deserved it.

Most players signed without reading, let alone understanding their contracts. They were desperate to become professionals. They were desperate to be paid properly. When the news broke, quietly at first, there were few headlines, and no front page stories. But then Tony Greig was stripped of the Test captaincy and Kerry Packer was summoned to London by the International Cricket Council for negotiations. He was portrayed as a barbaric monster, the Australian business version of a Thommo short ball. But on a live TV debate, Packer came out looking like the sensible one. He was more Lillee than Thommo.

When Packer met the ICC, he assured them they could have all their players back, if only he could get the TV rights he wanted in Australia. They said they couldn't do that – it was beyond their jurisdiction – and then they told him any player signed with him was banned from first-class cricket. The ICC started a war with a richer, smarter opponent; they were arrogant and stupid. They were after all, cricket administrators.

Packer took their blackballing of his players to court in England and won. In his judgement, Justice Sir Christopher Slade said that professional cricketers needed to make a living.

This was now Packer's circus, and the players were 'Test Pirates'.

The ICC's only victories over Packer were that he couldn't use the term Test (he called them Supertests), that he couldn't call his team Australia (he called them 'WSC Australian XI') and that he couldn't use the laws of cricket that the MCC had copyrighted (Richie Benaud wrote him up a new version). Packer also couldn't use the grounds – so he rented an Aussie rules ground called Waverley, the Sydney Showgrounds and a trotting track in Perth. For the pitches he hired the Gabba groundsman John Maley to invent drop-in pitches. It was genius from a horticulture perspective, but cricket fans have complained about them ever since.

They marketed the game like it was a heavyweight contest. It would be big hitters up against fast bowlers. Packer knew what kind of cricket casual cricket fans wanted to see. He promoted the pace of Lillee, Snow, Andy Roberts and Imran Khan. He organised his Supertests to be on the same day as the official Tests. The ICC had started the fight, and Packer was ready to bounce them out.

Instead, Packer's bouncers flew high over the ACB's head. Only 2000 people turned up to see the first Supertest at VFL Park in Waverley. VFL Park could be a grim place on the best day, miles from the city centre, a soulless, charmless stadium. Its carpark always had a post-apocalyptic feel about it, but never more than that day Packer found himself counting the cars as the game went on.

At the Gabba, Bob Simpson had been brought back from a 10-year retirement to captain the board's official Australians against India. It turned out to be the greatest Test series yet between the two teams, per-haps largely because Australia was so weak. On the final day of the series, it was one Test each and India needed 131 to win, while Australia needed four wickets. Australia won by 45 runs. The press was on the ACB's side; the fans loved having Simpson back; the Australians were winning. Packer needed something to happen.

Channel 9 might not have grabbed the hearts and minds of the fans, but what they did capture was cricket in a whole new way. The ABC seemed to have one or two cameras at the ground, and it wasn't a TV production, but a radio production with visuals. TV sports broadcasting at that time would try and replicate the feeling of being at the ground by leaving the camera at one end and having two old men drone on endlessly while you try to enjoy the cricket. It meant that, to paraphrase Packer, you had to watch a batsman's arse for half the day. Channel 9 brought in more cameras and covered cricket from a visual perspective better than anyone before it. Almost 40 years later, they still do.

You were closer than ever.

·

David Hookes was a good-looking kid. He looked like a typical Aussie teenager, and you could imagine him in old Super 8 footage riding on a skateboard, all long hair and smiles. In the Centenary Test he'd smashed Tony Greig for five consecutive straight boundaries. His instincts were to attack. It seemed like nothing could stop him.

Andy Roberts wasn't the first West Indian quick bowler, but he was the first of Clive Lloyd's new idea. Roberts never let the batsmen know what he was thinking. He wanted them to try to work him out, while he worked out their batting. He was fast. In less than two and a half years, Roberts took 100 Test wickets. He was quick at everything. The only thing he did slowly was his sucker ball bouncer. The sucker bouncer was the one he let you see. The next bouncer was the one you didn't.

Channel 9 starts on a close-up of David Hookes from a ground level. Hookes' long sleeves are rolled up perfectly. His unbaggy unofficial yellow cap is on his head. Shirt unbuttoned, of course. He taps his bat quite a lot, leaving it on the ground right until the bowler hits the crease. Tap, tap, tap. They cut back to a camera that is high behind the non-striker as Roberts gets close to the crease. The ball is delivered from that angle; it makes a sound on impact. As Hookes starts to fall, the camera changes to another angle that is slightly lower, but still behind the bowler, and it is zooming out to the hook shot. The next shot is from the close-up camera. This time Hookes is getting up from the ground, before falling down again. Viv Richards tries to grab him. Channel 9 then load up the slow-motion replay from the original angle. They cut back to Hookes on the ground. Another slow-motion replay is shown, this time from the position of the close-up camera, but far enough back to see Hookes' whole body while still seeing the ball hit, and also hearing that noise. Hookes is now up and bending over on what appears to be the same ground-level camera. They show the same slo-mo replay again. This time Richie Benaud explains exactly which side of the jaw the ball hit. Hookes is helped from the ground. A close-up of his bloody face shows us his pain.

This is cricket as we now know it.

Some think Hookes was spooked from there on out, the fearless boy wonder that never quite made it. But that day, and days like it, helped turn that series from Packer's circus to World Series Cricket, cricket so brutal that Ian Chappell says it was the toughest cricket of his career.

It also meant that players started wearing helmets. Players were being hit in the head far too often. The bowling had gone from fast, to superfast.

Patsy Hendren had used a protective hat in the 1930s. It wasn't very protective. Batsmen had at times also worn mouthguards. And they wore boxes – one of cricket's greatest jokes was that batsman protected their genitalia 100 years before they protected their brain.

The batsmen needed to evolve again. Dennis Amiss wore a helmet. A motorcycle helmet. It produced many problems, most notably that no one wearing them could hear a thing, and run-outs followed. Lillee smacked a bouncer into one that Tony Greig was wearing. Lillee made a knocking gesture, Greig did a shimmy. The game went on. No one was taken to hospital.

Amiss asked the manufacturer to modify an equestrian helmet, and from then on in, cricket changed again. At first the batsmen who wore them were considered cowards, but as time went by, everyone wore them.

Bouncers continued to intimidate, to play on batsmen's fears, but the ultimate fear, that a Test player would die, was put to rest.

The official version of the game won the first year, but the next year, as World Series Cricket got successful, the official team lost the plot. An England team captained by Mike Brearley came out for six Tests. England's professionals beat Australia's second-string amateurs 5-1. It was dull cricket. Dull might be overstating it. Geoff Boycott made 263 runs off the 1163 balls he faced in that series. That's not exactly Chapelli hooking Imran Khan, is it?

By now Packer had convinced NSW Premier Neville Wran to stop the ban on him using the SCG. The government even installed lights so they could play cricket at night, a novelty that drew the punters in. World Series Cricket had a catchy jingle that was the best cricket marketing anyone had ever produced. When they released 'C'mon Aussie C'mon' as a single, it went to number one. Packer kept innovating as well. Next was the coloured clothing. Australia had canary yellow; the Windies had hot pink. Just proving what a brave man Packer was. The ball was changed from red to white, without cricket ending.

The ACB fought fire with more Tests. Six wasn't enough, so their poor underpaid second-string side now had to play against Pakistan as well. More cricket wasn't the answer.

Packer by this point had more than 60 of the best players from around the world on contracts. Had he wanted to, he could have just taken over world cricket. Instead he did a deal with the ACB. He was given the cricket to broadcast, and he was also given a publicity deal with the ACB. Channel 9 and the ACB have never been parted since.

In Packer's circus there were 56,126 runs and 2364 wickets. Not one of them was considered first-class.

Kerry Packer went back to being a broadcaster. He now had players in the coloured clothes he favoured, playing far more one-day cricket in the lucrative day-night time-slot. Packer had marketed the game. Packer had profited from the game. Packer had changed the game.

Cricketers have been singing his praises ever since.

And cricket fans are still singing 'C'mon Aussie c'mon, c'mon'.

Chapter 33

DID HE SAY 'GROVEL'?

CLIVE LLOYD WAS stern. Something was on his mind. He was sitting in a bar with Viv Richards to discuss the tour. But Lloyd wasn't in a discussing mood. Jeff Thomson had terrorised his batsmen. Scared them. Scarred them. Lillee and Thommo had beaten them up on the field; off the field they said they were racially abused, and just generally abused. They lost 5-1. The crowd chanted, 'Lillee, Lillee, Lillee, kill, kill, kill,' and that's pretty much what happened. There had been calls for Lloyd's head. But he wasn't thinking of giving up. He was thinking about toughening up. 'Never again.'

The next Test after leaving Australia they won by an innings against India. It was the first of a four-Test series. They took in two fast bowlers, the medium-paced stylings of Bernard Julien and two spinners. Their spinners took as many wickets as their quicks.

Two Tests later, the West Indies declared to set India a 403-run target. India made it. With six wickets in hand. It was the second biggest chase in Test history, and it was a slap to the face. The West Indies played three spinners in that game, one quick and Julien.

Lloyd probably sat staring after that. His spinners weren't as good as India's, and he questioned their worth after that loss. The fourth Test was at Sabina Park. It was quick there. Really quick. Julien kept his spot, as did spinner Raphnick Jumadeen and Vanburn Holder. Fast bowler Wayne Daniels came in. Michael Holding remained.

Holding was the best bowler the West Indies had. He had played against Australia. He looked like a boy. He had doubtless pace and skill, but had not yet become what he would become: Whispering Death.

That started at Sabina Park. It was barbarism. Massacre. Bloodbath.

The West Indies sent India in. At lunch on day one India had not lost a wicket.

Under Lloyd the West Indies had just managed to beat India 3-2 in his first series. They had drawn with Pakistan in their second series. They had been annihilated by Australia. And now, in Lloyd's first series at home, at lunch on day one, there was a chance that after leading the series 1-0, and setting India a chase of over 400, the West Indies could lose the series.

Lloyd instructed Holding and Daniels to start bowling at the middle of the pitch. Three bouncers were aimed at opener Anshuman Gaekwad. Sunil Gavaskar received four bouncers, and a beamer, from around the wicket. The bowling got very hot. Very dangerous. Very beyond what many believed was right.

Yet, with all the hostility, all the danger, India lost only one wicket on that first day. Sunil Gavaskar, bowled for 66.

Perhaps Lillee and Thommo had shown Lloyd the way. Maybe the lack of spin penetration had necessitated a change. But the real reason the West Indies unflinchingly started bouncing India on that day was simply because had Lloyd lost, he might well have lost his job as captain. In the heat of the Kingston afternoon, with one of the all-time greats batting, and an obdurate blocker at the other end, Lloyd tried something that many captains had tried. The difference was that the West Indies then bowled that way for much of the next 25 years.

The pitch was also quite interesting; it was fast, but also, as sometimes happened at Sabina Park, unpredictable. On day two, Holding managed to get a ball off a full length to leap up at Mohinder Amarnath and have him caught at short leg. The bouncers the day before had already spooked the Indian dressing-room; now the pitch was playing its part as well.

Then there was the crowd. Sunil Gavaskar later wrote, 'And the spectators, to put it mildly, were positively inhuman.' And if you think 'inhuman' sounds off, he also said this:

To call the crowd a 'crowd' in Jamaica is a misnomer. It should be called a 'mob'. The way they shrieked and howled every time Holding bowled was positively horrible. They encouraged him with shouts of 'Kill him, maan!', 'Hit him maan!', 'Knock his head off, Mike!' All this proved beyond a shadow of doubt that these people still belonged to the jungles and forests, instead of a civilised country.

Racism aside, the Indians now felt they were under attack from every direction.

Gundappa Viswanath came in. He was the batsman India depended on when they were struggling. Which mostly meant when Gavaskar was out. The first ball he faced was a bouncer that veered back at him, flicked his glove and hit the fence so hard it made sane men shudder. Holding kept straight at him, hitting him on the glove again. This time it found a fielder. Viswanath's finger did not recover.

Gaekwad had already been hit so many times people stopped keeping count – until he was hit in the head, and started bleeding on the pitch. The bloodbath had begun. Brijesh Patel walked off with his lip opened up.

The scoreboard read 3/273. But it was written in blood.

Dilip Vengsarkar would go on to become one of India's best servants, playing more than 100 Tests in a career as a batsman mostly at first drop. Vengsarkar at this point was only 19. In two and half hours he made 39, but showed the sort of batsman he would be.

When Vengsarkar was out, Srinivas Venkataraghavan followed straight after, and Bishen Bedi declared, only six wickets down. Although, it was really eight wickets down, with two retired hurt. He explained: 'There is a limit to courage when you are facing bowling at 90 miles per hour. A lot of human beings would have conked out. I gave the umpires a piece of my mind. It became so painful to watch that I had to make the disgusting gesture of declaring in a six-day Test.'

Bedi was protesting the short bowling, but he was also thinking of the game. They had already bounced Venkataraghavan, who could bat a tiny bit. He had his wicketkeeper in, and then more importantly himself, and even more importantly perhaps, Chandra to follow. Chandra could not bat. Not at all. He ended his career with more wickets than runs. Normally bowling teams would have ended him within in a ball or two.

But in this situation, with the West Indies going for the throat, literally, why risk his fingers, his health or maybe even life?

India had faced short bowling before, but they had never mastered it. There was a solid reason for this: they played on the slowest and lowest pitches on earth, and they had not created any fast bowlers.

The West Indies' innings gave them a lead of 85. Every wicket the Indians took was with the three spinners from their quartet.

When India went back out to bat, they were already three wickets down, with Viswanath, Gaekwad and Patel all injured. The 12th man, Surinder Amarnath, also had appendicitis. India had to change their batting line-up. Madan Lal, a tireless slow medium seamer, who could bat a tiny amount, went in at four. When India were 5/97, they said they had no fit men to carry on batting.

Tony Cozier, the legendary West Indian writer and broadcaster called chicken:

Bedi's action was plain and simple. The Indians had had enough and were calling it quits. Bedi was conspicuous by his absence when the Indians took the field. All this did little to improve India's image, which had certainly got tarnished. It was a pity the series had to end like this because Bedi and his men had shown greater courage and determination than many other teams which have toured the Caribbean.

During their fielding, both Bedi and Chandra had been struck on the fingers, so it may have been just as simple as not having anyone left to bat. Considering neither man could really bat, and there were two days left in the match, it hardly would have mattered. India was beaten. Beaten up.

Polly Umrigar – the same Polly Umrigar who had backed away scared from Fred Trueman in 1952 – was the team manager. He called a press conference to complain about Clive Lloyd's tactics. *Wisden* said when 'the Indian team trudged along the tarmac towards their home-bound aeroplane at Kingston's Norman Manley Airport, they resembled Napoleon's troops on the retreat from Moscow'.

India was the first vanquished. There would be more.

•

'If they're down, they grovel, and I intend, with the help of Closey and a few others, to make them grovel.'

Tony Greig, the South African born captain of England, was speaking. He was talking up the series, trying to pump up his team, which had already been written off in the upcoming series against the West Indies.

The Windies heard a white man, a white South African man, a white South African man who was captaining England, say that he would make them grovel. Clive Lloyd: 'We resolved to show him and everyone else that the days for grovelling were over.'

Every single time Greig went out to bat, the West Indies bowlers stepped up a gear. He had put a target on his head – and an anchor around his team's neck.

The West Indies used spin, medium pace and fast medium pace alongside their quick bowlers in the first Two Tests. The score at that point was 0-0. The West Indies bowlers were aggressive, but they weren't as aggressive as Viv Richards, who had already hit a 232.

With the series still 0-0, it was only then did Lloyd actually go to three quicks, not even four. They had bowled short already, especially when Greig was batting, but the pitches weren't as quick as Sabina Park, and the batsmen were more used to short pitch bowling. Now they had three express pacers to intimidate with. And, oddly, a spinner.

Gordon Greenidge made 134 out of 211 in the first innings. England made 71.

It would be Close's last Test. Close was born in 1931. He played his first Test in 1949 and what he was doing out there in 1976, no one really knows. In the second innings he made 20 from 108 balls. His body had more than 20 bruises. Holding seemed to see him as a punching bag. The umpires stepped in. Perhaps they were just looking out for someone their age, but had they not stepped in he might have been broken. Brian Close was one of the toughest men to ever play Test cricket, but masculine pride doesn't stop broken skulls.

Close stayed as long as he could. He was essentially there to take as many quick balls as he could, mostly on the body, occasionally very close to his slow-moving head, hoping that the West Indies would get tired. They didn't. West Indies 1-0.

By the fourth Test, the West Indies had an all seam attack, with three legitimate quicks. The same line-up bowled in the fifth Test. With Daniel and Roberts doing the intimidating, Holding pitched it up. He took 14/159 in the match. In the series, Viv Richards made 829 runs, adding a 291 to his earlier double century.

The West Indies would eventually use four outright quick bowlers. Fast medium wasn't fast enough. They seemed to have a conveyor belt making doomsday quicks.

In four Tests that summer, Holding took 28 wickets at 12. He was from then on known as Whispering Death – because his run-up was so smooth, you didn't hear him coming. England didn't see either. 3-0.

Barbarism. Massacre. Bloodbath. Grovel?

Chapter 34

BRICKLAYER BUILDS NEW JERUSALEM

I will not cease from Mental Fight,
Nor shall my Sword sleep in my hand:
Till we have built Jerusalem,
In England's green and pleasant Land
　　　　　　　　– 'Jerusalem', William Blake

ENGLAND WAS NOT a great place to be in the late 1970s and '80s. Thatcherism had turned the country even colder than usual. There were race riots. A virtual class war. And the people were unhappy. It was cold and grey, and for a time, it looked like it wouldn't ever end.

The West Indies had taken supremacy in their sport. But there was still the Ashes. And they had Ian Botham. He was a hero, but even he couldn't beat the West Indies.

At Headingley in 1981, the Australian team had champagne in their dressing rooms. After the game, the English drank it.

Botham was the world's best all-rounder over his first 25 Tests. This is a world with Imran Khan and Kapil Dev in it. He averaged 40 with the bat, 18 with the ball. There was nothing he couldn't do. So England, with a leadership vacuum, gave him the captaincy. What followed was two series against the West Indies. England did well, compared with how they did later in the 1980s and '90s, but they still lost both series. Botham also lost all form with the bat, and all form with the ball. Botham lost a bit of himself.

In the first Test of the Ashes, Australia had won a scrappy bowlers' game. Lillee and Alderman took 17 of the wickets. The next Test was a draw and Botham made a pair. He was not asked to captain the third Test.

England brought back Mike Brearley. Brearley on the face of it was a throwback to England's amateur captain past. No one, Brearley included, would see him as a Test-level batsman. His batting average of 22 would have been low in 1881, let alone 1981. But Brearley knew how people worked. And although in previous generations Botham would have referred to him as Mr Brearley and carried his bags, in this generation, Brearley treated Botham like a talented genius.

One bowling spell under Brearley and suddenly Botham was back with a six-wicket haul. In his next knock he made 50 as well. But England was stuffed. So stuffed that the bookie at the ground offered odds of 500/1. Rod Marsh and Dennis Lillee were so amused by this that they got someone to place a bet for them. At 5/105, after a follow-on, and still 122 runs behind, Botham came out.

A former teammate of Botham once referred to him as 'a bricklayer who happened to be good at something else'. The bricks he laid next led people to refer to that team as the new Jerusalem.

Botham came out to bat without a helmet or cap at Headingley. His hair was much the same as any schoolteacher would have worn in that era. He had a sweater on, but the sweater didn't match his trousers. His face was covered in a well-manicured beard.

As the innings started it was classical batting: straight drive, cut, square drive, late cut. Establishment shots. England was gone. He was just cashing in a few loose balls.

His 50 was a slog through mid-wicket. Now his hair was wilder. He was spitting beside the pitch, holding his bat like an axe. He had slogged off the captaincy; he was no longer the statesman representing the establishment. He was Beefy again, the brickie with a bat.

Slog over mid-on. Sliced mistake just past the slips. Aerial over point. 'Absolute thoroughbred stroke,' said Christopher Martin-Jenkins for the BBC. Botham was now an animal at the crease. England had the lead. Another mistake missed the slips to the boundary. Another slog. Hundred partnership. Big smile.

Botham was now running down the wicket and smashing the Australian quicks back over their heads and into confectionery stalls.

The hundred was sliced between slips and third man. Botham didn't politely raise his bat at first; he put both his hands up like he had just slotted one for Scunthorp.

'On any other day,' said an objective Mike Brearley, 'they would have edged rather than missed, or edged more thinly, or the ball would have landed differently from one of the thick edges.'

The lead was only 129 when Botham ran out of partners.

Bob Willis didn't get the new ball. He wasn't even in the team originally. He was out of form, ill, maybe even past it. Willis couldn't stop bowling no-balls. Willis had to fight to get into the squad, had to fight to get into the team, and then had to wait for the new ball. In the first innings he took no wickets. Botham took an early wicket, but Trevor Chappell and the first innings century-maker John Dyson took the score to 1/56.

Willis had been bowling up the hill, into the wind, the idea being it would stop him from overstepping. But it wasn't working. He hated it. He thought he deserved better treatment. He thought he deserved to be in the team, with the new ball, running down the hill.

Bob Wills was a big Bob Dylan fan. Maybe he was thinking this when they made him bowl uphill:

> I ain't gonna bowl up the hill no more.
> No, I ain't gonna bowl up the hill no more.
> Well, I wake in the mornin'
> Strech my back and hope I'm-a off the chain
> I got a head full of ideas
> That are drivin' me insane
> It's a shame the way they make me wait some more
> I ain't gonna bowl up the hill no more.

The man with 200 Test Wickets and a whole heap of frustration came down that hill. If there wasn't wind at his back before hand, his anger summoned it. And he didn't bowl like an old man. He didn't bowl like a beaten man. He bowled like an angry man. He bowled like an angry man with 200 wickets.

Willis went straight at Trevor Chappell. Chappell lost the ball, and Willis was on his way. Then he removed two one-time Australian captains, Hughes and Yallop.

But Willis was at you. He was a whirlwind at the crease, all anger and awkwardness. He was hard to handle, hard to survive, and when in a mood like this, a bit deranged and wild. Willis was also fast. When Ray Bright was clean bowled, the stump leapt out of the ground. It is commonly believed that Australia can struggle with small chases. If you want to trace that belief back, Headingley 1981 was ground zero.

Ray Bright's broken stumps was the last wicket; Australia had lost. Botham and Willis had won. As had Marsh and Lillee on their bet. But it was Willis and Botham who drank the champagne. All of England drank it with them. It wasn't just a cricket victory; it was a victory for England.

English people still remember where they were that day.

At Edgbaston for the next Test, Australia needed 151. They had owned the game. But Botham bowled as he had batted at Headingley, and Australia failed again in the chase. England would end the series 3-1. Beefy Botham would become Sir Ian Botham.

A brickie. A footballer. A slogger. A knight.

The 1980s were a grim time in England, on the pitch, in the streets. Botham gave a country something. He was a brute, their brute.

Chapter 35

THE ONE AND ONLY VIV

But my hand was made strong
By the 'and of the Almighty.
We forward in this generation
Triumphantly.

— Bob Marley

VIV RICHARDS DIDN'T walk like other men. Like John Wayne's walk, on another man it would look ridiculous. His hips went out to the side. His shoulders looked too large for his body. His head would stay out of rhythm with the rest of him.

The way he held his bat wasn't like other batsmen either. He would often hold it up near his shoulder, shadow-boxing an invisible enemy. But when it was in his left hand, it was almost dainty. Like he didn't need his whole hand to hold it.

Batsmen from the beginning of time have gone down the wicket to do some gardening. A pat at the wicket. Out of all of them, only Viv Richards made it a declaration of war. Staring into the bowler's eyes, letting him know only one of them will survive this. Then the turn and strut. Even his arse moved aggressively.

At the crease, just before the ball, that was the respite. Other than some chewing of gum, he was serene. Just a man in cap. Chewing gum. About to kick your arse.

Then the bowler would arrive and his front leg would go across the stumps. You are not good enough to get me out, to beat me, so I'm going to plant my leg across the stump and then smash the shit out of you.

Bowlers were beaten as he walked out. Bowlers were beaten as he gardened. Bowlers were beaten by his mastication. Bowlers were beaten.

On his own he was aggressive as four of the strongest, quickest and brutish fast bowlers the West Indies could find. Yet he said, 'I felt I was an artist.'

Batsmen have been as good as Viv Richards. Batsmen have batted as fast. Batsmen have scored as much. Batsmen have been as confident. No batsman can be him. They want to. They all want to. But it's not a job you can apply for. Or something you can learn. That walk looks camp on another man. On him, it was gladiatorial.

Don Bradman averaged 103 batting at three. Wally Hammond averaged 74 there. Viv Richards averaged 61. The first two struggled with real quick short bowling. Viv ate it. The faster they were, the faster they went. The more aggressive they were, the harder he hit them.

In an era when batsmen evolved new protection to save them, Viv chewed gum. In 1976 Richards made 1710 runs in a year of Test cricket. He could not have made a bigger impact if he'd beheaded a bowler and dropped it in the Lord's long room.

Viv Richards faced Dennis Lillee, John Snow, Bob Willis, Ian Botham, Jeff Thomson, Kapil Dev, Waqar Younis, Imran Khan and Richard Hadlee. No mean list.

On the secret to batting he said:

Keep it simple, stay still, watch the ball. These fellas these days, they want to over-complicate this thing which is batting. Come forward, come at the face of the man against you and spring back if you must, to show him who's boss. Be the boss, man, because if you don't think you are, no one else will, true huh true.

Commentator Mark Nicholas tells a story of Viv's time in county cricket:

On strike to Malcolm Marshall in a county match in Swansea, something disturbed him. He pulled away with a regal sense of theatre and then walked – if we can call it that with Viv – down the pitch, past Marshall, past the umpire and towards the many steep and famous steps that brought pain or pleasure to the climb of returning batsmen. Suddenly, in no man's land, he stopped. 'Hey you, you, yes you,' he shouted with withering accusation to an alarmed spectator above the sightscreen, who was idly thumbing the pages of *The Daily Telegraph*. 'You got David Gower at slip, Robin Smith in the gully, Malcolm Marshall is bowling to Vivian Richards, and you reading the effing newspaper!'

Viv was the sort of man that even if he wasn't in charge, people would follow him. When he finally took the reigns, Clive Lloyd had laid a simple road map to success. Pick two skilful fast bowlers, top them up with two brutal fast bowlers, and make sure they bowl their overs slow enough that they can get through their whole day at full pace. Then let your batsmen bat. It was really that simple. But it needed a special kind of leader, one the bowlers would trust to have their backs, one the batsmen knew would be on the front line with them. Viv was perfect for that. It was Lloyd's strategy, the bowlers' speed and the batsmen's talent, but it was still Viv's team.

The team was molded in his image even before he was in charge.

There was something else with Viv. Something deeper. Viv was from a small island, Antigua. Viv was from a small cricket nation. And Viv was from a people who had been oppressed. Viv played cricket much in the same way Muhammad Ali boxed. Tupac rapped. Pele scored. Malcolm X spoke. All from different eras and different backgrounds. But there was this connection of men who had been oppressed and had then risen up.

This belief that they didn't have to worry about white rules. They were a force of nature, black, beautiful, breathtaking. Forget equals, they were better than anyone and they knew it.

When Richards bats, every shot is a statement. Not a protest, but a statement about who he is as a man. And that's not a cricket thing; you don't need to know or understand cricket to feel that something deeper is happening. It radiates from him. This magnificent combination of arrogance and regalness.

For Viv, this was real. This black expression. This beating the masters. Using the generations of anger built up in him. His batting was righting some wrongs. His batting was evening the playing field. His political contribution to the cause was hooking for six. And you can see it.

'If you are going to call me a black bastard, how observant of you to notice that I am black,' Viv snorted while holding the throat of an Aussie player in the change-rooms. 'But do you have the documentation to prove I am a bastard?'

Other batsmen made runs. Viv made statements. Viv was a statement.

Chapter 36

THE UNFORGIVEN

'I would rather die than lay down my dignity,' said Viv Richards when asked about the so-called Rebel tours to South Africa. Everyone who knew him believed him when he said it.

When 12 English cricketers suddenly arrived in South Africa for a series of unofficial matches in 1982, they expected to be given a slap on the wrist. The rebels had got it very wrong.

The media and politicians attacked them for breaking the sporting sanctions on South Africa and banned them from cricket for three years. The team was full of English Test players, most notably future England captains Graham Gooch and John Emburey, plus Geoffrey Boycott. They were easily beaten. In 1989, Mike Gatting led another tour. Later he would once again play for England, and then become president of the MCC at the same time they promoted the 'Spirit of Cricket'.

Journalist Frank Keating wrote upon their arrival back home, 'No more inglorious, downright disgraced and discredited team or sportsmen wearing the badge of "England" can ever have returned through customs with such nothingness to declare.'

A Sri Lankan side went. Sri Lanka had only just come into Test cricket. The rebel side they sent over was captained by their inaugural Test captain, Bandula Warnapura. They were smashed by the South Africans on the field. Smashed by the Asian and West Indian media off it. At home they were called treasonous. Future captain Arjuna Ranatunga originally tried to join the tour, but Warnapura said, 'You are not going anywhere. You are too young to go and you have a long career ahead of you.' It was Warnapura's best decision for Sri Lankan cricket.

Australia sent two tours. Both times Kim Hughes took a team with Ashes heroes Terry Alderman and Rodney Hogg. Former Victorian coach Greg Shippherd played, as did well-known commentator Mike Haysman. The Australian Prime Minister, Bob Hawke, called them traitors. They lost as well.

Many of these players still bear the scars of being a rebel. Some still try to defend their motives. Others just sort of shrug off their past.

The players who have suffered the most weren't from these three countries; they were all from one other team. The West Indies.

The West Indian rebel team included one of the fastest bowlers ever, Sylvester Clarke; 1979 World Cup final star Collis King; and one of the original fast four, Colin Croft.

And Richard 'Danny Germs' Austin, who only ever played two Tests. In his article 'The Unforgiven', Siddhartha Vaidyanathan paints a horrible picture of what happened to Austin, whom he encountered at Sabina Park during a Test in 2006:

> When Jerome Taylor, a fellow Jamaican, gets a standing ovation for his five-wicket haul, Danny cannot control himself. 'I could have done that,' he sobs. He begs for money at the end of the conversation and hugs you when he sees the 500-Jamaican-dollar note. He blushes when asked what he will do with the money. 'A bit of booze, a bit of crack.'

Danny Germs died while this book was being finished. He spent the last 32 years of his life in pain largely because of one mistake.

During the 2007 World Cup, Robert Craddock, the Australian writer, caught up with several of the players. There are too many who are now homeless and on drugs. Craddock tells a story from a West Indian cricket official about Herbert Chang, who played one Test for the Windies before going on the 1983 rebel tour. 'He wound down his window and Chang, clearly out of it, put his head through the window and moved to within a few centimetres of the man's face and said: "man, man, man, I just, I just wanna know which end I bowl from tomorrow."'

Franklyn Stephenson was a proper fast bowler, and a decent batsman. He once took more than 100 wickets and scored more than 1000 runs in a season of county cricket. To get there, he made two centuries in the last match, and added 11 wickets. He was a gun. He toured. And these days he struggles to get any coaching work. He never played a Test.

The most notable is Colin Croft. Croft would have been remembered as a legend. A brutal, fast legend. A man who bowled wide of the crease to aim the ball at a frightening angle at the batsman. In 27 Tests he took 125 wickets at 23. He was a monster. He could have been a legend. Instead he is the face of the unforgiven.

It wasn't long ago he was working in a supermarket.

Almost all the players were so traumatised when they returned that their lives never recovered, many spiralling viciously out of control.

Some have tried to claim that they actually helped. That black South African fans loved them. That they showed the white population that they weren't inferior; they even won. Plus they were part of the first bi-racial sporting event in South Africa for a very long time.

But while Mike Gatting can be forgiven by the rotten establishment and end up as the face of Lord's, the black players were held to a higher moral standard. Especially by players and media of colour. They knew what was happening in South Africa.

They knew.

And that is why they are the unforgiven. They were paid well, but they are still paying for it. Those that are still with us.

Chapter 37

A SUPERPOWER IS BORN

A T LORD'S ON a damp day in 1983, the World Cup final was being played. It was the third event in the UK, as no one had thought much about playing it anywhere else. India was in the final. They made a meagre 183, not even using up their allotted overs. Only the dashing Kris Srikkanth, one of the first real slappers in ODIs, made it past 30. The bowling line-up of Garner, Roberts, Marshall and Holding was simply too good. The West Indies would surely win without any real trouble.

Greenidge and Haynes were opening. Greenidge had made more than this score at Lord's on his own. And he'd done it against a quicker, and just better, bowling attack than this, and on a fifth-day pitch as well. Oh, and with a limp. But Greenidge was soon out. Haynes would finish his career with 17 ODI centuries. One of those was an undefeated 152. He was a champion of ODI cricket. He was out too.

Viv Richards was in no mood to think about defeat. He never was.

The names of Roger Binny, Balwinder Sandhu, Mohinder Amarnath and Madan Lal scared no man. How would they, even with the mastery of Kapil Dev, scare King Viv? After 27 balls, Viv was on 33. The only thing that would stop him seemed to be the small Indian total.

Then Madal Lal bowled a short ball.

Madan Lal ran in quicker than he bowled it. When he bowled a short ball, the game was at a pause while the batsman waited for it to reach him. Out beyond the Lord's square boundary there is Abbey Road. *The*

Abbey Road. Richards probably could have hit the ball there if he had wanted. While he waited for Lal's short ball, he probably thought about it. Instead he top-edged.

The cameras panned quickly to the deep mid-wicket stand. That is where the ball was expected to land when you dropped short to Viv. On the right of the screen you can just see Kapil Dev, and you can hear the crowd reaction. A fan runs out on the ground to celebrate with Dev. The King is out.

Dev took something like 18 steps. He had to run at close to full pace, while looking back over his shoulder. There was not a moment when it looked like he would do anything other than catch it. In his batting, he had failed trying to hit out. Dev only took one wicket in the final, a tailender once the game was all but won. But that catch, that catch. It won the match. It won the World Cup. It changed cricket.

Had Dev dropped that, India most probably would have lost that match.

Instead India was number one. Number one, at the home of cricket, against the greatest team the sport had produced.

From that day onwards, all sport, and most of life, took a backseat to cricket in India. It had not always been so. Football had been the premier sport in Kolkata. Hockey was a matter of national pride: India had won seven of eight gold medals at the Olympics at one stage. But now there are more cricket fans in India than there are people in all the other non-Asian countries combined. And that started in 1983, when Dev caught the ball that changed cricket.

Dev was a champion even before that. He made eight Test centuries and had a mullet that belongs in the Lord's museum. But his deeds as captain, as a batsman and as a bowler would never amount to anything compared with the athletic way he went to that catch, or the assured way he caught it.

Dev caught the World Cup and delivered a superpower.

Chapter 38

BLOOD AND SWEAT FROM BORDER; TEARS FROM HUGHES

'CAN YOU READ that?' Kim Hughes never actually said he was stepping down as Australian captain. He couldn't get through his statement to the cameras. The crying is what people remember.

The West Indies was the team that made Kim Hughes cry. They weren't the only ones to blame. His own form, bitchiness from his teammates and the media all played their part.

Australian captains since Bill Woodfull were seen as hard, unflinching men. That was the stereotype, if not always the truth. They had aggressive mannerisms, dominant facial hair and had their shirts unbuttoned to show their masculinity. Kim Hughes was crying. Kim Hughes was not a hard man. Kim Hughes was not Australian captain.

The man who replaced him may not have even had tear ducts.

Allan Border batted with a grimace. His shots were little jabs. Nothing flowed. Everything was a punch. A struggle. He batted like a labourer. Sweat and hard work. All the other Australians seemed soft compared to him, even the beer barrel–shaped, moustachioed David Boon. Border seemed like the perfect combination of attack while refusing to be beaten. His wicket was always more dramatic than other players', as you had to pry it from his hands while staring into his eyes.

Border's debut was during Kerry Packer's series. Most of the players from that era were not good enough, broken, or old. Border was none of those things. Border was a master of spin and a master of pace. His footwork wasn't always beautiful, but it was beautifully efficient.

His hook shot was always willing, and seemingly more consistent than other batsmen. And he scored runs overseas. He scored more hundreds overseas than he did at home, despite playing more innings at home. He also averaged well over 50 away from home.

Allan Border was made for tours. The dirtier, the sweatier, the more controversial, the better. In 1983/84 he was just another member of the team. It was still Kim Hughes in charge.

The West Indies bowling attack consisted of Wayne Daniel, Michael Holding, Malcolm Marshall and Joel Garner.

At Port of Spain in 1984, it rained most of the first day. So when Australia finally started batting, it was dark and dangerous. The West Indies had three wickets for the first 16 runs. That's when Border came in. By drinks the next morning Joel Garner had taken every single wicket in the top five, except Border's.

Garner was tall. He was a collection of yorkers and throat balls. He might have bowled on a length, but still the ball reared to the throat. He broke your toes, or your ribs, or your wicket. His bowling wasn't complex; it was a really tall, really strong man, bowling really fast.

If Garner isn't always automatically mentioned any time people are talking about the greatest bowlers of all time in Test cricket, it's probably because he was probably the greatest ODI bowler, or player, of all time. In ODI cricket he went at 3 runs an over, and took a wicket every 18 runs.

But Garner wasn't stopping Border, who kept going. Geoff Lawson and Dean Jones stuck around, but eventually Border was left with the tail. Border got an extra hour from the last three men. Australia made it to 255, Border to 98. Not out.

The West Indies quickly put on 468 and declared. They had three and a half sessions to beat Australia. Garner took the first wicket and that night Australia was already three wickets down.

The next day Border came in. Again all the batsmen left him. So Border shepherded the tail. He was used to batting with the tail.

At the MCG just over a year earlier, Allan Border was batting with the tail, chasing 218. They needed 74 runs to win when Jeff Thomson came out as the last man. It was nearing stumps, but Border and Thommo kept scoring runs, and at the close, they needed only 37 more. The next morning 18,000 people came to the ground. With four more needed,

Thommo nicked one off Ian Botham. It went flying towards the slips and Chris Tavare dropped a straightforward chance, but Geoff Miller took the spill. Australia lost by three runs.

At Port of Spain, the situation was different. Runs didn't matter. Time did. Rodney Hogg batted with Border for 53 minutes. But when he was out, that still left over an hour and a half for Terry Alderman. Alderman couldn't bat. He bowled beautiful gentle out-swingers that, eight years apart, completely baffled English batsmen in England. But Alderman truly couldn't bat. His highest score was 12 at that time. His batting average was six and in 23 of his 53 career innings he did not score.

Allan Border somehow got Terry Alderman through 105 minutes of cricket. And off the last ball of the day, Gus Logie presented Border with a ball he could hit to bring up his hundred. Allan Border had faced the West Indies at their best, at a time when no other Australian could handle them, and he'd not been dismissed in the match. He'd even outlasted Joel Garner, the natural disaster of fast bowlers.

In that series Border would score more than double any other Australian player. Garner would take 31 wickets at 16. There would be no more draws in that series. The West Indies would win all the remaining matches.

Allan Border would bat on and grimace. A few months later, it would be his team, not just in spirit.

Chapter 39

DAVID BEATS GOLIATH

THERE WAS ONLY one team that beat a strong West Indies team during their years of dominance – and it was the most unlikely team to do so. In the summer of 1979 the West Indies easily accounted for Australia, winning a three-Test series 2-0, one by an innings, the other by 400-plus runs. And they were then due to play New Zealand.

The West Indies turned up without Viv Richards, in the mood to have a bit of a rest from Australia, win some easy matches and then head home. They didn't fear the New Zealanders at all. Joel Garner's 'We've beat the Aussies, maan, and now we're gonna beat you' taunt on an ad didn't go down well.

At lunch on day one, the West Indies had lost four wickets. Three of them to Richard Hadlee. All three were LBW. The umpire's name was Fred Goodall. In the match there were 12 LBWS; Hadlee claimed seven, the West Indies took the other five. Hadlee added four other wickets to his total. Hadlee left his batsmen with 104 runs to get. When Hadlee came into the wicket the score was 6/44. Hadlee second-top scored, before Gary Troup and Stephen Boock managed an epic four-run partnership and won the game by one wicket.

The West Indies was 0-1, but the team was more upset with umpire Goodall than themselves. They felt like he was an annoying teacher who had to be part of everything. To be fair, Goodall was an annoying teacher who had to be part of everything.

BREAKTHROUGH

Forty years is a long time to wait for your first Test series win. When New Zealand did finally win a series, they did it in their own understated way. They had no champions in the team that won the only Test. In that Test, the top score was from a Pakistani, and so was the only five-wicket haul. They had a collapse of 4/4. When they were finally chasing the target of 82, they lost five wickets. And by doing it in Pakistan, their fans did not see it.

In the third and final Test they were playing in Dhaka when Glenn Turner made a stoic, almost comatose, 110, his first century in Test Cricket, over 440 minutes. In their second innings they went into the final day, the fourth, slightly in front, but with Turner at the crease. Soon after they were 8/108, with a lead of less than a hundred. Then Mark Burgess was joined at the crease by Bob Cunis.

Burgess played 50 Tests for an average of 31, but this was him at his best – an undefeated 119, helped out by tailender Cunis hanging around for almost two hours.

Cunis' surname inspired the line 'neither one thing nor the other'. That was also the truth about his career. He was a bowler who could scrap with the bat.

These are not two Hollywood action heroes; these are everyday humans in a foreign land with everything falling down around them and their dream of winning their first-ever series on the line. Two hours they batted. They added 96 runs. Put on a lead. Took out time. Gave some hope. Burgess made a hundred, his second first-class hundred. Cunis only 23. Which is neither one thing, nor the other.

Pakistan had two hours and 20 minutes to score 184. They shut up after losing four wickets – all to Cunis. And the crowd ran onto the ground, ensuring a draw.

Cunis' 29 runs and four wickets are among the most important ever by a New Zealander. It meant a draw, which meant a 1-0 series victory. After 40 years of trying.

Don Neely, a former first-class cricketer and cricket official later said, 'It's a pity this side hasn't had greater recognition. Perhaps their achievements were overshadowed by other world events in those tumultuous times, which saw men walking on the moon, as well as Vietnam and Woodstock.'

The West Indies had been acting like kids. The most memorable occasion in that first Test was when they thought they had a certain caught behind from Michael Holding. Not out. John Parker, the batsman, attended to his gloves, perhaps even resticking them after getting ready to take them off. Michael Holding then ran past him and kicked down his stumps. John Parker barely looked up. Goodall, the square-leg umpire walked in, looked at Clive Lloyd and said, ''Scuse me skipper, would you mind having a quiet word with your bowler? This is not on,' as he put the stumps back up.

To soothe them between Tests a local Christchurch radio station made a satirical calypso song.

The second Test actually went ok, until Goodall missed a caught-behind that almost took Geoff Howarth's thumb off. After tea, the West Indies wouldn't even come out of their rooms. They wanted Goodall replaced; the New Zealand officials said no. Twelve minutes later the team entered the field. But they dropped catches on purpose and let balls go to the boundary; they were staging an onfield stroppy protest. Hadlee exploited that for a hundred. That night the West Indies planned on going home, but their board would not let them.

The next day, after a rest day had calmed down the West Indies, Goodall managed to make them upset again. This time he missed a catch behind from Colin Croft to Hadlee.

Soon after Croft bowled a back-foot return crease no-ball. Croft walked up to the stumps and, like a two-year-old, flicked the bails off and just kept walking. Jeremy Coney picked up the bails to save Goodall the embarrassment. Next ball, Coney couldn't protect Goodall.

Croft, who was bowling so wide of the crease, as he usually did, that he was being called for no-balls, suddenly came so close to the stumps that he bumped into Goodall as he bowled. Goodall managed to stay upright, despite Croft's massive frame – six foot six and 230 pounds – elbowing him at full pace.

Croft wasn't even given suspended.

The Test ended in a draw. Goodall missed the next Test. That was a draw. New Zealand won the series 1-0.

At an awards ceremony a short time later, Goodall got himself in trouble with a remark about the West Indians: 'They could, I suppose, interpret what I said as a taunt. It was a flippant remark that could have been taken the wrong way and some people decided it was racist.' Those guys and their flippant remarks about West Indians.

There is no evidence to say that Goodall was a cheat. But there was plenty of evidence that suggested Goodall was not a good umpire.

It was an era of bad home umpiring. Jeremy Coney threatened to take his team off the ground in Pakistan when Shakoor Rana gave a horrible decision. In Pakistan Mike Gatting infamously screamed at Shakoor Rana (again). There were also fun facts such as Bill Lawry never once being out LBW in Australia in his entire career. Eventually, these sorts of problems would be fixed when neutral umpires were brought in.

None of that should overshadow what was a remarkable win for New Zealand. This was the second Test series New Zealand had ever won. Its first series win had taken 40 years to achieve. Then the next decade, the 1970s, went by without a series win at all.

The third Test against New Zealand ended on 5 March 1980. It was 3 May 1995 when the West Indies lost their next series.

Chapter 40

THE MOUSTACHIOED VILLAIN

THAT MOUSTACHE. THERE was no way around it. It was the moustache of a villain. It wasn't just the moustache. There were the sharp features of someone who would tie a young girl to a train line. And his eyes. They were supposed to look at you like that. Always.

Richard Hadlee seemed to pop out of a 1920s film and straight into the bowling crease.

Every move he made was calculated. Everything he did was about moving his case forward and bringing another man down. There have been many cricketers in this book, but perhaps none was more cunning, more devious, more skilful and more of one absolute mind than Richard Hadlee. The objective was to take more wickets, and score more runs, than anyone else. It made him successful, though not always liked.

The Australian crowds called him a wanker, as one, in unison; he made them channel their rage at him. It was the highest honour they could bestow.

Even when he was at his best, New Zealand could not warm to him. On two occasions Hadlee won a car for his performances in Australia, the first time he sold the car and the whole team took a slice of the profits. The second time he did not. He wanted the car. Some people never forgot that.

Everyone had an opinion on Richard Hadlee, but he was determined to take more wickets than there were people who hated him. He came very close. Never has a player been this good, and yet still remained so unloved by even his own fans.

The New Zealand public might never have warmed to Richard Hadlee, but they hated Australia more. Australia had treated them poorly since they arrived in Test Cricket. And then in 1981, Greg Chappell made it so very much worse.

By 1981 cricket had not overdosed on ODIs, but they were still thought of as fairly meaningless matches. Really until the 1983 World Cup, ODI cricket was still not much of a phenomenon. So the New Zealand match at the MCG should have been a forgettable match.

Thanks to the last ball, it wasn't.

Greg Chappell was the Australian captain. He was also the Australian coach. Under the new era of Australian cricket, as many games as possible were added to the schedule to give Kerry Packer as much content as possible. Australia had a team manager, a physio, and their players. The captain's job had grown to such a level that it was almost impossible.

All of this had turned Greg Chappell into a ticking time bomb. 'I wasn't fit,' he said later.

> I mean, I was mentally wrung out, I was physically wrung out, and I was fed up with the whole system. Things seemed to be just closing in on us, and I suppose in my own case I felt they were closing in on me, and it was a cry for help. I was sitting on the ground at deep mid-on, Brian McKechnie came in to bat, I'd never seen him before. The fact that he was batting number 11 probably suggested he wasn't that good, but at that stage I didn't really care. I hadn't thought about it before looking up and seeing him walk through the gate, and I thought I've had a gutful of this.

Chappell walked up to his brother Trevor and told him to roll the ball along the ground ensuring that McKechnie couldn't hit a six and Australia would win the match. It was a legal ball under the laws of cricket. The umpires discussed it, but couldn't stop it. Rod Marsh behind the stumps was angry. Brian McKechnie was angry. Trevor Chappell rolled the ball along the ground. Brian McKechnie blocked it, and then threw his bat.

Richie Benaud gave the Channel 9 viewers as much rage as he had ever used on air. New Zealand Prime Minister Robert Muldoon chimed in with 'the most disgusting incident I can recall in the history of cricket'.

Underarm. There are New Zealand fans who never truly got over it.

When in another ODI from 2009 Brad Haddin took off the bails with his hands, and then let Neil Broom think he was bowled, it all came flooding back. It is never far from the surface in Australia–New Zealand cricket relations.

The law was changed to prevent underarm happening again. Greg Chappell was given a support network, and the workloads of players have been monitored more closely since then. And it took the Australia–New Zealand rivalry from lukewarm to boiling hot.

The next year, 1982, New Zealand added a hero to their villain, a champion batsman to their champion bowler.

Martin Crowe came into world cricket and was instantly identifiable as a future champion. Like Hadlee, Crowe came from a cricket family, but unlike Hadlee, Crowe was almost instantly liked. By everyone. His technique was just delicious. Batting fans wanted to eat it up.

Martin Crowe was like a beautifully illustrated coaching manual come to life. He managed to play forward, and still late. He rotated the strike right up until the moment there was a ball he could hit for four, and then it went. His batting was calm and complete. There were no histrionics. He wasn't a man who got sucked in to conflicts. He just batted, perfectly.

When Martin Crowe pushes through point, you feel like you have seen Jesus.

Martin Crowe was so cool, that even kids in Australian cricket would dress like him. When he wore a white helmet, so did they. When Martin Crowe wore long sleeves, they asked their mother for a long-sleeve shirt. There is nothing his cousin, Russell, could do on a screen that would ever equate to what Martin did on the field.

He was Martin Crowe; he was perfect.

When reverse swing became a big deal through the skill of Pakistan, it was Martin Crowe who worked it out in a way that no one else could. They would bowl faster, they would swing the ball more, and he would just continue to beat them.

His batting average was 45, batting in what was one of the hardest eras. He had to face the West Indies at their best. Willis and Botham. The Pakistanis and their swing. Lillee and Warne. And then the South Africans showed up. Bowling has rarely been better. Crowe was there for all of it. Playing forward, playing late, playing perfectly.

When Crowe brought up his hundred in the 1992 World Cup against the Australians, an innings of straight drives you'd cry about and pull shots you'd want to be able to tell your grandkids about, the crowd swarmed on. So many kids. They loved him.

Hadlee's bowling was actually more perfect than Crowe's batting. His breeding as a cricketer was even better than Crowe's. Crowe had one brother who played internationals and a father who played first-class cricket. Hadlee came through the most royal line. That of Walter Hadlee, the former player, captain, chairman, selector and president of the New Zealand board. Walter was like the old guy at your local club. He started off playing, and ended up sweeping the floors and running the meetings. There was nothing that Walter wouldn't do for New Zealand cricket. Even when he had kids, he bred them for the cricket team. He also had sons Barry as an ODI batsman, and Dayle as a handy swing bowler.

Richard went beyond all of them. When he was young, he was properly quick. Every part of his action was devised just to get the most out of the next ball. His arms had no tell. His run-up had no kink. He ran straight at the target. At the crease he went into the most prefect side on-position. His front arm was exactly where it needed to be, and as strong as it needed to be. To get as close to the umpire as possible his right arm would come up over the umpire's head. His follow-through was so perfect that if he had a pen, he would have marked the same line on his trousers every single ball. By the end of his career his run-up was only 10 paces. He didn't need more.

Early on he'd tried to blast people with pace, but after struggling against the Australian team, who loved pace, his keeper Ken Wadsworth gave him some advice: 'At home you might get wickets by bowling fast and scaring batsmen. Australian batsmen are used to fast bowling, are not scared, and the bowler needs more skills than sheer speed if he is to get out good batsmen on the hard, fast Australian pitches.'

No religious extremist has ever taken to a dogma more than Richard Hadlee did to that advice. He became the skilled bowler of a generation. Nothing he did was wrong. Nothing.

When New Zealand combined this perfect hero and this perfect villain, they turned from the little team that might, to the little team that did. They had always had role players, they had always had triers, they had even occasionally had champions, but they had never had this mix of all of them.

They had beaten the West Indies. They won six out of 10 series. They beat India, Sri Lanka, England and Pakistan. It was a golden time. Their best of times. But they still had to beat Australia. Everything else was great, but there would have been an asterisk without beating Australia.

There were to be two back-to-back series between the countries. Each of three Tests home and away. The first Test was in Brisbane. Australia was in no way a great side. They were trying to build one. Allan Border had given them a professional outlook. He had dragged them up. He would not accept anything short of tough quality cricket. His leadership wasn't via subtle methods or tactical genius. He captained as he batted – a solid defence, an attacking instinct, and as though his life depended on it. Australia was starting to understand. And improve.

New Zealand won the toss and bowled. Vaughan Brown took his only Test wicket, caught by Hadlee. It was the only wicket Hadlee didn't take. His figures: 23.4 overs, 4 maidens, 52 runs and 9 wickets. Australia had made 127 runs off the remaining bowlers.

Then it was Martin Crowe's turn. You know what he did. He was perfect. For 328 balls he batted, he hit the ball through point like a poet, flicked off his pads like the ball deserved it, drove as nature intended it and pulled with complete control. Crowe ended on 188. To replace him, on came Hadlee. For a bit of fun, Hadlee threw in 54 off 45 balls.

The only thing that could stop Hadlee was Allan Border. Border was ably backed up by his spectacularly odd off-spinner Greg Matthews. Both made hundreds in the second innings. Eventually Hadlee had Australia done, and he took the final wicket of the match, his 15th. Border stood at the other end, his hands were in the teapot position even before the last wicket. He was 152. New Zealand was 1-0.

Crowe failed twice, once a run-out, in the following Test, and Australia scampered home with four wickets in hand. Hadlee took only seven wickets.

The third and deciding Test went like this. Hadlee took five wickets. Crowe made 71 runs. Hadlee took six wickets. Crowe was not out on 42 when the winning runs were scored.

Hadlee took 33 wickets in the series; Australian bowlers took 40 altogether. Hadlee took just over one-third of New Zealand's wickets in his career.

Allan Border would have to be talked into not quitting the captaincy. New Zealand had broken Border. They had almost ended an era before Border could build it. He stayed on and Australia won the 1987 World Cup. But not before losing the return Test series in New Zealand. To Hadlee. To Crowe.

The Kiwis' golden era would continue for two more series. They would end up winning nine out of 14 series. After beating Australia, they would then travel to England and win that series too.

In the deciding Test, Richard Hadlee would take 10 wickets. Martin Crowe would be not out at the end. The Villain and the Hero. Perfect alone. Perfect together.

Chapter 41

BLACKWASH

MALCOLM MARSHALL RUNS in fast. His arms move fast. His deliveries move fast. And Andy Lloyd hits the ground fast.

It was the last ball that Andy Lloyd ever faced in Test cricket. He spent his next few days in hospital with blurred vision. He didn't play again in first-class cricket until the following year. His Test career lasted 30 minutes. He is the only opener in the history of the game who was never dismissed.

Lloyd was wearing an arm guard, a chest guard, a thigh pad and a helmet. Against Malcolm Marshall that wasn't enough.

This was the first morning of the series that would be dubbed 'Blackwash'. At lunch, England had lost four wickets, and one batsman forever. Marshall hadn't taken a wicket, but he'd set the tone.

Malcom Marshall was one of a kind. At five foot nine, most modern bowling academies would kiss him on the head and throw him away. Skiddy bowlers can be handy, at times, but they need to be so much more skilful to just survive. Marshall was.

His run-up came from mid-off; it was angled to the point of parody. And it was a run-up. Few bowlers have ever approached the crease that quickly. Then he bowled front-on. The coaching manuals disagree with that, but Marshall managed to swing the ball, both ways, without the traditional action. His height was supposed to be a hindrance, but if you are short, and you bowl fast, you actually have a big advantage. When you bowl short, the ball is hard to get away from.

All the West Indian quicks had their own kind of bouncer, much like the very best leg-spinners all have their own kind of wrong'un.

Roberts had the slower and faster bouncers: one to set you up, the other to finish you. Holding had the effortless bouncer that you saw no evidence of until your self-preservation reflexes kicked in. Joel Garner's bouncers often weren't bouncers; they were just vertical length balls.

All were tough, but survivable. Marshall's bouncer was aimed for maximum damage. The skiddy nature meant that it wouldn't fly by, you couldn't get out of its path. It was a heat-seeking missile and it was locked on you. It was as if it knew your fear and wouldn't let you go. If you took your eye off it, it cannoned into you. Arms and shoulders took a huge beating. Heads were in trouble.

Marshall was just always at something. If it wasn't your body or stumps, it was your technical flaws, or mental ones.

And if you were the captain, Marshall lifted again. So did all the West Indies; they believed in the 'knock the head off and the body will fall' theory. They tried to knock off the head of a lot of captains.

In the Blackwash series, the leader was David Gower. Gower was effortless grace at the crease. He was dainty and sublime. His batting was like a dream. The West Indies crushed dreams.

Gower with the bat was very much a cricket ingenue against the West Indies. Against the softer and gentler teams, he was a stylish Test batsman; against the West Indies he was more of a smear. In that series he passed 50 once in 10 innings. He averaged 19. The beautiful blond curls atop Gower's manicured head looked great as the West Indies placed it on the steps of Lord's.

Then, his captaincy was taken down. Gower was 1-0 down, and England was having a good Test. Marshall had taken a six-wicket haul, but England had scored more in both of their innings than the West Indies had in their second innings. Botham had taken an eight-wicket haul, made an 81, and had his waddle on. England was confident enough to give the West Indies a bit of a nominal chase of 342 to win in five and a half hours.

Gordon Greenidge was limping. He had a thigh injury. From this day forward there are sane English cricket fans who don't like it when a batsman has an injury. Greenidge did that to them.

Had he played today, Greenidge might have chosen to play for England, and not the West Indies. He played for Hampshire before Barbados and many, including those in the West Indies change-room, often thought of him as English. But he didn't play English-style cricket. Like many of the great West Indians, he was a natural player who learnt refinements to his game in county cricket. Playing in England day in and out as a professional seemed to turn many English players into drones. But for the West Indies players it took off the rawness that needed to go, and gave them the sort of experience and game that meant they could play anywhere and win.

When the ball was outside off stump, Greenidge played it like it had slept with his sister. There was a square drive early on in his Lord's innings in that second Test. The ball is short and wide; it deserves to be hit, craves to be hit. Greenidge launches into it, and there is a moment where it feels like the ball is on his bat and on the boundary at the same time. As if Greenidge with the bat could prove quantum physics, or disprove relativity. Even Richie Benaud, who is allergic to hyperbole said, 'Shot. That's hit the fence now.'

Desmond Haynes, the Haynes in 'Greenidge and Haynes', was run out when the score was 57. Then Gomes and Greenidge played until all 341 runs were scored. In 66.1 overs. On the last day of a Test Match. Against Bob Willis and Ian Botham.

The normal rules of cricket science did not apply to this team.

England never looked like stopping them in that innings. They never looked like stopping the West Indies. The West Indies won 5-0. They blackwashed England. They blackwashed cricket.

Chapter 42

THE LION OF LAHORE ROARS

A FORMER CRICKETER FALLS off a forklift and it makes the news world wide. It wasn't just a cricketer. It was a political leader with 20 million devotees. At one time, he was one of XI.

Back in the early 1970s he was just an educated cricketer, bowling a bit of medium pace, batting a little bit, and looking good doing it. But Imran Khan was never content. So he turned that medium pace into pace like fire.

By the time he was playing against Australia in 1978/79, the world knew who Imran Khan was.

In the first Test, at the MCG, both teams struggled in the first innings. Imran Khan bowled very fast against an Australian team with almost all its stars playing for Kerry Packer. In the second innings Pakistan made 353, which meant Australia needed 382 to win.

Australia, or Australia lite, did quite well. Dav Whatmore, before he became a World Cup winning coach with Sri Lanka, was the only Australian out when they crossed a hundred. But then something odd happened. Andrew Hilditch moved across his stumps when he was 62 and then tried to leg glance a ball that faded away from him. It clipped the outside of leg stump. The commentators called it a peculiar dismissal.

Graeme Yallop, the accidental and unwilling Australian captain, was run out not long after, but then Allan Border and Kim Hughes put on a huge partnership. At tea on the final day, Australia had beaten the new ball, needed less than a hundred, and had their two best batsmen at the crease.

Then Sarfraz Nawaz came back on. He was no Imran Khan. He had even shortened his run, and slowed down his already pedestrian pace. He bowled Allan Border. Graeme Wood was caught behind next ball. Peter Sleep was clean bowled. Kim Hughes, never one to defend, decided that with Sarfraz getting all these wickets, the best thing to do was to attack, and found mid-on. Next over Wayne Clark was bowled playing back to a ball he couldn't understand.

Then, a no-ball. One run.

Rodney Hogg was LBW. When Alan Hurst wasn't out first ball, the crowd cheered. Next ball, Hurst was caught behind.

Australia had been 3/305. They were now all out for 310. Sarfraz had had 2/85. He now had 9/86.

That number now adorns one of the walls of the MCG as part of an art exhibition.

Most of the Australian batsmen had helmets. They were prepared for Imran Khan's scary pace. They would survive that. At the other end a man bowled as if his hip needed to be replaced, shuffling in with a sideways action and bowling just above medium pace. The ball veered in dramatically at the stumps and, when he wanted it to, also went away. All this swing was late. And combined with a low-bouncing Melbourne pitch, it became impossible.

'The Australian newspapers,' Sarfraz later said, 'reported that I was the most talked-about person in the country the day after the Test.'

Batsmen had evolved to protect themselves from bouncers. But as they did, Sarfraz Nawaz showed the world reverse swing. Their heads were safer; their leg stumps were not.

Years later, when talking to Osman Samiuddin and Peter Oborne for their books on Pakistan cricket, Sarfraz would deny that his 9/86 was from reverse swing. But the grainy footage of Sarfraz is unmistakable to modern cricket eyes. The ball went Irish. Reverse.

Back in the 1960s at the Mozang Link cricket club of Lahore, Sarfraz and Salim Mir opened the bowling together. One of them, Salim probably, first worked out that when the ball stopped swinging, if you roughed up one side significantly and kept the other side smooth, the ball would swing the opposite to the conventional way. And, if done correctly, it would swing violently, like the ball had a grudge against the batsman.

That is how Sarfraz took his last seven wickets – like the ball was on a private mission to hit pads and stumps – and the batsmen were just helpless.

Salim Mir might have invented, or co-invented, reverse swing on those lonely days watching Pakistani batsmen carve the runs, but he wasn't great at it. His first-class career was eight wickets at 40.

Sarfraz's career only got better. He was signed with Northamptonshire before he played Test cricket because he could, conventionally and non-conventionally, swing it both ways. But unlike Reggie Schwarz, who upon learning of the wrong'un taught everyone he could and built an army of wrist-spinners, Sarfraz kept it to himself. And it wasn't until the mid-70s that he would teach Imran Khan. And it wasn't until 1982 that Imran perfected it.

India was sent in at Karachi by Imran Khan. They were then bowled out very cheaply. Khan, bowling very fast, took three wickets, and also ran out Gavaskar off his own bowling with a piece of athleticism that involved running and turning and hitting the stumps. It was a fast bowler in perfection. And yet, in the second innings, he would top that.

Pakistan had a massive lead. India had managed to build a steady platform with their two greatest batsmen of the era, Gavaskar and Vengsarkar, moving the score slowly but surely as they fought for the draw. Then, Imran.

Gavaskar is back and across; he is so cautious he might as well be batting in a radiation suit. But the ball doesn't care; it just goes through him. It was 199th career wicket of Imran Khan. The 200th was against the great Gundappa Viswanath, who left a ball miles outside off stump, and lost his off stump. The third wicket in that spell was Mohinder Amarnath. His was a shocking LBW outside off stump, but by this stage the umpire was probably hypnotised by the reverse swing.

Imran kept hitting the stumps, kept swooping, kept being majestic. India lost 6/12 as Imran dismissed Kapil Dev. Three of their all-time greats, all swept aside, blown away, embarrassed, gone. Imran would come back later for Vengsarkar as well. 8/60.

It was during the 1980s that Imran's batting came along as well. By came along, read he turned himself into one of the world's best batsmen.

And from 1980 to 1988 Imran took 236 wickets at 17. As captain, with the bat he averaged 52. Martin Crowe and David Gower, with their endless grace and dripping skill, couldn't average 50 with the bat. It was fewer flowing locks, open shirts and the pure sex of his bowling, but Imran was a proper batsman, despite being a party batsman for almost the first 10 years of his career.

In the 1980s Imran Khan was as close to cricket perfection as human eyes had ever seen.

And had he not existed, Pakistan cricket would not have grown into what it did. Imran's all-round skill was only part of it. Pakistan grew cricketers with such freakish talent that you could barely believe they existed.

Javed Miandad could bat. In his soul, he could bat. His mind could bat. His mouth could bat. And his hands, well, they had a soul, mind and mouth of their own. Miandad would beat the bowler, would beat the captain, would beat the field, and then he would tell everyone how he beat them.

His batting style was perverse as, unlike most batsmen, he seemed to want the wicket to be bad. He wanted to run into the burning house. He needed that adrenaline to get him to be great.

Miandad was the first batsman to find and exploit the gaps in ODI fields. Captains would spend most of their day moving cover 20 feet to the right and left as Miandad picked up endless twos, before he got bored and just started hitting boundaries. He played to his own tune, and it was a beautiful, sophisticated, mad symphony that only existed in his head.

Abdul Qadir also played cricket his own way. Spinners had virtually been ended by the West Indies. Wrist-spin was dead. There was the odd flare-up from India, but it was crushed eventually. Cricket is a stats game – but Abdul Qadir was above stats. Abdul Qadir was the keeper of the flame. While the West Indies displayed cricket's most brutal masculinity, Qadir danced like a beautiful fairy. A jaunty cricket wizard. Not worrying about stats, Qadir could stalk his target for hours. Moving the batsman an inch an over for a session, showing them his two obvious wrong'uns, and then, when he had them standing where he wanted them, thinking they knew what was coming, he'd bowl his secret finger wrong'un, and watch them get bowled.

Then there was Saleem Malik, a batsman with a bag of tricks. Mushtaq Ahmed, enthusiasm and skill of wrist. Zaheer Abbas, once dubbed the Asian Bradman. Ijaz Ahmed and his axe grip. The parsimonious Iqbal Ahmed. Mudassar Nazar the slow low battler. And the pace and sideways movement of Aaqib Javed.

This is a team that should have smashed pretty much everyone, and even scared the great West Indians. Instead, it bumbled. Their Test record wasn't poor; it just wasn't good enough for a team this good. In fact, had they not had a magical couple of weeks, there would be nothing other than individual brilliance to remember this team for.

The 1992 World Cup was like the dawn of cricket's new era. ODI cricket in Australia had been about coloured clothing and white balls for a very long time. But the world cups were whites and red balls, like the rest of cricket. The 1992 World Cup was different. It felt like, for the first time, a real event. There were nine nations playing. To spread the game, it was played around big cities and regional places. New Zealand and Australia both embraced the tournament. The uniforms are still the most fetishised of all cricket strips.

The series captains' photo is a sight to behold. Dave Houghton, the best Zimbabwean batsman in history. Kepler Wessels, a man tough enough to brave the Australian shield system and then get a game for Australia before leading his country, South Africa. Mohammad Azharuddin, the word's most stylish batsman. Richie Richardson, the new Viv Richards. Aravinda De Silva, Sri Lanka's greatest player. Martin Crowe, New Zealand's greatest batsman. Allan Border, the father of Australia's greatest generation. Graham Gooch, a man who got better and better with age. And Imran Khan.

Pakistan's World Cup started shambolically. The team had travelled out early, which showed foresight they so rarely applied. But when they were out there, they were horrible. Javed Miandad had been left out of the side because of, depending on who you believed, injury, injury and form, or politics played by Imran Khan. He used his own politics to get back into the side when in every warm-up Pakistan didn't cross 200.

Miandad arriving brought no joy though, despite the fact he batted well – as Waqar Younis was sent home with a back fracture.

Wasim Akram and Waqar could win a World Cup on their own. When Wasim bowled, the ball had a mind of its own. It could be placed on the same spot, repeatedly on a good day, but it also leapt up, cut left, cut right, swung in, swung out. It was as if it was being operated by a remote control. His run-up was reportedly 17 paces, but it felt like six super quick steps and a left arm that was invisible to the eye. He was the combination of every single tape ball bowler in Pakistan's street cricket history. When Wasim bowled, it felt like anything could happen.

While the West Indies was still about endless brutality and pace, the Pakistanis were about unseeable swerve. Imran Khan might well have birthed two perfect weapons.

Waqar Younis arrived as a child, but a fully grown man. For five years, the only thing that slowed down his deliveries were stumps and toes. His superpower seemed to be that his torso could detach from his waist, turn all the way back and then hurl the ball from a wind-up that mortal spines could not maintain. You knew where he was going to bowl it, how it was going to get there, how fast it would come, and what would happen if you missed it. Still, you were out. From 1990 to 1994 Waqar took a wicket every 32 balls in Test cricket. No one has ever done better for that long. Ever.

So with Waqar out, Pakistan was missing something special.

Pakistan played like a broken team. They won once in their first five games, against Zimbabwe. They were bowled out for 74 against England. Imran was in and out of the team with injury. Ijaz Ahmed was turned from steady batsman to horrendous slow-medium bowler. Wasim took wickets, but could not control the two white balls being used in the match. When Imran was out of the side, it seemed like no one else wanted the poisoned chalice of the captaincy.

Pakistan's sixth game was at the WACA. Had they lost, their tournament was over. Imran Khan stood in their change-room wearing a white T-shirt with a tiger on it. He gave a speech. Some players listened and were inspired. Others tuned out and mocked him. But he spoke to them all for 20 minutes, telling each one how talented they were, how special they were. Then he pointed to the tiger on his chest. The hunter. The warrior. The survivor.

Imran might as well have been pointing to himself.

Here was their greatest player, telling his team he thought they would win the World Cup, but that they had to play like a cornered tiger.

Then he walked out in front of the world, wearing what looked like a $5 T-shirt to the toss, and said to Ian Chappell, 'I want my team to play like a cornered tiger, you know, when it's at its most dangerous.'

By the end of telling Ian Chappell this, Imran was smiling. He knew how ridiculous this was. He knew it was his last chance.

Aamer Sohail made 76, Pakistan's only score above 50 in the match, and was caught first ball off a no-ball. Aaqib Javed and Mushtaq Ahmed were both the most inspired by Imran, and they combined for seven wickets as Australia were well beaten. The next day Wasim picked up the paper and Imran had told the press, 'I don't care how many no-balls Wasim bowls, I just want him to bowl fast.'

Against Sri Lanka in the next game, Imran steadied the batting line-up by moving himself to number three.

In the change-room, one-on-one, to the TV cameras, through the press and out on the ground, Imran was doing everything he could to inspire his team.

In the end they needed Australia to beat the West Indies for them to qualify for the semi-finals. They did. They had a celebration meal, and Wasim signed and dated an autograph for a taxi driver telling him they would win the World Cup.

•

They started their unlikely semi-final by bowling to Martin Crowe.

Crowe had become a cult figure of the tournament. His decision to let Mark Greatbatch slog at the top of the order would eventually change the way all ODI openers batted. His decision to open the bowling with Dipak Patel, a wily off-spinner, was seen as a masterstroke as well. Then there was his batting. Crowe might have had no knees to speak of, but his touch in that tournament was amazing. So while the rest of the Kiwis hung on, he smashed the ball everywhere. Crowe scored at better than a run a ball 91 from 83, and was only taken through a run-out.

New Zealand made 264, the biggest total made in a game not including Zimbabwe or Sri Lanka that tournament. New Zealand was so confident that Crowe didn't field, as he had injured his hamstring and instead watched from off the ground.

It's a decision that still haunts Crowe to this day.

This was Pakistan's first-ever World Cup semi-final. This would be their biggest ever chase in World Cup Cricket.

With Imran playing the anchor role, Pakistan was 4/140 after 35 overs. A simple chase now. A monster then. Inzamam ul-Haq walked out. That morning he had asked not to play. He felt his form was poor, and that he was unwell. Imran had told him he was going to play. When Inzamam walked out, Miandad said he looked like he had seen a ghost.

Only 31 balls later Inzamam brought up his 50. Miandad was not out as Pakistan won the match with an over to spare.

In the final, Imran continued to talk about tigers, and now everyone listened. There was no laughing or smirking now. Pakistan really believed they would win; Imran had made them believe.

A crowd of 87,172 people was at the MCG for the final. England was the form team. Derek Pringle, one of England's failed new Bothams, was swinging the ball nicely and Pakistan decided to sit on the game.

Imran Khan had nine runs from the first 16 overs, including a drop from Graham Gooch. After 25 overs, Pakistan was 70 runs. They batted themselves into a corner. That is when they became dangerous. Imran, Miandad, Inzamam and Wasim all started swinging and by the end of the innings they had taken the score to 249.

With England four wickets down, Neil Fairbrother and Allan Lamb put on a decent partnership. Lamb was a staggeringly talented batsman who never truly got the most out of himself in Test Cricket. In ODI cricket, Lamb could play. He got on the nerves of the bowlers: his arrogance was always right at them, and he knew how to hit the ball. Once needing 18 runs of a final over from Bruce Reid in an ODI, Lamb only needed five balls.

So Imran brought on Wasim. Wasim had already bowled round the wicket to the right-handers earlier in the day when he took the wicket of Botham. It wasn't something left arm bowlers were known for.

The ball Wasim bowls is fast and angled in at Lamb. It is on a perfect length, a divine length. It is the exact length where batsmen are not sure whether to come forward or go back. Add to that Wasim's pace, his angle, and then, just a little more magic, the ball moves away from Lamb. Not a lot, but at his pace, with this angle, it only needs to do a little. Lamb is groping for a ball that he will barely ever see. He's clean bowled. Even the Pakistanis stop to watch the ball on the big screen.

Chris Lewis came in to bat. Lewis was a mega-talented English all-rounder who could never make the most of that talent. Years later he would be incarcerated for his part in a drug syndicate. At the MCG that day, he entered Wasim and Pakistan's legend.

Wasim starts this one wide. Very wide. But from the moment he puts it out there, it starts to move in. It's the most typical Wasim Akram ball. The ball doesn't just swing, it manages its own destiny in a madcapped energetic way. It's an orb of light more than a ball. Fluttering. Dancing. Lewis gets on the front foot and pushes towards it, but the ball zips past him quicker than he can see. It takes a bit of inside edge for dramatic effect and zaps into the stumps. This is reverse swing.

This is Wasim's reverse. Sarfraz's reverse. Pakistan's.

But it was all because of Imran. This might have been Pakistan's cricket's greatest day. Even Pakistan the nation's greatest day. It was also one of cricket's greatest.

Imran Khan, the lion of Lahore. The cornered tiger of 92. He bowled. He batted. He led. He gave us Pakistan the cricket nation.

No one man has ever had a bigger say in his nation's cricket. Now he wants a bigger say in how his nation is run. Imran has already conquered the world – Pakistan should be a cake-walk.

Chapter 43

TAKING ON THE WINDIES

AUSTRALIA ALWAYS BELIEVED in itself the way other cricket countries didn't. They thought their way was best, which mostly meant it was better than England's. As Ian Chappell once said, 'Look at what England have done and do the opposite.'

The West Indies dismantled good sides, but they never really had to with Australia, who was already dismantled. Allan Border was on the change-room floor with pieces trying to make them fit.

Australia had gone eight straight series without a win. They had lost to New Zealand in a series for the first time. Then lost another to them. They had won only two of 18 Tests in the '80s against the West Indies.

The last win was in Sydney in 1989. Allan Border took seven wickets with his generic left-arm finger-spin. He then made 75 in a partnership of 180 with David Boon. In the second innings he took another four wickets. And then hit the winning runs. The West Indies was already 3-0 in the series at this point.

When Australia went to the West Indies for 1990/91, they won another Test. When they were already 2-0 down, they won the last Test.

The West Indies was arrogant and awesome, but they weren't stupid. They would have noticed that although Australia was losing to them, they were building something. And the West Indies had changed. They still had the same belief, but they had a whole different set of men. This was the third phase of their dynasty.

Curtly Ambrose, Courtney Walsh, Ian Bishop and Patrick Patterson were now their four main bowlers. They had Brian Lara and Carl Hooper in their batting line-up, and their captain might as well have stepped out of 1974.

Richie Richardson could have been grown in a test tube by scientists trying to find the ideal West Indian batsman. They said he was from Antigua, but is it possible for two batsmen who had his and Viv Richard's talent to come from such a small place?

As the batsmen of the world put helmets on, Richardson put on a white, then maroon, floppy hat. To this day, he is the only batsman in Test cricket to truly look badass in a floppy hat. He also had the swagger. He didn't have hips like Richards, but he had that feel, that look of, 'seriously, you're going to bounce me?'

Entire coaching aids were made up of his shots. His feet and hands moved like they knew what to do even before his brain had instructed them.

With his hook shot he seemed to be almost hooking it off his face, just an inch or two from his nose, but he also never seemed to miss it, or mishit it, or do anything other than smash the hell out of it. He was a force. Richardson also loved playing against the Australians. He made more hundreds against them than he did in his entire career against everyone else.

It felt like the Windies' dominance would never end.

Australia was finding a cricketer every couple of years who was very good. Few were great, none was Border. But David Boon became very dependable, as did Merv Hughes, despite looking unfit for cricket. Craig McDermott, when he played, was a proper strike bowler. Bruce Reid, when he played, was even better. Mark Waugh floated in. Ian Healy even looked like you expect an Australian wicketkeeper to look. Mark Taylor was there as well. And Steve Waugh had just turned from attacking enigma to a gladiator. It was not a team of superstars, but a quality team. Who believed.

In the first Test of this 1992/93 series at the Gabba, they did not look scared or scarred. They went in like they were equals. At stumps on day five, they were two wickets from victory.

In Melbourne, they added a young man who had played four Tests. Had taken as many wickets. Had a bowling average of 96. Was chubby.

Had this bleached blonde hair. And would have worried no West Indian, ever. In the first innings Mark Waugh stroked a century, Border punched one.

On day five, with 359 to get, the West Indies was 1/143. It looked like business as usual. But then this kid, bowled a short one, that kept low, really low, and Richardson was bowled.

We were about to enter a new world. The ball had kept low, not because of the MCG pitch, but because Shane Warne had bowled a delivery that was not even in modern cricket's vocabulary. The commentators just assumed at first the ball had kept low. The ball had been snapped out of his hand with backspin, like he was clicking his fingers and magic came out.

Shane Warne brought back leg-spin, he brought back the flipper. He changed cricket's language.

After two Tests, Australia was 1-0. In the third, thoughts that the new West Indies wasn't good were smashed through point, and backward point, and cover point. It was a flat pitch, as the fact that only four batsmen in the match made single figures, and one of them was run out. But all that really did was give a young man the stage.

Brian Charles Lara was on 35 at lunch when the phone rang in the change-room. It was Sir Garfield Sobers, still the holder of Test cricket's highest score, 365. He told Lara: 'This is your day, keep on batting.'

At the age of 18, playing for Trinidad, Lara had played his second first-class match. Malcolm Marshall and Joel Garner were bowling. Trinidad was 2/14 when Lara came to the crease. No one else made a 50; Lara made 92. Almost every time Brian Charles Lara hit a boundary, it was as if he was saying the next generation was pretty good too. At Sydney he did that 38 times. When he was run out for 277, he had just started to count down to Garry Sobers' world record. It was his first Test hundred. In his third, he would score 375 and go past Sobers' record. When his record was taken from him, he went one better and scored 400. In first-class cricket, he has a 501 as well.

Not even Lara could change the scoreline. Australia led 1-0, with two Tests to play.

After two days, West Indies had the lead, had an Adelaide pitch and three days of play left. But instead of clipping up a big lead and bowling Australia out, they fell apart.

When he arrived on the scene, Craig McDermott had been heralded as the saviour. A man who would take over from Dennis Lillee, form a partnership with Bruce Reid, and bring Australia back to glory. In a 12-year career, McDermott only got on the ground for 71 Tests. Bruce Reid, only 27. Reid played in the first Test of the series. Then they never played Test cricket together again.

McDermott was in career-best form. The summer before he took a 10-wicket haul. The summer after another. He was hungry after missing more than two years of cricket, and his body was standing by him. The West Indies was 3/63. He had the three, and one of those three was Lara.

Then Tim May came on. He bowled 41 balls. The West Indies scored nine runs from him. He took five wickets. He hadn't even expected to play. Let alone take 5/9.

Now Australia only needed 186. To win the test. To win the series. May and McDermott sat down to watch their batsmen chase on a fourth-day pitch.

The West Indies used five bowlers. Kenny Benjamin was the fourth quick, and Carl Hooper bowled a few overs of off-spin. The other three were Curtly Ambrose, Ian Bishop and Courtney Walsh.

Allan Border was the man for this chase. He had spent a whole career being bullied, beaten and targeted by the West Indies. Here he was, the leader, a champion, he had 10,000 runs in his career, and almost as many scars from battle. This was his final chance to get back at them. He knew at his age, this might be the last one. If they lost at Adelaide, the next Test was at the WACA. The only pitch more Sabina Park than Sabina Park.

In front of him was Ambrose. No one knew much about Ambrose other than he was young, fast, tall and deadly. Ambrose was virtually unplayable when at his best. But more importantly, Ambrose was stone cold. The best thing you could do with Ambrose was survive. You didn't want to make a sudden move, or in any way upset him.

The West Indies knew Australia had improved. But they still wanted Border. They needed Border. Ambrose went at him. In 17 balls, Border made one run, was bounced repeatedly and was hit on the helmet.

Then there was a short of a length ball that was straight, it looked, upon pitching, a normal ball but it bounced up and came back at Border. Border was in mid-air, head to the side, hands pushing at the ball, no idea what was coming up at him, and somehow the ball hit the bat and found short leg. Border had faced well over 50,000 first-class balls by this age. No player had ever played more Tests than Border. And in his entire career, he wouldn't have faced a handful of balls better than that.

Shane Warne was the eighth wicket, Australia had barely passed 100.

Tim May joined Justin Langer, who was playing his first Test. Langer spent a whole career punching above his weight, scrapping, counter-attacking and generally trying to survive at Test level. Here, he had to do something that Allan Border and Steve Waugh couldn't do – stay out there. At tea, Langer and May chatted. Langer said: 'We're gonna make a fist of this.' They still needed 80 runs.

With 42 left, Langer went out. He'd made a fighting 50, but now May was left with McDermott. Neither were terrible tailenders. May had always been able to stay around. And McDermott, well he was not as steady, but he had been a pinch-hitter at times in ODI cricket, so he had an eye.

In their change-room a ball was thrown from the right to left hand.

May truly believed, 'I kept saying to myself, It's Australia Day, it's my birthday; of course, we're going to win.' When Craig McDermott picked a gap, he would bellow 'yes'. May kept playing extravagant drives without any foot movement.

That ball from the left hand to the right hand. They could do it.

McDermott's career was interesting. He once suffered a twisted bowel. He once suffered Border's wrath. 'You fuckin' do that again mate, you'll be on the first plane home. You fuckin' test me mate and we'll see'.

The man who said that, was the man throwing the ball between his hands in the change-room.

The Australians were all superstitious. Once the partnership got going, no one was allowed to move in the change-room. Border was stuck there, on the balcony, pacing with his hands. Back row, on the right. He refused to smile. He had played the West Indies before.

McDermott knocked a ball up towards mid-off. For a moment, the ball stopped being flicked from hand to hand. Richardson flew in, he was vertical, and moved inhumanly fast. But it fell short.

May turned a ball off his ribs; Desmond Haynes was placed for just such a shot. It goes wide of him, May thinks of two, two will tie, they stay with one.

Border is now flicking the balls between his hands at a great pace. It's a stress ball, and if he gripped it any tighter, he'd squash it flat.

After the second-last delivery Walsh looked over at Richardson, 'He looked a bit hesitant. He looked like he wanted to say something to me and he didn't. I just sensed something was going to happen'. Walsh's ball was straight at McDermott's trunk. McDermott was a big man, but tried to pirouette away from it, turning his back on the umpire. There was a noise.

It was Australia Day. But it wasn't Australia's day.

The next noise was Allan Border. Throwing the cricket ball on the balcony.

1-1.

Everyone knew the West Indies could now be beaten. Allan Border didn't give a shit. He just wanted to beat them.

At the WACA, Ambrose took 0/24 in his first spell. In his second, he took 7/1. Ambrose took Border for a golden duck. Border faced four balls in the match. Border's dream was over.

Someone would end the West Indies dynasty, but it wouldn't be the warrior who faced them 31 times. Border would play 156 Tests. He would average 50 with the bat. He would build a team that became the next dynasty. But he would never beat the West Indies in a Test series.

Chapter 44

MINNOWS – AND WORLD CHAMPION

CRICKET NEVER IGNORED a country quite like it ignored Sri Lanka. Sri Lanka, or Ceylon, as it was then known, had a cricket history going back to the early 1800s. It was a stopover for Ashes tours, and New Zealand tours, and occasionally an add-on for India and Pakistan tours, but that is all.

The Colombo cricket club was formed in 1863. It took 98 years before 'natives' were allowed to become members. The rivalry between the Royal College and S. Thomas' College – the battle of the blues, styled on the Eton-Harrow posh boy contests – began in 1880. These two schools to this day get crowds of sometimes over 20,000 people to see schoolkids play.

Pick up a Sri Lankan paper from any time in their history and the paper will be full of cricket. Not just their cricket, not just Test cricket, but odd cricket stories. Wes Hall injury news. Club tours of Indians in Australia. Editorials about grounds, prices and the team. In Sri Lanka, train stations would announce the first-class scores to passengers as they waited for their trains. This was as pure and devoted a cricket nation as any before it.

And the men who ran cricket waited until 1982 to allow them to stop being a stopover and become a Test nation.

Colonel Fredrick Cecil Derek de Saram watched their first Test in 1982 against the English. He had captained Ceylon, as Sri Lanka was called then, in the 1930s. He also led a coup, a bad one, in 1962.

He made a century against the Australians in first-class cricket. Clarrie Grimmett and Chuck Fleetwood-Smith were in the attack. In first-class cricket he averaged 40, and had a top score of 208. When he watched Bob Willis open the bowling to Bandula Warnapura all he could think was, this is 40 years too late.

Keith Fletcher, England's captain, didn't think Sri Lanka were as good as a county side. He worried about the pitch, and as he had been in Sri Lanka the last time when it was still Ceylon, he struggled with the name. Frank Keating wrote about his many speeches, 'He regularly had his team and us pressmen giggling into our handkerchiefs, for Keith could never stop himself calling it, not Sri Lanka, but Sri-lon as in: "ow a'appy we are to be Sri lon".'

That first Test, the only one in the series, started, as David Frith put it, 'with a whoop of the newborn: a delightful and daring half-century from schoolboy Arjuna Ranatunga. At 18 years 78 days this precocious left-hander ranks among the youngest of Test debutants, none of whom could possibly have batted with more flair and assurance.' England had a five-run lead after the first innings.

At close of day three, Sri Lanka was 3/152. England had a huge heart-to-heart about how they couldn't lose to a team in their first Test. But, the next day, Sri Lanka just collapsed largely of their own making. Only the great Roy Dias went beyond 50, scoring 77 out of 178, a lead of 170. Sri Lanka had no great bowling depth, so England chased down their total with seven wickets in hand.

Sri Lanka's continued exclusion at least allowed them to enter Test cricket with players the quality of Dias. Dias was near 30, and probably close to his peak as a batsman. In Tests he would average 36 with the bat, but for a new team, it was enough. With him and Duleep Mendis, another solid player around the age of 30, it meant that Sri Lanka wasn't the easybeats that the previous Test newbies had often been. But it was the new brigade. First Arjuna, and then another batsman with kamikaze flair, who sent them flying.

India was the World Cup champion in 1985 when Sri Lanka invited them to tour. Unlike Australia, India was quick to welcome their neighbours to Tests. In 1979 it was India that Sri Lanka had beaten in the World Cup that started them on their Test adventure. In 1982/83 they played a one-off Test in India that was a draw.

This 1985 tour was a strong side. Kapil Dev had Kris Srikkanth, Mohammad Azharuddin, Ravi Shastri, Dilip Vengarakar and Sunil Gavaskar in his side. In the first Test, Arjuna Ranatunga made a hundred. Sri Lanka dominated, and they ended up needing 123 runs in 11 overs. They got half way there, after eight overs, four wickets down. But the match was called off as bad light had come in, and Sri Lanka had to concede they couldn't score 62 runs in three overs.

Sri Lanka started the second Test well. Their keeper, Amal Silva, made a hundred, the wise old heads of Mendis and Dias made 51 and 95. And when their swing bowlers troubled India, they went into the second innings well in front, and wanting quick runs for their declaration. In the first innings, Sri Lanka had batted a young man at seven. This was only his third Test, and he had not yet proved he belonged. In this innings they promoted the kid they called Mad Max to number three.

For 33 minutes, nothing happened. Not one run. Then, carnage. Aravinda de Silva went berserk. At one stage, he and Dias scored 64 runs in six overs. De Silva scored 77. Nine fours, two sixes. Dias made a calmer 60 at the other end.

Now Sri Lanka had to finish the job. India slipped to 7/98, but Kapil Dev was still in. Dev was angry at the umpires, he was angry at his batsmen, he was angry at his board. Kapil Dev is a lion when he's angry. No other Indian batsman had made 30, Dev was on a mission. Sri Lanka started to get nervous, they had run out of time last Test. If they ran out of time again, India could easily find their form for the last Test. For 85 minutes Dev batted with Laxman Sivaramakrishnan. Laxman had a broken thumb, but he wouldn't leave his captain's side. And only then as the last hour was about to be called, did he leave.

In the third ball of the last hour, Rumesh Ratnayake held the ball back, Kapil pushed at it, then Ratnayake threw himself. Almost every single Sri Lankan held their breath as he dived across the pitch. Almost all of them dived with him. The moment that ball stuck in his hand, Sri Lanka had won a Test. They had beaten India, beaten Dev, they were Test victors. His teammates piled on top of him. Had they been able to, so would all of Colombo.

The players screamed, the spectators cheered, the commuters waiting for their trains cheered.

The third Test had Sri Lanka chasing 377. Dias made 106, Mendis 124. When they went out, they aborted the chase. They took the draw, barely, by three wickets. They had won a series. They had beaten India. They had beaten India, in a series. It had taken them three years.

It had taken them more than a hundred years.

Years later Aravinda would walk to the wicket in Wellington. The score would be 2/41, New Zealand had already been bundled out for less than 200. It was a bowler's wicket, everyone said so. When de Silva was out, Sri Lanka had amassed 454 runs, de Silva had 267. New Zealand tried to bounce de Silva, de Silva decided to hook them. His first hundred only took 124 balls. Then he opened up his off-side play, which at its best mocked bowlers. If de Silva wanted to hit the ball on the off-side, you knew about it. De Silva broke the record for a Sri Lankan batsman, and held the ground record for two days, before Martin Crowe made his 299 in the second innings. By then the pitch had flattened out. Or, Aravinda had just made it feel that way. In the 0-0 series, Aravinda had scored 493 runs at 98, a long way from Colombo.

Coming into the 1996 World Cup, the Sri Lankans had developed a couple of things that would help them. Chaminda Vaas was a left-arm medium-pace swing bowler of rare skill.

In another series in New Zealand in 1994/95 Sri Lanka had their first series win away from Asia, winning 1-0. In their win Vaas had taken 10 wickets; de Silva helped out with a 60. They also added the controversial unorthodox off-spinner Muttiah Muralitharan, who had been called for chucking in Australia. They had revolutionised the one-day opening position by throwing two dashers at the top, their sloggy keeper Romesh Kaluwitharana and their stylish pirate Sanath Jayasuriya, the true successors to Victor Trumper. Plus, Arjuna Ranatunga was all grown up, and out, and had turned into an angry man, a great tactician and leader.

Australia and the West Indies decided to miss their games in Colombo during the early part of the tournament, which meant Sri Lanka had a dream run. They could play exactly as they wanted, with freedom. They had already won the biggest battle when Ranatunga had made such a fuss that Murali was not blackballed despite being called for chucking. They didn't believe he chucked, and they definitely wouldn't be giving up their best spinner on the basis of some Australian umpires. Arjuna was clear, Sri Lanka would not be bullied.

Ranatunga took only two seamers into most games. They relied on spin. Spin hadn't been a factor in one-day matches that often. One off-spinner, maybe even two, but Ranatunga took in four. Murali and Kumar Dharmasena were the front-liners, with de Silva and Jayasuriya bowling a lot of overs. In the final their spin quartet bowled 37 overs.

When the top order failed, de Silva came in. He joined the stonefaced Asanka Gurusinha, a man who had, on occasion, batted with sunglasses on. He was Sri Lanka's rock. At the other end, de Silva was the rock star. His innings was full of class. He played the right shots every time he needed to. His cover drive went where he wanted it to go. He worked the ball to leg with ease. He built an innings. This wasn't berserk, this wasn't kamikaze, this wasn't Mad Max. This was a rhapsody of ODI batting. Australia had Glenn McGrath and Shane Warne. They were the number one team in the world. They were the bullies. The champions. The team that had previously revolutionsed ODI cricket.

But they didn't have de Silva.

Australia would change the whole way they thought about one-day cricket after that. They had been beaten by a master, from a country they still thought was a minnow. Sri Lanka wouldn't be bullied. Sri Lanka wouldn't be beaten. They passed Australia's total with 22 balls to go. Asanka Gurusinha screamed 'Now we are the world champions, and pretty soon we will get up there in Test cricket as well.'

In 1981 they might as well not have existed. Fifteen years later they were the best team on earth.

Chapter 45

NINE FLAVOURS

RHODESIA HAD PLAYED in the Currie Cup, South Africa's domestic competition since 1905, on and off. They never won a Currie Cup, but their cricket had improved over the years. In the 1970s and '80s their players made it through to county cricket. And by 1980, as Zimbabwe, they entered world cricket. Not that that many people noticed.

It was only in 1983, when they beat Australia in the World Cup, that people noticed. It should be pointed out that the Australian team had Dennis Lillee, Rodney Marsh, Jeff Thomson and Allan Border in it. Duncan Fletcher was captain of Zimbabwe, he would make 69 not out and take four wickets. He enjoyed embarrassing Australia.

During the 1992 World Cup, Zimbabwe struggled hard, but they gave up close games against India and Sri Lanka, and looked like going home early. Against England they batted poorly. So poorly that Geoff Boycott had made a special trip to Zimbabwe captain Dave Houghton to tell him just how useless Zimbabwe batsmen were.

He was right, but the English batsmen were even worse. They were undone by Eddie Brandes, a large farmer who looked nothing like a professional cricketer, but who took 4/21 bowling his 10 overs straight. England would go into the final, but Zimbabwe would go into Test cricket. Only England opposed their promotion.

Their first Test went about as well as they could have hoped. Dave Houghton won the toss. Kevin Arnott faced the first ball. The Flower brothers, Andy and Grant, both made 50s, and Dave Houghton made a hundred. They made very slow and steady pace, but went past 400. It was a top-class Indian attack. Javagal Srinath, one of the best Indian seam bowlers in history, and Anil Kumble, the third-highest wicket-taker in Test match history, joined Kapil Dev.

India's reply made them look more like the debutants, they stumbled to 5/101, and for a time looked like a team of Shastri, Tendulkar and Azharuddin would be forced to follow on. Thanks to Manjrekar and Dev, that was not the case. But Zimbabwe had their first draw. Not out at the end of the game was Dave Houghton and Andy Flower. Zimbabwe's master and apprentice. Houghton would only get the chance to play 22 Tests, but he would average 43 in them.

Andy Flower was already on his way to being the greatest player Zimbabwe had ever had. And he is, to this day, the most important Zimbabwean cricketer to have ever played.

•

'The new era which is dawning in our country, beneath the great southern stars, will lift us out of the silent grief of our past and into a future in which there will be opportunity and space for joy and beauty.'

Nelson Mandela was free. The ban on the African National Congress had been lifted. And apartheid was officially ended. Of course many South Africans could still not vote yet, but the country was changing. South Africa was brought back into cricket's bosom.

Ali Bacher, who had been their last Test captain, never let the flames of cricket die. And with so many South Africans playing in county cricket, they hit the ground running. Bacher convinced the India board to host South Africa for three ODIs. A hundred thousand people showed up, Allan Donald took a five-wicket haul, but India got over the line.

Their first Test was in the West Indies. There had been fears that there would be hostility and boycotts. There were. The hostility was on the field and the crowd boycotted because local boy Anderson Cummins wasn't picked. The crowd in Barbados actually seemed to warm to what essentially was a white South Africa team, with only Omar Henry to provide any inkling this was the new South Africa.

Andrew Hudson made a hundred. It was not exciting; it wasn't Barry Richards, but it was a Test hundred, and a good one. South Africa was well set in the game. By stumps on day three, it looked like the West

Indies would not win. They had already lost to South Africa in the 92 World Cup; they did not want to do it again.

Jimmy Adams (known as Jimmy Paddams for the way he played spinners) batting with Courtney Walsh and Patrick Patterson put on over a hundred. Still, South Africa needed only 201 runs on what was now a good enough pitch that two ordinary tailenders could handle it. At stumps on day four, South Africa was 2/122. Champagne was bought by Meyrick Pringle, who also told Brian Lara, 'Tomorrow, after the win, South Africa is gonna have a big party.'

The next day was far from a party. The West Indies refused to lose. Curtly Ambrose and Courtney Walsh took either end. Walsh, 4/31. Ambrose, 6/43. South Africa lost eight wickets for 26 runs.

South Africa got doused in Test cricket reality while the West Indies drank their champagne.

South Africa went on to beat India and was now a bit more used to Test cricket. That was lucky, because they had six Tests, three away and three at home, to play in Australia for the 1993/94 series.

After the first Test was a draw, Shane Warne took 12 wickets in the second Test. All Australia had to do was chase 117 and they would be 1-0 up. At stumps they were 4/63. But Mark Waugh and Allan Border were there. Two balls into the day, Border received a ball from Allan Donald.

It was Donald who was most talked up by people when South Africa was brought back. He was a hipster cricket fan's best friend. A South African who had been hidden in exile that only the really cool people knew about. Warwickshire had seen the best of him. Young and hungry, and quicker than hell. He bowled like a quality England seamer, only 15kms quicker.

That is why the second ball of this day, which Border left, hit the perfectly placed seam and came back into off stump. Border stood there, confused at what had happened, looking back as if a bird had flown by and taken the bail off. Australia's chase mimicked Border's confusion.

Damien Martyn was the only batsmen to stay in, but he hit a ball to a cover fielder with only a few runs to get and had to wait 2256 days for his next Test.

With five runs left to get, it was Fanie De Villiers, a fast medium toiler, who took a catch from his own bowling, completing his sixth wicket and beating Australia.

For some reason, that only the schedulers at the time will understand, a million ODIs were played in between, and four weeks later the third Test was played, Australia won easily. Both teams shared a Test in the return series as well. Going into the last Test, either team could have won.

Australia struggled to score in their first innings. They ended up on 269. South Africa then batted for 205.2 overs. They were in by lunch on day two, and almost made it to tea on day four. In all that time, and despite the fact that for much of it they were completely in charge of the game, and had a lead, they scored at barely two an over. It may not have been possible, but it felt like at times some of the South African batsmen's strike rates went into the negative. To an Australia that had built their game around attacking and going for the win, this was very odd. South Africa were just happy with a 1-1, or even 2-2, total series result.

In disgust, Australia batted out the draw. No one was angrier than Allan Border, in general, or in that game. He faced his final 166 Test deliveries, scoring 44, and making everyone at the ground, or in the world, know exactly how he felt. His face went into a mega-grimace.

The South Africans were back, and they were good, you didn't need to see the look on Allan Border's face to tell you that. Test cricket felt more complete.

•

South Africa was back. Zimbabwe was in. Sri Lanka was a champion. Bangladesh and Kenya were seemingly next on the list. Pakistan, India and New Zealand found their voice. England had heroes. Australia evolved the sport. Women were being encouraged to play. Disabled and blind cricket were finally being pushed. The West Indies gave us our greatest ever dynasty. Cable TV showed us so much cricket. Cricinfo gave us every scorecard.

Test Cricket now came in nine of the most delicious flavours. There were champions, legends, icons, villains and heroes in every team. Cricket had never been played as well, in as many varying styles, in so many parts of the globe. The ICC allowed all Test nations to be equal at the board. The World Cup spread the game.

It was beautiful; it was more golden than the previous golden era, which was vanilla in comparison.

The sport that a few kids playing on the streets centuries earlier had planted had been mistreated, kicked and stood on, but it had grown into something beautiful despite everything that humanity had bowled at it.

Chapter 46

END OF AN ERA

GEOFF BOYCOTT HAD told the world that something massive had changed. Boycott at the time probably didn't know he was announcing the end of an empire. He made some jokes about old men, and mentioned his famed floppy hat. But he didn't quite put it together.

Richie Richardson wearing a helmet was sending us a sign. The West Indies we knew was gone. Just wearing the helmet was enough for his home crowd, home country, home ground, to boo him. Other West Indians had worn helmets. Even some of the original batsmen. But Richardson wasn't a normal batsman. He was the keeper of the flame.

Richardson took 40 balls, before and after stumps, to make a run. Here was their dasher, their hooker, their leader, shuffling around the crease like a 43-year-old Leicestershire opening batsman in April. What had he become, a makeshift opener, with a helmet? There was no aggression, no pomp, he was swagless.

Anyone walking into the ground late would have asked who the opening batsman was. Richie Richardson had become just another player. The West Indies, just another team.

In the first session of the series, a Test earlier, Australia had the West Indies 2/6, Richardson hit out. Badly, as it happened. He was out, caught for a duck. But the session itself was exactly as you'd want the opening of a heavyweight bout to be.

Australia arrived in the West Indies in 1995 full of hope, and for the first time in over 20 years, belief. Then Craig McDermott was injured, as he often was. Damien Fleming was injured, as he often was. Australia had lost their opening pair. But the West Indies was missing Desmond Haynes through a contract dispute. Had things been different, the first morning would have been Fleming and McDermott bowling to Haynes. Instead it was the erratic-as-hell Brendon Julian and steady-as-a-locomotive Paul Reiffel up against Stuart Williams and Sherwin Campbell. Julian took Williams. Reiffel took Campbell. Julian took Richardson.

Then Brian Lara and Carl Hooper came to the crease, and within an hour Shane Warne was bowling, with a long-on. The West Indies had taken a few good jabs to the head, but they were fighting back with right-hand leads. The partnership was exciting and dangerous, but like all good things, it wasn't meant to last forever.

When the West Indies tail came in to bat, Australia's second-change bowler, a youngster with a 12-year-old's haircut, bounced them. Here was Australia's fifth best seamer bouncing the greatest fast bowlers in the world. Walsh and Ambrose were bounced at times, but not often, and not before they got the first shot in. This Australian team was about to show them it took the first shot.

In the second innings, that youngster Glenn McGrath took five wickets. Australia won by 10.

Due to rain, the second Test was ruined. Both teams had a chance to win on the final day.

Curtly Ambrose had taken three wickets in two Tests. This was as unacceptable as Richardson's helmet. Curtly was one of the great West Indian fast bowlers; he must rip out throats, now. A green pitch greeted him at Port of Spain, Richardson was quick to send the Australians in. Australia made it to 128, Ambrose had 5/45, and Steve Waugh remained not out.

'What the fuck are you looking at?' is what Steve Waugh said during an Ambrose stare at him. Even through the carnage, as the wickets fell everywhere, Waugh was not willing to back down.

Three years earlier Dean Jones' teammates had almost killed him when he fired Ambrose up by asking him to take off his white wrist bands in an ODI against Australia. Ambrose went on to destroy Australia in that match. Now, here was Steve Waugh, in the middle of a collapse, on a green pitch, poking the bear.

Australia was just as good, and aggressive when they bowled. The West Indies made eight more runs than Australia. McGrath took 6/47. But Australia's batsmen failed again, and the West Indie's cruised to a win.

One all. One to play.

The last Test started with Richardson trying to prove he was still a force. While the Australian bowlers chipped away, Richardson made a strong hundred out of only 265 runs. In the past, that hundred might have been enough. Australia would have just doubted themselves enough for the West Indian bowlers to pounce.

This wasn't the broken Australia and the champion West Indies of the '80s. Australia did not back down. A partnership between Steve and Mark Waugh, Australia's fraternal twins, made 231. Both Waughs had always been accused of struggling with the short ball. Mark preferred to back away and dance. Steve preferred to take the hits and fight. That day, they both succeeded.

Mark, 126. Steve, 200. Steve had more bruises on him than the 43-year-old Brian Close in 1976. The difference was, he also had 200 runs.

The last innings was a formality. The West Indies was beaten, even they knew it. Not one of their frontline batsmen made over 20. The last four wickets fell to one man. He bowled leg-spin. The West Indies reign had been ended by the one thing they had turned their back on. Allan Border even allowed himself a small smile.

In 15 years the West Indies never lost a Test series. They were giants. Of cricket, of sport, of culture. In 19 years, the West Indies fielded three different generations of cricketers. They were kings. Giant kings.

Giant kings of cricket's most beautiful and brutal empire in cricket's true Golden Era.

Never again. Never. Again.

Chapter 47

THE GRINCH WHO STOLE CRICKET

'THE WORLD IS anxiously waiting for heroes' says the speaker. Behind the speaker is a wall covered with names and busts of important men. The speaker stands at a podium. There are hundreds listening to him. All dressed in grey, all young, all men, all white. They are at South Africa's third oldest school, Grey College Bloemfontein, a school so elite it has its own handshake.

'Are you going to be one of them?' the speaker says as he looks into the crowd. A young boy stands out in the crowd. Across his face it says, 'Destined for greatness'.

A montage of great South African cricket victories plays out. Stumps are broken. Boundaries are hit. Blonde women cheer in the grandstand. And a man fist-pumps at his own magnificence. He carried a nation's hopes, the screen tells us.

Nelson Mandela appears on the screen, 'I must congratulate in particular captain Hansie Cronje, for the excellent manner, in which he has led the national team'.

This is a trailer. The film is called Hansie. It was written and produced by Hansie Cronje's brother, Frans, and is very much a born-again Christian redemption story of how you can be saved after your greatest sin.

Hansie Cronje's greatest sin was fixing cricket matches, and encouraging young men who looked up to him, as Dale Steyn once said 'as a god', to also fix matches.

Cricket's greatest era was ended by criminals, bookies and cricketers.

Cronje was a criminal, he committed fraud as he represented his country. In sporting terms, he was a traitor. A Judas. He stole hope and dreams.

Writer Telford Vice once said, 'Part of the pain is the fact that a South African was at the centre of the scandal. We had, not many years before, thrown off the yoke of apartheid and been welcomed back into the world as prodigals. After being untouchables for so long we were everybody's favourite cricketing nation. At least, that's what being South African felt like back then. Cronje took that from us. He ended the innocence we were indulging in when we called ourselves cricket people. He was, and remains, the Grinch who stole cricket.'

Hansie would later say that the devil made him do it. It seems that in the realms of imaginary creatures, the devil is stronger than the spirit of cricket.

But it wasn't just the South African captain involved; the Indian and Pakistan captains were also caught. Saleem Malik had offered Mark Waugh and Shane Warne money and it was Mohammad Azharuddin who had first brought Cronje into the filthy lucre world. That is three Test captains out of nine Test teams. Of the three of them, it was Azharuddin who was the loss. Cronje was a good bat, an ok medium pacer and an attacking captain. Malik was a good attacking batsman.

Azharuddin was a beautiful batsman. Ian Chappell would refer to his good shots as 'the artistry of Azharuddin'. He painted pictures with the bat. Even bastards can be beautiful. So still, so smooth, so crisp. He was like the best beer you've ever drunk. Until you realised he'd pissed in it.

But how much of it all was a lie? Courtney Walsh would bowl just short of a length two balls in a row. Both just outside off stump, both left alone by Azharuddin. The next one, Walsh hits the same area on the pitch, but he's wide of the crease; this time Azharuddin plays, finds the edge and is taken by Jeff Dujon. Was that a great bowling tactic, or just a bookie's plan?

When Justice Malik Muhummad Qayyum's report into match-fixing came out, the Pakistan team, and much of the entire world, looked on the take. It was as if you thought you'd been watching Bugs Bunny for years, and suddenly it was a violent Japanese anime.

Other sports weren't perfect. Performance-enhancing drugs were so deep in certain sports you weren't sure if you were cheering the steroids or growth hormones. In the 1988 Olympics 100-metre final, according to legend and rumour, there was perhaps one clean runner, but they were all doing it for the glory of gold. In cricket, they weren't fixing for glory or cheating to be legends; they were cheating for money, cheating to lose. Hansie Cronje did it for a leather jacket.

Cricket's greatest era had been vomited on, dragged through the mud, and made to feel less special. All the games that followed felt different. The hope and glory had been replaced by fear and resentment. Paranoia became a common cricket emotion. Before, five quick wickets would have brought joy or heartache; now they brought suspicion.

The fixers, even the ones who were never caught, turned the thing that we believed in, the thing that we watched as an escape from the world, and made it just another tawdry news story.

Pakistan was hit the hardest. Look at Pakistan the nation. It was a new country, looking for an identity. Known on the world stage barely at all. It had hockey and squash stars, and politicians. But it had Imran Khan, it had that team of '92. No cricket fan could watch Mushtaq Ahmed's wrong'un and not smile. Waqar Younis' yorker was the most amazing delivery since Fred Spofforth's swerve. And Pakistan was named in Qayyum's report for suspicious activity.

Later on the Pakistan Cricket Board would admit that had they acted on every player they were suspicious of, they would no longer have been a team.

That was how cricket was run: instead of trying to thoroughly rid itself of fixers, and more importantly look at the causes behind why players would risk their careers and reputations, and even freedom, they instead focused on the smaller issues.

Players would not have access to mobile phones, for instance. Even now when fixing occurs they find ways around that through messages from kids with autographs to different coloured towels. There was also the ICC's Anti Corruption and Security Unit, which, while being run by people who truly wanted to stop fixing, is hardly an episode of *The Wire*. They can't wire tap, can't subpoena records, and can't send in undercover agents. They simply have to hope that the player is not coached well enough by the fixers. Or that they find a crumb, which they usually then have to pass off to a real investigative service.

At that point what could have happened was looking at why $100,000 and a leather jacket was enough for Cronje to put his career on the line. Cricket was already making good money by the late 1990s. But other than the Australian and English players, no one else was making it. The cricket boards weren't paying the players what they could have been, and that made so many more players susceptible.

Cricket had always been a game of betting. Since the game went from kids on the street to adults on grounds, the laws were devised around betting. There are few better sports to bet on than cricket. Each ball can be a bet. Each over. The batsman's total. The partnership total. When the dismissal will come, the type of dismissal. First-innings results. Score before lunch, tea, end of day, in a bracket, in the first over. It just goes on and on. Betting formed the game, and fixing has been in the game longer than all players started wearing whites.

William Lambert was the first man to score two hundreds in a first-class match, but it was a game between England and Nottingham in 1817 for which he is most remembered. Because both sides agreed to lose the match. Fans of the rebel Indian Cricket League of only a few years ago might remember similar games. Batsmen played horrendous shots as early as they thought they could get away with. Fielders threw overthrows consistently and catches weren't just dropped; they were guided to the ground. Nottingham, unfortunately for them, won the game, but lost the money.

Lambert left the ground with a brown envelope, and his teammate, Lord Frederick Beauclerk, was furious. First at having a broken finger from trying to save deliberate overthrows, and also at the result. He reported Lambert to the MCC, who banned Lambert for life. A few years later the MCC would ban bookies from the ground.

Whether caught or not, players have fixed cricket matches through almost the entirety of cricket's history. What happened in the late 1990s was that no one could ignore it anymore. Even if they wanted to.

Chapter 48

THE NEW PROFESSIONALS

CORRUPTION WASN'T THE only new thing in cricket. Professional-ism would soon follow. England had professionals for almost all the years of cricket, but it was Australia who truly went professional first, as quick as you can say 12-month contract.

Australia took to it quickly. They built academies. They added coaches. Their players were on contracts. They no longer had to work jobs. They got a percentage of cricket's revenues.

The academies added analytics. Software. Cameras. Bio-mechanics. Books. Hyperbaric chambers. KPIs. Hitting zones. Pitch maps. Units. Twitch fibres. Hydration. Recovery time. Ice baths. Bat speed. Coach-ing aids. Dieticians. Physios. Leadership seminars. Opposition analysis. Psychologists. Virtual reality. Fielding coaches. Cross fitness. Spread-sheets. Range hitting. Computer-generated bowling machines. Athletes.

Cricketers became cricket athletes.

Australia had always been a forward-thinking sports country. Academies, training facilities, institutes, overseas coaches, government funding and the best of sport science was what turned a small country into a top-five Olympic country. The weather helped, as did the aggression and hard work that seems to fuel Australian sports. The entire mix meant that while much of the world was relying on old methods, Australia was pushing sport forward.

The Australian Institute of Sport was opened in 1981; six years later the Australian Cricket Academy was founded. It is where the macho moustache of Australian cricket met the white lab coats of bio-mechanists. But perhaps the greatest thing was young players were now trained like professional athletes. They stayed together, cricketed together. They built trust and skills. And, as we call it in Australia, mateship.

The cricket board was important here as well. Not only had they built a cricket academy, but they were also in the process of making their domestic cricketers professional. This meant instead of losing players to real jobs, and losing players to injuries, and just losing players to bad form, players could be retained, retrained, rehabilitated. It was not a perfect system, but it was the best system, by a distance, in cricket.

Without Shane Warne and Glenn McGrath, Australia would not have taken over the world. But they also existed at the right time. Shane Warne was beyond professional; he was a freak of nature. He was outside what cricket thought possible. He didn't get a degree from the cricket academy – although he certainly learnt things at the academy – before he was asked to leave.

McGrath was different. While he had a brain that just seemed to hear a cricket tip, store it, and perfect it later, this was all helped by the academy. A few years ago the Australian Institute of Sport picked the 21 greatest athletes to come through their system; Glenn McGrath was on that list. He would have found his own way, but they made it easier, and because of that he got better.

McGrath isn't as sexy. There is no musical written about Glenn McGrath like there is about Shane Warne. But McGrath does have a song about him by the Melbourne band TISM, 'The Parable of Glenn McGrath's Haircut', but even that is about how the nerdy kids are the ones who become successful. McGrath had a perfect wrist position, got amazing bounce, and spent most of his career looking like the guy who you picked on in grade five.

Conditions didn't matter to him. Whatever was happening, McGrath would turn up and take wickets. He took 563 Test wickets. If you ask him about one of them, he'll tell you where, who and how he took it. There have been many great bowlers in Test cricket, but McGrath is the closest to a walking bowling encyclopedia that cricket has ever had.

When McGrath partnered with Warne and the other academy graduates, Australia went forward and destroyed.

In two separate runs, with different captains and coaches, Australia managed to win 16 straight Test wins. The great West Indies never went past 11. No one else has gone past nine.

The West Indies built an empire. Australia was trying to build a production line.

Steve Waugh is the important cog in this. Waugh was one of the original children of Allan Border. He learnt his cricket through that horrible period for Australian cricket, and also rebuilt his own game, very much modelled after Border. A solid defence, few shots, and a punchy demeanour. By the mid 1990s, he was one of the best batsmen in the world. Waugh was made to wait for the captaincy. Mark Taylor took the role first. When he did take over, he brought his own personal brand of professionalism, his attacking theory, and Allan Border's stunning bastardry, to make a team that only ever thought of winning.

They would try and mentally disintegrate opposition teams. They often did.

Adam Gilchrist is a nice man. But what that nice man did to the bowlers of the world was a crime. A batsman who could keep, he was brought into Test cricket straight from hitting the world's best bowlers out of parks in one-dayers. And here we have two important things. Test cricket was no longer about putting a price on your wicket; it was about bashing as many runs as you could from the opposition. And wicket-keepers were no longer specialists who could bat a bit; they now had to be heavy, scary monsters who could make a major impact with the bat.

The impact of Gilchrist was so big that almost no cricket team since picks the best keeper; they all pick the guy who can keep a bit, but bat a lot. The more explosive the better. Wicketkeepers went from match-winners with the gloves to match winners with the bat. Gilchrist hit the ball so hard he hit cricket into a whole new era. His disciples now smash sixes and drop regulation catches the world over.

There have been many big hitters of the cricket ball, but none like Gilchrist, who hit hard so consistently and so fearlessly. His brain told him he was a wicketkeeper, so that his batting didn't matter. But it mattered to every cricket selector in the world.

Australia also had Ricky Ponting. Ponting was the gravel in the gut of Australian cricket. He might have been an academy boy, a professional cricketer from his teens, and one of the new generation. But Ponting was hard. Willing to face Curtly Ambrose with a helmet off even when the rest of the world had theirs firmly on. At the Oval one day, Ponting went in to silly mid-off, and didn't wait for the helmet. The ball struck him in the face; he spat out some blood and just got on with it. When Ponting was batting, it wasn't for records or style, it was to win the match.

These are just the champions, legends. It doesn't include Damien Martyn, who could play back foot through the covers like a concert violinist. Jason Gillespie, Australia's first Indigenous player, a bowler so fast, and then so good, that for periods of time he outshone Warne and McGrath. Matthew Hayden, a heaving bat of finely tuned muscle. Brett Lee: no player has bowled as fast for as long. Mark Waugh, yawn, flick through the leg side, repeat. Justin Langer, who went to war every time he batted. Colin Miller, a self-made spinner who beat them all for Test player of the year. Damien Fleming, an out-swinger posing as a man. Michael Clarke, man with the magic feet. Michael Slater, a crown jester who hit the ball like a bullet. And Stuart Macgill, the world's greatest understudy.

Australia played 42 test series in their golden run.

The results were Australia, Australia, India, Australia, Australia, Australia, Australia, Australia, India, Australia, Australia, Draw, Sri Lanka, Australia, Australia, Australia, Australia, Australia, India, Australia, Draw, Australia, Australia, Australia, Australia, Australia, Australia, Australia, Draw, Australia, Australia, Australia, Australia, Australia, England, Australia, Australia, Australia, Australia, Australia, and Australia.

Thirty-four series wins. Between 1992/93 and 2008/09 they didn't lose a home series, and only drew two. Professional, clinical, ruthless and aggressive. They ruled the new cricket world.

Chapter 49

A NEW DIMENSION

A ND IT WAS a new cricket world. Even women's cricket was being moved towards professionalism.

There were two women professional cricket teams in 1890. 'The Original English lady cricketers' were split into the reds and blues. They were recruited through a newspaper ad and played against each other for crowds of between 15,000 and 20,000. The women were not allowed to play under their own names and the good times ended when the all-men organising committee left, taking all the money with them. But 120 years later, women's cricket is finally becoming professional again. Somehow, during that large gap and in the face of little money, little promotion and blatant sexism, women's cricket has survived and is even flourishing. When Charlotte Edwards started her career she had to wear a skirt, women could still not be MCC members and her dad paid for her blazer. Today she is a professional cricketer. She leads her country. She walks into schools in the UK and says to girls, you can have a career playing cricket.

Claire Taylor decided in 2001 to give up her well-paid job to try and become the best batsman in the world. The ECB gave some support, but she wasn't supported the way a male cricketer would have been. It was a struggle for her. And although she was obviously talented, she had her own, almost hockey-inspired, technique that caused its own problems. As the years went by, her batting kept improving, and with it so did England's cricket. In 2009 the English women won the World Cup.

Later in the year, they won the women's world T20 as well. They were the best team on earth, and Taylor was the best batsman in the world. She was also made one of *Wisden*'s cricketers of the year, the first woman ever to win that honour.

The Sri Lankan women played the English team in the last Women's World Cup. Sri Lanka had never beaten a major side coming into the tournament, and England was the world champion. England made 238 and it seemed like it was enough. At five wickets down, Eshani Kaushalya came in and took seven balls to get off the mark. Then Kaushalya hit out. She took the spinners back over their heads, slogged when she had to, and the England women completely lost the plot. With one over left, they needed nine.

Starting with a single to short fine leg to Surangika, Sri Lanka needed eight to win from five balls, and Kaushalya was on 49 from 39 balls. Instead of showing any nerves, Kaushalya smacked a six over square leg. She celebrated like she had won the game, when in fact they still needed two from four. England dropped Kaushalya next ball, and then ran her out the next.

Scores tied; Surangika was on strike. First ball she bashed one straight to point; no run. Now the game was set up perfectly. Nine wickets down. Scores tied. Last ball. A game televised around the world. Even the neophytes who hated women's cricket couldn't hate this.

All this was still a world away from what happened off the field, where Sri Lankan Cricket eventually finally confirmed the rumours that the men in charge of the game had extorted sex for positions in the side.

That is just a horrible fact of life for some of these women's cricket pioneers. But when Surangika hit the last ball for six, her first ever international six, to win the first-ever game against England for her country, these women had more of a voice.

The final of the same tournament saw Australia play the West Indies. And Ellsye Perry, in front of millions on the TV, showed how serious the women were about cricket.

Ellsye Perry is an amazing athlete. She scored the goal of the tournament in the Women's football World Cup and she was a fast bowling all-rounder. Perry shouldn't have played in the final. Australia had a potential replacement in Holly Ferling, who had done so well that Perry needn't have been tested. But she is a star, and she wanted to help win the World Cup for her team. Australia took a gamble on her fitness. With the bat, Perry's injured foot held up. She slogged her way to 25 off 22, the only Australian batsman with a strike rate above 100, and woke up an innings that was dipping into a coma.

When she came on to bowl, the West Indies had handled the new ball well. They'd built a platform, not lost a wicket, and still had Stefanie Taylor and Deandra Dottin, the West Indies' star hitters, to come. Australia needed Perry.

Instead of steaming in and firing through the openers, Perry barely got to the crease for her first attempt. She pulled up, limped and looked worried. As did every other Australian player. It didn't look like she'd get through a ball, let alone an over. The second attempt was much the same. It ended in no delivery, pain and worry.

It was then that the captain Jodie Fields shot a look off to the dressing room. It wasn't a happy look. Australia's gamble was about to cost them 10 overs of a strike bowler, and Fields was suddenly trying to work out how she was going to make up for that. Perry could have limped off.

But Perry refused to give up. Her third attempt was painful to watch; it was someone hurting, someone who didn't trust her body, but somehow she delivered a ball. Nothing great, but one more than looked likely. Her teammates screamed their support. The ball was left alone and went through to Fields, who kept the ball and ran up to Perry. It was the briefest of chats, perhaps just mindless support. Fields knew how important every ball Perry bowled was. It was the difference between West Indies having a chance to win, and not. Whatever was said got Perry through the over.

With her sixth ball, Perry took Kycia Knight with a dodgy LBW. Perry's seventh took the edge of West Indies gun Taylor, but the evidence on the catch at slip was inconclusive. Perry's 10th ball, she had Taylor out caught and bowled. Perry's 15th was Natasha McLean's wicket. After three overs Perry had 3-2-2-3.

Perry might have limped her way through it, but it was the West Indies who never recovered. She could have stepped back from there.

She wouldn't allow herself to become a passenger. Perry kept giving it her all. She raced around for run-outs, dived to stop singles, threw herself into the air unsafely, unwisely and ungainly to catch Deandra Dottin. And continued to bowl.

Perry bowled her entire 10 overs, often limping in between balls or overs, but she just kept going until Australia had won the World Cup. In her last over, Perry bowled a bouncer. It was a special effort, courageous and skillful.

Ten days later the X-rays showed that Perry had a broken leg, a stress fracture in her distal left tibia. She had won a World Cup on a broken leg.

Australia, New Zealand and England are pushing through professionalism. Sri Lanka, whose men's team is only barely professional, enlisted its women cricketers into the armed forces so they could train as professionals and receive money while doing so. The West Indies has talented players, but they have trouble paying their men, let alone their women. South Africa, after many years, is finally taking women's cricket seriously. The Ireland women's team is getting almost as much support as the men. In Pakistan, women are often discouraged from sport, but their women keep playing. India, despite their billion-dollar turnover, have only just now made the move towards women being professional cricketers. But the women's game is joyous.

Chapter 50

HE DIVIDED THE WORLD AND UNITED A COUNTRY

ANOTHER MAN WOULD be called joyous. He would change the way people thought about cricket, and would become one of the most controversial cricketers and important national icons this game has ever produced.

When Allan Border first faced this bowler, he missed several balls in a row, and came down the wicket to talk to Ian Healy and told him he was having trouble picking this leggie. Healy informed Border that he was actually an off-spinner.

No one in the history of the game had ever bowled anything like Muttiah Muralitharan.

The first thing you notice about Murali is his eyes. They're so big. So alive. Like he can see things that other people can't. His run-up and grip are normal for an off-spinner. As he hits the crease he could be any spinner, but there is nothing that prepares you for what happens next. His arm goes inside out.

Almost every bowler in the history of the game, even the underarm lobbers, have bowled with the underside of their arm facing the batsman. Murali bowled with the back of his arm facing the batsman. He was cricket's first back-to-front bowler. He inverted bowling.

Murali had morphed off-spin and leg-spin. He had found a way to bowl off-spin with his fingers and his wrist. He got the bounce and energy of leg-spin and the consistency of off-spin. Murali had a great bowling mind. His victims didn't come one at a time, but in big hauls, like a fisherman using a net instead of a line. Murali took five wickets in an innings 67 times. He was like a wind-up toy of destruction.

Murali would look at the pitch, find his line, and then just keep going until all the batsmen were gone. His ball would leave his side-on wrist, go up, then drop down like an anchor, before spinning every bit as much as Warne, perhaps more. His skill wasn't the hunt or the plan; it was in the execution.

The game wasn't ready for an inverted bowling action. Chucking, they said. The accusation never really went away. It just flared up at times.

Cricket has been harsh on those suspected of chucking. Troy Corbett was playing for Victoria at the same time as Murali. He wore shorts when playing limited-overs for Victoria, as Victoria thought that would bring in crowds. In eight List A matches, Corbett gave up 197 runs, took 18 wickets at an average of 10.94 and a strike rate of 23.5. Then Corbett never played again. Never. Not once. Why? Because he was suspected of chucking. That is all it took. Corbett was never tested, or even called for a no-ball. He, and his shorts, just disappeared. That is how it was done.

Tony Lock, as in Lock and Laker, would admit that over time his action degenerated into chucking. The Windies' Sonny Ramadhin wore long sleeves when he bowled, which he later admitted was to stop people from seeing his arm bend at the elbow. Ian Meckiff, the last man out in the first tied Test, was called for chucking and then slowly pushed from the game.

What Murali really gave us, other than 800 Test wickets, a World Cup victory and a delightful smile, was the knowledge that we actually have no idea if someone is chucking. When Arjuna Ranatunga refused to lose the greatest strike weapon in Sri Lankan and cricket history, he changed the game for the better. Now, it's possible that Murali's action may not pass modern-day testing, but it gave us testing. It took it away from home umpires, racism and rumours. It became about science. As it always should have been.

When Sri Lanka played Australia in 1995/96, it was perhaps the first time people paid any attention to them. Their one-day cricket would do that, only a short time later, but they were for the first time seen as a proper touring team, and on Boxing Day, they played some decent cricket against a better team.

That is not what people remember. They remember Darrell Hair sticking out his right arm and calling Murali for chucking. They remember the crowd, mostly bay 13, screaming no-ball every time he bowled.

They don't remember the awkward pause from the crowd when he was called for a no-ball, and everyone murmuring and whispering that they thought it was for chucking.

It was Murali's action that caused the first outcry, but it was another man's invention that really bothered the cricket world.

Saqlain Mushtaq was another who changed cricket. Off-spinners went from, as Gideon Haigh calls it, 'cricket's rubbish skill' to one of the best forms of attack in cricket. Saqlain's ball was a doosra.

There was a story that Jack Potter, the Victorian batsman from the 1960s, had a magical off-spinner that went the other way. Jack Potter may in fact be the ultimate mystery spinner, as he never even played a Test, hardly bowled at all and was rumoured to have shown Warne the flipper. According to Richie Benaud and Wally Grout, Potter had an off-spinner that went the other way. Yet for all the talk, stories, and interest, he took 31 wickets in 104 first-class games at an average of 41.

Decades later Saqlain Mushtaq bowled the same ball. His wasn't a party trick; it was a Test match mystery ball. If Murali was a monster before he found a doosra, he was a planet-sized behemoth afterwards. Saqlain never got to that level. He was the Pixies to Murali's Nirvana, the inspiration to the biggest band on earth. Eventually Saqlain would just fade away from cricket; by the end he was so inspired by his own invention that it consumed his off-spin. He became a two-bit trickster, and he battled injury. He took 200 wickets, but he had the talent for 500.

The problem with this doosra is that it is unnatural in a normal bowling delivery, and that means it has to be flicked out. And it's in that flick that the problem comes. Cricket has now, largely because of Murali, decided that a 15-degree elbow flex (more of a rotation, really) is ok for an international bowler, as that is the point a bowling action starts to look illegal to our eyes. But a doosra is almost unbowlable, at a Test quality standard, when those rules are applied.

So as the doosra spread in use, so did the dodgy actions that bowled it. Australia and England tried to coach it out of people. Other nations seemed to have many different bowlers willing to bowl it. The problem was that often players would bowl it before they had tried to stop their elbow from flexing, and often there was no testing at the level below international cricket. So instead of being a brand new weapon to help off-spinners, the doosra became a blight on the game.

While the flipper had been a ball so hard to deliver that only a handful of spinners had ever mastered it, the doosra was easier to bowl, but just as hard to do so legally.

Saqlain invented this ball in the mid-'90s, and in the mid-2010s it still haunts cricket. And cricket still doesn't have the answers when it comes to chucking. Until suspected chuckers can be called in games, with a scientific method, and the stigma of chucking is removed, meaning that all that happens is a no-ball is called and nothing more, then we will not have got it right.

Most bowlers don't chuck on purpose. Most bowlers probably chuck the odd delivery without even knowing it. And the worst thing is, if we condemn everything that is new and outlaw it from the game, then we don't know what we are missing. When the first round-arm bowlers came on the scene, they were called chuckers. If we'd outlawed them we'd have missed out on our entire game.

But people like Troy Corbett deserve a chance: they deserve rehabilitation and a fair trial. Troy Corbett lost a career without even a hearing.

If we'd outlawed Murali, we also would have missed out on so much.

Whether you think Murali chucked or not, it is worth considering this. Sri Lanka has been plagued by civil war virtually throughout its entire history. During most of Murali's career Tamils were committing terrorist acts and the Sri Lankan government was trying to virtually wipe out their entire gene pool. They had an island paradise, and both sides covered it in blood.

Murali is a Tamil. For most of his career Murali was the only, or one of few, Tamils in the team. In 2007 that Tamil player was given his own stamp by the Sri Lankan Post office.

In a time of war, Murali was an inspiration for all of Sri Lanka.

Chapter 51

ALONG CAME KENYA

K ENYA PRODUCED MARVELS while the world wasn't watching. One was a skinny 17-year-old who played against Zimbabwe in 1980. One day he was proudly wearing his blazer in his backyard in Mombasa as his parents took his photo; soon after he was taking a wicket with his first ball in international cricket – that of Duncan Fletcher.

Sixteen years later the same boy was in the World Cup, Kenya's first as an independent team. Formerly one of the four nations that made up East Africa in the 1975 World Cup, Kenya was now a cricket nation on its own, and by 1996 the team had made it on its own.

Kenya's fourth game was against the West Indies. Their team included Richie Richardson, Brian Lara, Shivnarine Chanderpaul, Jimmy Adams, Courtney Walsh, Ian Bishop and Curtly Ambrose.

Kenya had to fly from Patna to Delhi, then to Mumbai, and then take a bus to Pune. They didn't reach the ground until late the night before the match. When they did, they found a green pitch. They thought they would be killed.

Kenya made 166. The joke in the dressing room was how many overs the West Indies would need to win. But once they took a few wickets, things changed. The 17-year-old kid was now a 32-year-old man. Aasif Karim took 1/19 off his eight unchanged overs. The team forgot who they were playing, and the West Indies never even got close. It was the biggest upset in World Cup history.

After a disappointing 1999 World Cup, in which Aasif Karim was now 36 and the Kenyan captain, they were overlooked to be the 10th team in Test cricket. After 19 years of service to Kenyan cricket, Aasif Karim was forced to step down from his position as captain.

In 2003, they played at home. Before the tournament their players almost went on strike. Their two star players, Maurice Odumbe and Steve Tikolo, were fighting for control of the team. So Kenya cricket begged the now 39-year-old insurance broker to come back. Aasif brokered peace between the team and the board, and Kenya was one of the hosts of cricket's most prestigious tournaments. They beat Canada. They had a walkover, due to security concerns about traveling to Nairobi, from New Zealand. They beat Sri Lanka. They beat Bangladesh. And then to qualify for the semi-finals, they beat Zimbabwe as well.

Here was a team that almost went on strike because their board simply had no money to pay them. That had players who would soon be banned for years for match-fixing. And yet, for just that tournament, they managed to overcome the internal politics and problems that had so often held them back.

Kenya as a cricket team was a joy. A beautiful mix of West Indies and Asian cricket. Their star was the chubby cavalier Steve Tikolo, who will forever be known as the greatest batsman outside Test cricket. In that tournament they also had two spinners. One was the young leg-spin of Collins Obuya who, against Sri Lanka, in their second greatest upset, took the wickets of Hasan Tillakaratne, Aravinda de Silva, Mahela Jayawardene, Kumar Sangakkara and Chaminda Vaas. His day job was selling fruit at the side of the road.

Their other spinner was Aasif, who bowled well despite not having played a game for Kenya between World Cups. Against a rampaging Australia, who would win the tournament barely a week later, he bowled unchanged for 8.2 overs and took 3/7. Five of those runs came in his last two balls.

Kenya had made the semi-finals of the World Cup, with no Test status, with no professional cricket, with no functioning board, with no first-class structure and with a retired amateur 39-year-old. They should have become a Test nation; they should have used that to go on to great things. Instead when Aasif Karim retired again after the semi-final loss to India, Kenyan cricket walked into the sunset with him. This time, there were no second acts.

Chapter 52

THEN BANGLADESH
AND ZIMBABWE

B ANGLADESH WON THEIR Test place by defeating Pakistan at the '99 World Cup, a curious result considering Pakistan made the World Cup final. Mohammad Isam once referred to Bangladesh as 'the happiest country to gain Test status'. In their Test history, which began in 2000, they have won series against Zimbabwe and a team of strike-breakers playing as the West Indies. It is certainly a better record than New Zealand had at the start of their journey, but this is a different world, and Zimbabwe and Sri Lanka certainly looked a lot more at home in Test cricket than Bangladesh.

Bangladesh has had players of talent, but no players of substance. No everlasting warriors. No Test winners who roam the earth making teams respect them. Shakib Al-Hasan has been their greatest player, but not a great. A man capable of taking a five-wicket haul or making a Test hundred. His Test batting average is 38, and bowling is 33 despite the fact he is their all-time leading wicket-taker. He is a proper cricketer. But has also had trouble with authority.

Tamim Iqbal has serious talent, and made hundreds in Lord's and Old Trafford on his first tour there as a 21-year-old. But five years on it is still that tour that he is remembered for, despite being their all-time leading run scorer by the time he was 26. Mominul Haque is averaging over 50 after 15 Tests, and he is the fresh hope.

Over 2014 and 2015, they won 10 straight ODIs at home, made the World Cup quarter-finals and qualified for the Champions Trophy.

But even then, instead of continuing their bad run, they had a setback: Australia refused to tour there for safety concerns and, yet again, another potential flicker of hope was blown away. In Bangladesh cricket, there had been flickers before.

They thought they had one on 7 September 2001 when Mohammad Ashraful became the youngest man to make a Test century, at 17 years and 61 days. Bangladesh had found someone special, someone fearless. Their Aravinda de Silva. A player who played Bangladesh-style cricket.

The difference was de Silva had other players beside him. By the time Ashraful was 23 he was the captain. Habibul Bashar had been captain, and despite the fact he was not really a Test match batsman, he was a fighter, and could make a 50 and, early on, held the team together. Once he left the team, Ashraful was given a young team and was trying to rebuild his batting, which had dropped off. It was a disaster. When Ashraful played his last Test, even the selectors seemed to apologise, and he ended his career with a Test average of 24.

Ashraful is only 31 right now. Unfortunately he is sitting out cricket for eight years after being involved with the Bangladesh Premier League match-fixing.

One day, Mohammad Ashraful will hopefully be a terrible story in their glorious cricket. As always with Bangladesh, hopefully is all you can say.

Zimbabwe, starting in 1992, built a team that Bangladesh would have longed for. Alistair Campbell was leading them, and his game was nothing spectacular, but he was clearly a decent batsman. Grant Flower, not as good as his brother Andy, but a solid player. Paul Strang, a leg-spinner with good control. Neil Johnson, could open the batting or bowling in ODI cricket. Henry Olonga, a fast medium bowler who could play. And Andy Flower. And Heath Streak.

It was impossible not to like Heath Streak. He put so much into everything he did, on a cricket field. He bustled like no one before him. It was all about effort, and working hard, and trying hard and doing whatever it took. A bowler good enough to average less than 30 with the ball over 60 Tests, and over 20 with the bat. Streak was whatever you needed him to be.

Zimbabwe had something special in Streak. They were something special.

Andy Flower certainly was. Zimbabwe probably has never truly appreciated how lucky they were to be given a batsman of his talent just as they started their adventure. They have certainly never had a batsman as good as Flower since. Flower was a player in almost religious control of his game. If it had a flaw, he moved it on. At first he was a player who handled quick bowling well, but later he became one of the world's best players of spin. Throughout most of his career he never really played with other batsmen of Test quality.

The 1999 World Cup was probably Zimbabwe's greatest achievement, when they made the super six part of the tournament.

They beat Kenya, India and South Africa. In their second-last game, Australia made more than 300, which in 1999, was a massive total. Instead of folding up, against the team that would win the tournament only a week or so later, they hit out. Neil Johnson just kept hitting the Australians everywhere. They could not stop him; eventually they just tried to get him off strike. Zimbabwe couldn't get past 259. Johnson made 132 not out. There is an image of him holding his helmet and bat in the air when he made his hundred. That innings, and many days like that from Zimbabwean cricketers, made fans around the world adopt them as a second side.

The 2003 World Cup should have been a party for them. They were at home, and co-hosting cricket's biggest tournament. They had now been in the top level of ODI cricket, one way or another, for 20 years. Heath Streak was in charge, but it was clear he would rather not be. Quotas for the number of black players had come in, and they weren't paying the cricketers properly. Years later Streak would say that he was told to downplay the white players at all times while talking up the black players. Robert Mugabe was now firmly in the dictator phase of his reign; a year before a protester had been killed outside an ODI at Bulawayo.

People were worried. England asked whether the tournament should still be played there on moral grounds. But it was, and only England didn't play their match in Zimbabwe, and that was for security concerns.

Before the first Zimbabwe match, a statement was handed to the press from Andy Flower and Henry Olonga where they said they would wear black armbands to 'mourn the death of democracy in Zimbabwe'. Flower wore his when he went out to bat, and Olonga wore his on the balcony in full view of the cameras. Olonga said, 'If guys want to take me out they can. They know where I live.' In South Africa at the time there was a genuine fear Olonga would be killed. The Zimbabwe minister for information, Jonathan Moyo, called Olonga an 'Uncle Tom'.

The black armbands made way in a compromise; they became black sweatbands. People in the grounds wore them as well. Olonga was not picked again, and eventually was forcibly removed from the Zimbabwe team bus. When the same was to happen to Andy Flower, the players threatened to strike, so they had to let him play.

The black armbands could have been worn for the end of Zimbabwe as a quality cricket team. From that day forward they have been terrible.

The only bright spark in their cricket history since then was when Charles Coventry briefly held the world record in ODIs for a 194 against Bangladesh in Bulawayo. They banned themselves from Test Cricket, and the major Test nations shun them still. They instated the youngest ever Test captain Tatenda Taibu. During a contract dispute his wife's life was threatened. Taibu stood down shortly after and left cricket altogether before he was 30. Even their long-serving cricket official Peter Chingoka, described by many as the most cunning man in cricket, left them recently.

In the 2015 World Cup, Brendon Taylor made 138 from 110 balls, in Zimbabwe's last game of the tournament. Then he took up a county cricket contract. Taylor had been their best cricketer since Flower and Streak. He started his career when the rest of the senior players had been stood down. He is a solid batsman of clear international quality. But there was no point playing for Zimbabwe anymore. They weren't getting any better, they weren't paid decent wages and the team had been going nowhere for most of the previous decade.

Robert Mugabe once said 'Cricket civilises people and creates good gentlemen. I want everyone to play cricket in Zimbabwe; I want ours to be a nation of gentlemen.' If only.

Chapter 53

HEALING SOUTH AFRICA'S WOUNDS

THE 2003 WORLD CUP was supposed to be a magical time in South African cricket. Hosting the game's premier event, with a side full of champions, it was sitting on top of the world. And about to crash.

South Africa didn't make it to the last six. It was another mistake due to rain, and when punchy wicketkeeper Mark Boucher, whose career would ultimately end when he was hit by a bail in the eye, hit Murali for six, he believed that his team had enough for the Duckworth Lewis revised total. He defended the next, and last ball. He was wrong. They needed one more. The match was tied. They had needed to win. South Africa left the tournament as a bad joke.

The South Africans were upset. So Shaun Pollock was dumped as captain. It was stupid and reactionary. Cricket administrators are nothing if not adept at offering sacrificial lambs.

Former South Africa coach Bob Woolmer said during that World Cup, 'There is a vacuum in South African cricket. South Africa is not producing the type of cricketers it used to anymore.' It wasn't just Woolmer thinking this. Allan Donald and Rhodes were done. Gary Kirsten was next.

It wasn't a vacuum, but a monumental chasm. And it needed to be filled.

A vetting committee to help find a captain was formed, with a silly title of the national professional selection advice committee, or something like that. They didn't have many options. Kirsten was not going to last long. Mark Boucher was a wicketkeeper. Jacques Kallis was a run-scoring machine who had to be prodded to bowl, and was not a man to lead other men. All they had was a young lad who had presence. And an odd technique.

At the crease Graeme Smith was squat. The squat looks like that of a club cricketer, not an international batsman. But his body is every inch the modern cricket beast. So is the massive shoulder that his massive jaw is virtually on top of, clearly visible beneath a massive helmet. The elbow guard is pointed straight at the umpire. His toes bobble up and down. There are two precise slow taps of the bat. Knees bent, back hunched over like he is too big for his equipment. Too big to even be that good at batting. He holds the bat like only he could lift it, not so he can swing it, but more so he can drop it on the ball.

In his first Test, at Newlands in 2002, Smith faced Glenn McGrath. McGrath the seasoned veteran who still looks like a boy, bowling to the confident boy with the man's body. In any sort of hand-to-hand combat, McGrath would likely be crushed. But with the ball, against a young kid thrown in at number three, McGrath wins often. Caught Ponting, for 3.

In the second innings Smith fights back. He turns balls to the leg side from off stump with that twist of his arms that looked like it could never work, and practically never failed. When facing Shane Warne, he'll lean forward, eager to show he is not afraid of Warne. When the ball suits him he'll race at Warne when he gets some air, stamping his feet at the ball and lifting Warne over mid-on with a beautiful lack of elegance. Eventually Warne will take the brash kid's wicket. Caught behind, by Gilchrist, for 68.

That kid making his Test debut was dismissed twice, by four legends of the game. What was clear then was that he had this immense presence. Monstrous confidence radiated through him.

Smith would be the new captain. Smith would be the youngest captain of his country. He had not been named in the World Cup squad. Instead he captained Western Province in a warm-up against the national side. And won. Thirty-five days later Smith was captain of his country. He had played three World Cup games, coming in after Jonty Rhodes went out injured.

Smith had barely played outside South Africa – a few ODIs in Sri Lanka – and he knew little of international cricket. But Smith knew he wanted to conquer it.

Only a few years later Graeme Smith was the most successful captain in South Africa's history, the man who took his team to number one, who slayed Australia and burnt down English captains. Some never liked him for his abrasive nature as a young captain, but without it, no one would have ever noticed him. Hansie took a potentially great team after apartheid and betrayed it, ending in disgrace, banned for life for match-fixing, and dead, victim of a plane crash. Smith took a team in the shadow of a fixer and made it the number one Test Team on earth.

But in 2011 South African crowds booed Graeme Smith. It came after losing the World Cup game against New Zealand. Smith did almost everything he could for South African cricket, but even he couldn't bash his way through their World Cup wobbles.

By the time Smith retired, he had been in charge for 4006 days.

He had longevity, results and integrity. He certainly spent years trying to prove that left-handed batsmen aren't actually more aesthetically appealing than right-handed batsmen. But he deserves to be respected as brutal, an ugly monolith of world cricket, the large guy who was always there.

Since the age of 10, Smith had been saying he wanted to captain his country. He put his goal to be captain on his fridge, and he accomplished it.

It was that single-mindedness that drove him as a batsman, that drove him as a leader, that pulled his country back to the top, after racism and criminals tried to ruin a great cricket nation.

Chapter 54

MURDER ON TOUR?

I T'S JUST AFTER 11am on 18 March 2007 in Jamaica's Pegasus Hotel. The white tiles of room 374 have vomit on them. A man lies naked on his back, his legs splayed. There is blood in his mouth. There are whispers of tracheal damage.

The coach of Pakistan's national cricket team is dead, 17 hours after their most embarrassing loss in their history – to a cricket nation that most never knew existed.

Cricket was played in Ireland at least as far back as the 1730s in Dublin's Phoenix Park. Clongowes Wood College was playing cricket in the 1820s, and had its own local playing regulations – that you couldn't be out if you dragged on, and that the long stop could stop the ball with his coat. It was the school of Joyce. Colin Farrell played junior cricket. Samuel Beckett played two first-class games. Even the boyband Jedward has played cricket.

In 1855, Ireland beat the Gentlemen of England. At that stage cricket was the biggest sport in Ireland. WG Grace visited heaps of times. Ireland's debut as a first-class team was in 1902 when they beat a London county side that included Grace.

John Wisden took a seven-wicket haul against them. In 1865 they even had their own version of *Wisden*, John Lawrence's *Handbook of Cricket* in Ireland. In Sir Stanley Cochrane they had their own version of Kerry Packer and Allen Stanford, who built a ground, brought in big teams, paid county stars to play and also built a railway line into his ground. Cricket was a major part of Ireland.

The problem was, in Ireland, they never set a formal, or even a semi-competent informal governing body. But the Gaelic Athletic Association was formed in 1884. It started off by structuring the country's sports, creating competitions that still exist today. It then went about attacking the other sports.

In 1901, the GAA brought in law 27, which banned GAA players from participating in or watching the English sports of rugby, football and cricket. If you played these foreign games, you would be banned from hurling and Gaelic football. The true Irish sports.

According to Ger Siggins' book *Green Days: Cricket in Ireland*, former Ireland head of government Éamon de Valera was at a cricket game once when he picked up a cricket bat and showed some decent cricket skills. A photographer ran over with a camera. The Fianna Fáil founder dropped the bat straight away. He knew that a photo like that would mean he wouldn't be invited to Croke Park, the home of Gaelic football.

It's in Irish literature as well as politics. 'In the soft grey silence he could hear the bump of the balls: and from here and from there through the quiet air the sound of the cricket bats: pick, pack, pock, puck: like drops of water in a fountain falling softly in the brimming bowl,' wrote James Joyce in *A Portrait of the Artist as a Young Man*.

But cricket did survive, in the shadows, and other than bowling out the West Indies for 25 in 1969, Irish cricket was just ignored. Then in the 2007 World Cup, 16 teams were invited. Ireland was in the middle of setting up an independent cricket board, in many ways, the game's first. They were finally trying to do something with the sport. They shared office space with mountaineering, who had a bigger office, and more staff. But Ireland had a passion for cricket.

Ireland's first match of the 2007 World Cup had Zimbabwe needing nine runs off the last over to beat them. It was a truly horrible over of cricket from pretty much everyone involved, and after Andrew White's six balls were bowled, the scores were tied.

In the Setanta documentary *Batmen – The Story of Irish Cricket*, there is footage taken just after that match of coach Adrian Burrell telling his side that they can also beat Pakistan. His captain, Trent Johnston, is behind him, topless, playing with his chest hair.

During the Pakistan match it was captain Johnston, an Australian who had moved to Ireland years before, who gave the speech. It was the sort of speech many Australian and Irish sports legends have made before. Angry, passionate and direct. He suggested that if the players didn't want to go back to their day jobs straight away, working as postmen and buying fabric, they had better win the game. It was, much like his cricket, blunt and effective.

In that game it was Johnston who hit the winning runs. A dirty slog to the leg side from a ball outside off. On St Patrick's Day Ireland had won their first World Cup game, and a whole country found out it had a cricket team. At the 2011 World Cup, Kevin O'Brien, Irish-born and bred, would make 113 off 63 to help chase down England's 327. In the 2015 World Cup, the West Indies made 304, Paul Stirling, Ed Joyce and Niall O'Brien scored 92, 84 and 79 not out, respectively. Ireland's success was due to the passion of a few dedicated cricket people and focused independent governance over cricket's closed-minded attitude. But that didn't help them gain Test status.

But the really dark side of their success in 2007 was lying on the floor of that hotel.

Two days after the death of Woolmer, the chief Jamaican detective declared he was 100 per cent sure it was murder. Rumours said Woolmer had argued with his team in the hours before his death. The initial coroner's report was inconclusive. The pathologist suggested the death was asphyxiation from strangulation. Woolmer's food is checked for drugs. Reports suggest natural poison may have been used. Or weed killer. Or snake venom.

The Pakistan team had a reputation for match-fixing. Match-fixing is run by organised crime syndicates. Organised crime syndicates strangle and poison people. Was Bob Woolmer killed because he caught his team fixing? Pakistan were 1/20 on against Ireland. The Harlem Globetrotters rarely have odds like that. If there was any game to fix, it would be the one where former World Cup holders Pakistan played, and lost, against what was still an amateur cricket team.

The Pakistan team was DNA tested. It turns out that Mushtaq Ahmed, now the assistant coach, had passed on champagne bottles to Woolmer. The captain, Ahmed and a manager are taken aside as they are about to leave the country and questioned.

But then the Jamaica Constabulary Force confirm that Bob Woolmer died of natural causes. The chief detective changes his mind, as does Lucius Thomas, the police commissioner. 'No substance was found to indicate that Bob Woolmer was poisoned.'

Then, six months later, an inquest that had called 50 witnesses over five weeks takes four hours to deliver an open verdict.

When Younis Khan was captain of Pakistan's 2009 World T20 winning side, he dedicated it to Woolmer: 'Woolmer was like a father figure to us.'

'He lived for the game and succumbed to the game,' said Allan Donald of his friend and mentor. A man who coached South Africa and Pakistan. Who spread the game around the world. A man of cricket.

Chapter 55

THE GHOST WHO BATS

A T 8.39AM ON 3 March 2009, 12 men with AK 47s, grenades, rocket-propelled grenades, claymores and explosive charges stormed the Sri Lankan team bus on the way to Gaddafi stadium for day two of the Test against Pakistan. Six Pakistani policemen and two civilians were killed. Six of the Sri Lanka team, and two backroom staff and one umpire were injured.

Kumar Sangakkara said, 'I don't regret coming here to play cricket because that's what we have been doing all our lives. That is our profession.' It was a beautiful thing to say, but he said it just after people had died and his team mate Thilan Samaraweera was having a bullet removed.

Pakistan's cricket future was lodged in Samaraweera's thigh. But, they never gave up. One man, more than most.

Younis Khan is sweating. Every part of his skin is wet. His shirt is clinging to him. His bat is raised. There are a few cherry marks on it. He holds that bat lightly in his hands as his 100 is celebrated. His eyes look tired. He has just beaten Australia. He has conquered the aggression of the Australian wolf pack. This old man, this warrior, this legend has done it in an empty stadium. Another empty stadium. Khan is a legend. But he haunts empty stadiums. In the United Arab Emirates. Empty because of those terrorists. He's a cricketing ghost.

Khan had a list of things happen in his career that players like Daniel Vettori and Ricky Ponting just didn't have to worry about. Things such as the Pakistan Cricket Board. An inept political board that banned women cricketers for supposedly faking sexual harassment, and backed Multan Cricket club chairman Maulvi Sultan Alam as he sued them. One of those women, Haleema Rafique, later drank acid to commit suicide. She was 17.

In 2009, Khan was made captain, but resigned after there was a Senate inquiry into match-fixing. He was cleared, but insulted. In 2010, the PCB banned him indefinitely. The ban was because of his role in the 'infighting which brought down the whole team during the tour of Australia in January' that year. The ban was lifted three months later. During the worst time of Pakistani cricket, nothing was permanent, except Khan at the crease.

He has seen Tests forfeited for ball-tampering, cancelled for match-fixing, for terrorism; he's had teammates go to jail and the opposition shot at in his country. Khan has also had to overcome so much death. His father died during a tour of Australia. A brother died during a tour to the West Indies. He lost another brother, and a nephew. Then there was Bob Woolmer.

When the Peshawar school attack happened in December 2014, where 132 schoolchildren were killed, the PCB decided not to postpone a meaningless one-day against New Zealand. It could only be a decision based on fiscal realities. Khan had seen enough. He wanted the game postponed, just as a Test had been postponed for Phil Hughes' death. 'How do you play a match when your spirit is not in the game? That is our state of mind right now.'

New Zealand won by 7 runs. The PCB made their money. Khan made 103. While Rome burns, he bats.

Occasionally, people may not be happy with Khan's public statements, or his ODI form, but he wouldn't be a Pakistani cricketer if some people didn't irrationally hate him. Or love him. But most just love him. He has ridden above the nonsense.

It is early on day four, 24 February 2009. Dilhara Fernando finds a short of a length spot where the ball can just do something. It jags back. Khan is on the back foot. He misses the ball.

Maybe he was tired from the 313 runs he had mostly made the previous day. Maybe he didn't have his eye in. Maybe he got that one great ball. That one ball was the last that Khan faced on a Pakistani Test pitch. The next Test was in Lahore. Sri Lanka batted first. Salman Butt was slow to move and ran himself out. Instead of Khan coming out, stumps were called. He was to come out in the morning. But there was no morning. The Sri Lankan team bus never made it to the ground.

Pakistani cricket has been in witness protection ever since. Khan is in that limbo. He has been made to bat behind glass, in a television cage.

Khan has the most Test centuries by a Pakistani. He has five double centuries in Tests. He has scored a hundred against every Test-playing nation. He holds the record for most catches in Test cricket for Pakistan. He averages more than 50 at home. He averages more than 50 away. He averages more than 50 in the neutral limbo. He has the highest average of any Pakistani batsman in history.

Younis has never played in a five-Test match series. Javed Miandad had the opportunity to play in seven five-Test series.

There are some who don't believe that anything less than a five-Test series is a real Test series. To them, Khan's career isn't real. He has not been tested enough. He has scored more than 500 runs in two three-Test series. Against Australia in 2014 he made 468 runs in two Tests. Maybe the five-Test series would have seen him worked out. Maybe a bowler who came at him week after week for six weeks would finally find the chink in his armour. But no one has worked out Khan.

He is a legend. You can't read the stats any other way. You can't watch him and think any differently. Pakistan's homeless status means they can't make the money they should. Teams don't have to play Pakistan. They do it because they can't get a date with England, India and Australia. Over a quarter of Khan's Tests are against Sri Lanka.

Of the 100-plus Tests he has played, three were in Australia. Matthew Sinclair has played five in Australia. And if you don't know who he is, that's the point. And if you do know who he is, you already knew the point.

Khan is a legend – and by legend, an unverifiable story handed down by tradition and popularly believed to be accurate. Cricket's first TV-only star.

After batting like few people ever have against Australia, he fronted the press. 'It would have been fantastic had all this happened in Pakistan before my own people.' Or just people.

There are so many images of Khan raising his bat, smiling on the way off the field, winning a Test, saving a Test, or just enjoying his time out in the middle. Almost all of them have no people behind him. Often, he is the only person in the shot. When he made 177 not out to help Pakistan chase 377 against Sri Lanka in 2015, the stadium was again virtually empty.

A champion in isolation. A victim of other's crimes. A batsman in a cage. He exists. He bats. But in many ways, he is the ghost who bats.

Chapter 56

A COUNTRY RE-BORN

ENGLAND HAD BUILT a team under Duncan Fletcher's coaching and Michael Vaughan's excellent leadership. Coming into the 2005 Ashes they had won seven of their last nine series. But the last time they played Australia they had lost 4-1. They were still the embarrassing team they had been since 1989.

It is important to remember how bad England had been. The country that invented the sport, evangelised the sport, revered the sport and administered the sport, could barely play the sport. They won only eight of 28 series in the 1990s. In one summer they had five captains. *Wisden* considered them the second worst Test team, in front of only Zimbabwe, in 2000.

In the Ashes since 1989 Australia had won 4-0, 3-0, 4-1, 3-1, 3-2, 3-1, 4-1, and 4-1. That's 28 wins to 7. Many of the seven had come after Australia had already won the series. England were just rubbish.

During the 1990s it got so bad they drew a series against the Zimbabweans, and lost at home to the Sri Lankans. It was a very good thing that Bangladesh wasn't given Test status at that point.

But that had all changed. Since that last Ashes defeat England had found a settled batting line-up. They discovered a talented bowling attack. Fletcher and Vaughan were good with tactics. They truly believed they were a shot.

They beat Australia in a T20 match. That, according to them, gave them confidence that they could beat Australia. Given that Australia showed no real care for T20 cricket for even a few years later, that should have meant nothing. But England was desperate to cling onto something, look for signs, so they held on to that.

Daniel Harris wrote in *The Nightwatchman*, 'But before the 2005 series, everyone hoped that things would be different, except really, they knew that they wouldn't, except secretly, they hoped that they might, except secretly, they knew that they wouldn't. But they might. But they won't.'

England had spent their last few years copying many of Australia's methods. They had academies, they had centralised contracts, they had a backroom staff full of analysts, psychologists and specialist coaches. After inventing professional cricket, they had now started to catch up to the new professional level. The other odd thing England did, was they dropped a proven performer for a dashing newcomer.

Graham Thorpe had played a hundred Tests. In the early part of the summer he'd made half-centuries against the Bangladeshis. The Australians respected him far more than most English players. Graeme Thorpe was a tough nugget of batting. Test average of 45. Thorpe was dropped.

In his place was Kevin Pietersen. A South African-born batsman with a stupid died stripe through his hair and a technique that looked like a camp Viv Richards on too much sugar. The safe and English bet was to pick Thorpe. England didn't do that. They went with the in-form younger man who could win them matches.

They were going for it. They were really trying to win the Ashes.

Second ball of the series, the enigmatic Steve Harmison bowled to Justin Langer, and he hit him. Right on the arm. Soon after, Harmison cut Ponting's face with a bouncer. Ponting's face was made of granite, and yet there it was, actual human blood. England had made it bleed, and if we believe our Predator folklore, if it bleeds, we can kill it. Something was happening. At lunch, five Australians were out. This was all shown in prime time in Australia, without a warning.

In 40.2 overs, Australia was out, 190.

An hour later England was 5/21. Glenn McGrath took five wickets. In England's second innings McGrath took 4/20. Kevin Pietersen made 57 in the first innings and 64 not out in the second. England's gamble had paid off. England had still lost by 239 runs.

It was hard to see how England could beat a team with McGrath in it.

At Edgbaston, the ground was under attack from a cyclone and a tornado meaning that it was miles behind where it should be for a Test match according to the curator. Twelve of the last 13 Tests had been won by the team bowling first. It was cloudy, and England hadn't batted well in either of their first two innings. But John Inverarity, a West Australian cricket legend, and Shane Warne, thought that Australia should bat first.

That seemed the even more logical way to go about it when something that would change the entire series happened. McGrath rolled his ankle on a cricket ball on the morning before play.

McGrath was out. Ricky Ponting won the toss. He chose to bowl first. Ponting was under attack from a cyclone and a tornado. England brought up their hundred in 22.4 overs. Marcus Trescothick and Andrew Strauss took advantage of the ball never going off the straight. They took advantage of the fact that Jason Gillespie was past his best. They took advantage of Michael Kasprowicz getting his shock call-up. They took advantage of Ponting.

England scored 400, in a day, before the second new ball was around.

Matthew Hayden faced one ball, but Ricky Ponting was on a mission. He had made a mistake, he didn't like making mistakes, he didn't like losing, and he came out swinging. When Australia was 88, Ponting was 61. Then he was out to Ashley Giles, a left-arm finger-spinner often laughed at by Australia, the country, the fans, the media. Had Ponting not gone out, Australia might have still dug their way out. They might have ended with a lead.

Then the next turn happened, it happened in reverse.

Since the moment that Sarfraz Nawaz showed the world reverse swing, Pakistan had taken it around the world. They were outstanding at it. And they were often told that they were cheating when they used it.

Here is the secret about reverse swing: you can get the ball to reverse without any illegal methods on the right day, with the right kind of outfield. But what really helps is scuffing up one side of the ball and leaving the other one perfect. Almost every cricket team in the world has done it, bowlers know about it. People inside the game know about it. Most of the press know about it. They just sort of ignore it, because, reverse swing is cool. Right up until England mastered it, it was still considered cheating. Now it is a part of the game. That said, when the ball started reversing in this series, many Australians still considered it cheating.

Australia had not mastered the art. They had less reason to than other teams. McGrath and Gillespie took all the top order wickets they needed, before Warne and Brett Lee polished off the middle and tail. Sometimes McGrath just took all the wickets. It meant that unlike other sides, they hadn't spent hours with an old ball doing little, so they hadn't spent as much time working on it.

There were stories, from Marcus Trescothick's book and from other places, that suggested the reverse swing was caused by Murray Mints. If that is true, then every single cricketer in the world would use them. They don't.

But whatever England did that series, the ball did reverse swing. Most importantly it was done at pace by Simon Jones and Andrew Flintoff. Simon Jones was a proper quick bowler, whose career was ruined by injury. He was in Australia for the tour before his leg planted in the turf and he ruined his knee. While being stretchered off someone in the crowd had a go at him.

As a karmic retribution it was Simon Jones' reverse-swinging yorker that took the wicket of Justin Langer. And then the tail had to deal with him and Flintoff. They didn't.

England came out and started slapping the ball around again, and right before stumps Warne came on. Warne was bowling around the wicket, trying to make the most of the rough.

Here, at Edgbaston, with his team well behind, he had a chip on his shoulder and saw a chink in England's armour. Perhaps to make a statement to England, and his captain about the toss, he came around the wicket to the left-handed Andrew Strauss and ripped a ball from the rough outside off stump.

Well outside. So outside that there is no reason to fear this ball, or to play the ball. It hit leg stump. It was like the ball had a personal grudge against Strauss and it was determined to embarrass him. It was a perfect magic trick, there was a puff of dust, then something happened behind Strauss as he was watching his off stump.

At least Strauss had an idea of what could happen.

●

When Shane Warne came on to bowl his first-ever ball of Ashes cricket back in 1993, Mike Gatting was the batsman. Richie Benaud was your commentator. 'He'll bowl to an orthodox field for a start. There's a slip. A short cover. Three other men on the offside saving a single. Three on the on and deep backward square.' Warne is marking out his run in his long-sleeve shirt. It's decently buttoned up. He has zinc on the end of his nose, and his bottom lip. There is a big hop at the end as he marks out his run-up.

Mike Gatting is tending to the pitch. Ian Healy is shadow-keeping to an imaginary ball. Gatting looks at the field. Warne bowls a couple of looseners out to mid-on. The crowd is having some fun at Old Trafford, chanting something at someone. Allan Border moves deep backward square just a little bit finer.

'First Ball in Test cricket in England for Shane Warne,' says Richie. Gatting is batting with his toes outside leg stump, and an open stance, ready for a big spinning leg-break. There is a slight hesitation before Warne sets off, then five normal walking steps, followed by three quicker ones and a small leap. Then a leg-break.

The ball does something odd after it leaves Warne's hand. Before it lands it starts to drift towards leg, then it dramatically moves even further, going well beyond leg stump.

Gatting has seen it all before. Handled Qadir. Scored heavily against Indians in India. He knows that Warne can spin it, so he opens up his stance, and gives himself room. He sees it drift, even further than normal, and his bat is drawn to the ball. He does not over-commit. He does not under-commit. He plays a perfectly reasonable shot.

It's the ball that doesn't play fair. It's the ball that reacts weirdly. It's the ball that rewrites cricket. The ball lands a foot outside leg stump. The ball then hits the outside of off stump.

'And he's done it. He's started off with the most beautiful delivery.' Healy and Mark Taylor leap in this creepy unison, like they had this choreographed. They run to Warne, who has a fist clenched near his face in celebration. Gooch is stonefaced behind them. Dickie Bird is shivering like he's just seen a ghost.

Gatting stares down the wicket for the longest time, trying to work out what has just happened. When he leaves the crease he looks back over his shoulder a couple of times, and gives his best 'I don't get it' face and shrugs his way off. 'Gatting has absolutely no idea what has happened to it.' Benaud pauses. 'He still doesn't know.'

That ball. The ball of the century. Make it the ball of a millennium.

Since Warne retired, many have tried to work out why Australian cricket couldn't produce another quality spinner. The truth lies in one certain fact; Shane Warne is literally a freak of nature.

When he was young Warne had to drag himself around by his arms when he had a leg condition. He built up his shoulder and wrist strength more than anyone in a gym could. Then he built his mind. If a normal leg-spinner, or spinner, bowls a short ball, a bad ball, or just a poor ball, they get down. Warne makes the batsman think it's part of a plan, like he knew they were going to do that, in fact, like he wanted them to do that. He looks at them as they have just smashed his ball over midwicket and makes them feel like they have stepped into a trap.

Warne used leg-spin like it was a bouncer. 'You hit me, and I'll rattle you next ball,' and he would, because he believed he would, and he was a freak.

•

The thing is, 12 years on, so many balls, so many replays, so many highlight packages, so much analysis, and yet, the same thing happened to Strauss. Not just the same result, but the same face, and the same look back. They never knew that had just happened to them. They still don't know.

England and Strauss were stunned by that ball, and the many that followed. They ended up 9/131 when Flintoff and Simon Jones came together.

Flintoff looks likely to go down in history as a better cricketer than he was. That is completely down to this period in time. When Flintoff could bowl at 90 miles an hour, and make Test match runs. When he was at his very best, as England won all these series, he took 110 wickets at 27 and made 1998 runs at 43. In his overall career he averaged 31 with the bat and 32 with the ball. But Freddie Flintoff was never about numbers. He was about being Freddie.

Freddie, like Botham before him, had presence. He knew where the cameras were, he knew what to give them. He knew how to perform for them. And when games needed to be won, Freddie was never far away. He wasn't an all-time great, but he was a superstar.

Australia should have been chasing down 240 at most.

Flintoff had hit 38 off 60 when Jones came in. The next over he hit Kasprowicz for two sixes. A few overs later he takes 18 runs off three deliveries from Brett Lee. One of the sixes left Edgbaston. Warne did get Flintoff out, but not before Flintoff had put on 51 for the last wicket and made 73 himself.

Australia now had to chase 284.

Australia had not started well. They had five batsmen in the top six with double figures, but no one could go on. Shane Warne entered with a young Michael Clarke who was fresh off a boisterous 91 in the first inning's at Lord's, fresh off a hundred in his first ever Test in India, and generally fresh. Warne had clearly decided that Australia was not going to be beaten in this series. If he couldn't do it with the ball, he was going to with the bat.

Clarke and Warne guided Australia to stumps, and also closer to the target. Then Clarke received a slower ball from Steve Harmison. A leg-spinner it looked like. Not that Clarke seemed to pick it, he was completely beaten, and England needed only two wickets the following day to win. Australia needed 105 runs.

It should have been easy, but Shane Warne wouldn't let go. And with Brett Lee, they put on 40 runs. Warne then trod on his own stumps, not from a quick short one at him, but from a full ball down the leg side. Now Michael Kasprowicz walked out, Australia still needed 62.

What took place below took an hour. One, four and no-ball, one bye, one leg-bye, two, one, no-ball, four, four, one, four, four, one, two, one, one, one, one, two, four byes. Flintoff hits Lee on the finger and Lee receives medical treatment, one leg-bye, four, one. Jones drops Kasprowicz, five no-balls, one, one, one, one, one, and one.

Australia need four runs to win. Michael Kasprowicz defends one well.

Next ball Steve Harmison bowls a bouncer. Richie Benaud screams, 'Jones, Bowden, Kasprowicz ...' The short ball took off, Kasprowicz played it like a pack of wasps was coming at his face, the ball does appear to have taken his glove. In what almost feels like slow motion Geraint Jones the wicketkeeper comes around to almost leg slip and takes the catch not far from the ground. Bowden does not hesitate.

Brett Lee goes into a squat at the non-striker's end. Freddie comes over and puts his hand on his shoulder and says something.

It will be remembered as one of the most sporting moments in cricket history. Ricky Ponting never won the toss and bowled first again. It's 1-1.

The third Test, McGrath was back. He bowled as if his ankle didn't want him to be back. Shane Warne took his 600th wicket at the ground on which he bowled Gatting, Old Trafford. Australia dropped catches and bowled Vaughan off a no-ball, England went past 400 again.

Australia collapsed in their innings. Simon Jones and his reverse swing were too fast and too much. It was only another innings from Shane Warne that gave Australia any hope at winning or drawing. He made 90 despite the fact the rest of his batsmen couldn't get past 40.

McGrath took five wickets in the second innings, and to do so he bowled more overs than Lee and Gillespie combined. England declared giving Australia a target of 423. Australia had not gone past 400 in the series.

About 43,000 people turned up at Old Trafford for the last day. Old Trafford can only hold 23,000. Australia should have lost. Ricky Ponting seemingly wouldn't allow it. Still angry from the toss, the last game. Still angry that McGrath was injured. Still angry that the ball was reverse swinging so early. Still angry that the ball was reverse swinging so much. Still angry that Ashley Giles had taken his wicket. Still angry.

Ponting went out to bat in the second over of the day. Ponting was out the 93rd over of the day. He had made 156. Had any other batsman even contributed 50, he might have been able to have a go at chasing down the England total. Instead he stood his ground until a slip-up right at the end. Then it was four overs of Lee and McGrath.

It was in his third Test that McGrath was facing Fanie De Villiers at the SCG, Australia just need him to stay in for four more balls, let McDermott have a swing at the other end. McGrath instead pushed the ball back to De Villiers. This time he would face nine balls, and Australia would draw.

Australia celebrated that draw like no one could ever remember them celebrating a draw. But it gave the English more confidence that this wasn't the Australia they were used to.

McGrath missed the fourth Test with injury. Australia dropped Gillespie. Kasprowicz came back in, and they picked Shaun Tait. A few months later Tait would bowl perhaps the greatest, weirdest, widest spell in domestic cricket history and take 6/41 in 10 overs, while bowling 14 wides. Another game he took 8/43. They called him the Wild Thing because Australian cricketers love the film *Major League* and because he was massively fast and massively erratic.

Tait did bowl fast, although not as fast as he would five years later when he would be clocked at over 100 miles per hour. But he also bowled erratically. Ponting brought himself on, and took the wicket of Michael Vaughan. England went past 400, again. Flintoff made a very good hundred, and Australia followed it up with another scratchy innings.

They were 259 behind, so England enforced the follow-on. It was, for most Australian cricketers, the first time they had ever been asked to follow on.

Australia did not have a batsman make over 61. But with Simon Jones injured, Australia clawed their way back into the match. Ponting was run out by the substitute. Ponting then started abusing Duncan Fletcher on the balcony as he went off, believing that England's tactic of resting their bowlers and using young fielders instead had cost him his wicket. But that wasn't the case. Simon Jones was injured and would never return to Test cricket.

Trescothick hit out, scoring at better than a run a ball. Warne needed one ball to dismiss Trescothick. He needed a further six to take Vaughan as well. In his fifth over Strauss was gone as well. And Warne had 5-2-7-3.

England kept losing wickets. At seven wickets down, they needed 13 more runs. Ashley Giles was a spinner, mostly in name. Here he was, batting with Matthew Hoggard, a quality bowler and batsman of an incredibly desperate nature. They were facing Brett Lee, who was bowling pure pace, and Shane Warne, who was bowling utter magic. Ashley Giles faced 17 balls, 14 from Warne. Had he made one mistake, his team would probably have lost. Instead he made seven runs, the last two, a flick on the leg side, won a Test match.

England were 2-1 up. All of England seemed to be following the series.

With Jones injured, England replaced him with a batsman, not a bowler. Paul Collingwood, their nuggety prodder, who despite not having the talent for Test cricket, got there through sheer will and hard work.

Thanks to an Andrew Strauss hundred, England went beyond 300. On day two, despite being no wickets down and well on top, Australia happily took the light and lost a bit of time from the game. From that moment onwards, it felt like Australia versus the clock, as much as Australia versus England.

On day three there were only 45.4 overs, both Matthew Hayden and Justin Langer made hundreds. And on the morning of day four, Australia was bowled out six runs shy of England's total. Australia was a team that had never really known how to come from behind, and it seemed like England didn't know how to win. Again, almost half the day was lost to rain, wet outfields and bad light.

Day five, it could have been anything. Shaun Tait took a wicket, Geraint Jones's stump was slaughtered. But the other nine wickets were three to McGrath and six to Warne. In the dressing-room they still would have talked about believing. They would have pumped themselves up. But a part of them would have believed that this wasn't their series. What are the odds that Jason Gillespie would lose all form, that McGrath would stand on a cricket ball, that every seemingly marginal call would go against them, that Ashley Giles would hit the winning runs, and that the ball would reverse swing so early?

Warne's brain didn't think that way.

That day, he ran into another man whose brain didn't work as normal players' did. Pietersen wasn't the star player for England, Andrew Flintoff was. Flintoff took over 20 wickets and made over 400 runs. Pietersen had been at best, an exciting bit player. When he strode to the wicket that last day, he was probably the least capable English player to bat out a draw. McGrath was on a hat-trick. Australia had three early wickets. Pietersen's first ball ended in slip, but it was off his shoulder, and rightly given not out. A few balls later he edged a leg-spinner from Warne, that was deflected by Gilchrist and wrong-footed Hayden.

Brett Lee started the 30th over with a straight full ball that Pietersen drilled back along the ground to the boundary. When Lee went full and straight again, Pietersen was just a bit late, just a bit tentative, and the ball flew off the edge straight to Shane Warne. Warne by this point was having the series of his life. His finger and shoulder were no longer pure magic, but his brain was at its very sharpest, and while his bowling attack floundered, he took 40 wickets in five Tests. And his batting was almost as important. He outscored Simon Katich, Adam Gilchrist and Damien Martyn. Warne had also taken five catches.

As the ball flew to him, at pace, with great carry, right at his eyes, Brett Lee jumped into the air. It was instinctive, this was a simple edge, straight to Warne. Brett Lee knew Australia had their fourth wicket. In those few nanoseconds that it took to reach Warne, it looked like Australia was going to steal this; this was going to be the Ashes that Warne won.

Then it was the Ashes that Warne dropped.

The ball hits Warne's hands right in front of his eyes, and it bounces, his left hand reaches for it, but it is, and will forever be, out of his grasp. Gilchrist stops celebrating and stares at nothing. Warne runs after the ball that almost hits the helmet and gives away a five-run penalty. Ponting looks at the ground and walks back to his place at slip. Warne flicks the ball from hand-to-hand, and wonders how it happened. This isn't how it was supposed to be.

Pietersen is sheepish. He might have got a bad call first ball and been given out. He could have been caught already. He almost ran himself out. And now this.

Three balls later Pietersen is facing Warne. Warne tries a flat quick leg break, Pietersen slog sweeps it into the stands in the shadows of the same gasometer that Grace played in front of.

Then Pietersen hooks. Over fine leg, short of fine leg, in front of fine leg. They were the shots of a man who had now decided if it wasn't Warne's day, it was his. At one stage he almost spooned a short ball straight to a fielder, but he didn't. Another was a sweep almost into his foot that landed at slip, but it bounced first, just. There were centuries of English batsmen who would have shut up shop after each near miss. Pietersen wasn't English. That was always one of his main strengths.

The rules of English cricket never applied to him, he was a frustrated South African off-spinning all-rounder. He came to England and upset and inspired people with this style of batting that involved taking on bowlers and not focusing on whether he would lose, but assuming he would win. When he guided the ball through the covers to run a two, he scored the first of his 23 Test hundreds. Almost all of them scored his way, in his style, not English, not South African, but pure Pietersen.

McGrath took Pietersen's off stump eventually, for 158. Off 187 balls. Hell of a way to start a career, hell of a way to draw a Test, hell of a way to win one of cricket's greatest ever series.

England celebrated that win for a very long time. But behind the drunken bus-top rides and pissing in the garden at 10 Downing Street, something else changed. Cricket went from a free-to-air spectacle, to a cable TV product. Like all those years before, cricket had taken over their country, and at the height of its popularity it had then been fenced away from those without the adequate means to afford it.

England would win the World T20 four years later, their first ICC win. Six years later they would be ranked number one in the Test world. But neither team would ever produce the pure joy of that 2005 win.

Glenn McGrath's ankle gave cricket one of its greatest series. England hasn't stopped talking about it since.

Chapter 57

TAKE NO PRISONERS

Kiwi cricket went to sleep after the brilliance of the 1980s – until Brendon McCullum changed all that. That is what he does. Brendon McCullum is a force, he changes the direction of things.

Stephen Fleming had been a great captain, in rare air at the top of the game. But Fleming only ever had a team of decent players, and very rarely, anyone above that. Shane Bond was for a short time the best fast bowler in the game, but his body couldn't maintain that. Then there was Chris Cairns, their charismatic all-rounder, who flirted with greatness, and ended up accused of match-fixing by his teammates.

Without Bond, but with Cairns, Stephen Fleming lead a 0-0 all draw against the Australians, one of only two series Australia did not win at home in their great era. But for almost 20 years, very nearly beating Australia was one of their highlights, They were good in one-day cricket, making a few more World Cup semi-finals and even winning the Champions Trophy (which at the time was really no big deal at all). But they were just a team that existed, making no real impact on cricket at all.

When McCullum took the Test captaincy, he changed New Zealand's cricket history, and left destruction everywhere. Ross Taylor was sacked, confused, and upset. Martin Crowe told the world he had burnt his New Zealand team blazer. New Zealand coach Mike Hesson made a mess. New Zealand Cricket admitted mistakes had been made. Kiwi fans were furious.

When McCullum arrived in South Africa for his first series as the Test captain, none of this had passed. In Cape Town January 2013 he won the toss and batted. By lunch, South Africa was batting.

South Africa had scored five times the runs, lost seven fewer wickets and ended the game, and series, in one day. There were still nine days of cricket scheduled to come. Somehow they lost the next match even more brutally.

After that series, the team brains trust gathered around a beer. They decided that their team was, as the fans had said, a bunch of overpaid franchise prima donnas. Putting their effort into IPL and treating the national team like a nuisance, annoyance. McCullum decided to change that. They would attack. They would play as hard as they could. They would do anything they could to win.

In 2009 McCullum was among the world's highest-scoring batsmen in T20s, yet, after 42 Tests, McCullum had never made a hundred against a team ranked in the top eight. He was averaging 31 with the bat. He was brash and fun but not the marrying kind.

In McCullum's 43rd Test he made 115 in a total of 619. In his next 10 Tests, McCullum made hundreds against Bangladesh and Australia.

A few months later, in 2010, he would be the first batsman to make 1000 international T20 runs. Not long afterwards, McCullum decided that he would give up keeping in Test cricket. After three hundreds in 10 Tests, McCullum had backed himself to be a Test batsman. His batting average in Test cricket at that time was 35. McCullum just gambled.

After four series since taking over the side, McCullum had won not one Test series. They won the fifth series, when Ross Taylor, the man McCullum had moved aside, made 495 runs.

Then India travelled to New Zealand. In the first Test, captain MS Dhoni sent New Zealand in, and just after drinks in the first session, McCullum came to the crease with the score 3/30. One hundred and four overs and three balls later McCullum was out. He had made 224. New Zealand won.

In the second Test, New Zealand was five wickets deep into their second innings and still more than 100 runs behind. A win for India would draw the series. The problem was McCullum. It would be for the next 775 minutes.

When he arrived on day five, 281 not out, so did as many New Zealanders as was possible. There were queues outside the ground just to watch him. Queues, on day five. Queues on day five of a Test in New Zealand. For one man.

For decades New Zealand cricket had been earnest. It had been dour. It had been clever. McCullum made it dynamic. He made it exciting. He made it unmissable. There were better cricketers than him around, but no more watchable.He demanded you watch everything he did.

•

Brendon McCullum is in mid-air. He is above the ground, above the ball. Floating. Flying.

The ball is heading for the boundary. McCullum sticks his hand down just before his body hits the ground. He stops the ball, but his hand, his shoulder, and most of his spine are on the padded triangle. The ball dribbles off slowly. McCullum crashes into the LED advertising boards behind the rope. He gets up wringing his hand.

The match is against Bangladesh. It is the last of New Zealand's World Cup 2015 group games. No matter the result, they will finish top of their group. The game means nothing. McCullum doesn't play like that. He doesn't think like that. He doesn't lead like that. He flies into danger. Sometimes he crashes.

McCullum was the second New Zealand batsman to score 6000 Test runs. McCullum was the first New Zealand batsman to ever make more than a thousand Test runs in a calendar year. In New Zealand's history there have been 19 scores over 200, and McCullum has made four of them.

But it was the triple-century New Zealand wanted. Martin Crowe had left them with a broken-hearted 299 all those years ago. Now they wanted more, at least one more. And the lazy prima donna franchise whacking boy gave it to them.

McCullum brought people back to the games, and kept them there. After another series win, and a come-from-behind draw inspired by a better than run-a-ball double hundred, in 2014 McCullum was named one of two New Zealanders of the year. Not for his cricket, but because he stood up to fixing. He dobbed in one of his heroes, Chris Cairns.

By the time the 2015 World Cup came around, McCullum was no longer just New Zealand's fearless leader, he was the world's most popular cricketer. The New Zealand team was adopted by most of the world as McCullum told his bowlers to take wickets, told his batsmen to hit sixes, and annihilated England in such a way that even grim hardcore dour English cricket types had to smile.

During that World Cup, the country that spends much of its time looking down at cricket, ignores it for rugby, and has a frustrated relationship with the national side, suddenly became an obsessed cricket nation. Had McCullum stood on the bow of a ship and declared war on Chile, most of New Zealand would have followed.

McCullum would charge into an oncoming truck to save a run for his country. He would face Mitchell Johnson naked holding a cucumber if he had too. And if needed he would place every single person in New Zealand around the bat.

Every moment was a powerplay when McCullum was involved. It was his World Cup, even as he lost it three balls into the final. Had he hit Mitchell Starc out of the attack, he could have won it as well.

That was his team, few captains in cricket history built a team more in their own image. McCullum drinks his own Kool-Aid, and everyone else follows. McCullum runs into burning houses, and everyone follows. McCullum attacks, New Zealand follows.

When Australia hosted the World Cup final, it was Australia versus Brendon McCullum. The man who could take Australia's whole World Cup away. After the first two deliveries, he had still not hit the ball. The MCG was salivating as one. The whole ground felt moist. Eager. Desperate. Lustful.

McCullum didn't run, charge or hurl down the wicket. He stayed in his crease. Starc didn't hoop the ball. It isn't a Wasim Akram ball. It didn't have a devious mind and a cunning plan. It was straight and full, and it faded back.

McCullum played it like a man who had just played and missed twice. McCullum was late. McCullum was wide. McCullum was out.

The MCG reacted like it had won the World Cup. You could feel the stands shake. You could feel the shake in every person. You could feel the concrete erupting. The MCG had just won the World Cup.

New Zealand kept fighting, they kept attacking, they kept flinging themselves.

'The greatest time of our lives,' was how Brendon McCullum described the World Cup. New Zealand went undefeated in seven Test series at the same time. It was perhaps the greatest time of New Zealand cricket. It was an almost. But their greatest almost.

Chapter 58

HEROES FOR HIRE

IN THE 1990S, if a Test batsman like Brendan McCullum failed, it was because the one-day game had ruined their technique. In the 2000s, the fault lay with a whole new format of cricket.

The birth of T20 was like many things in cricket – a way to make more money from cricket fans. Especially those fans who didn't have much time. The world was quicker, so was cricket. England's cricket board made it into a friendly little after-work game that ended up in a few drinks and some cricket.

The first international was played between Australia and New Zealand. Neither team took it seriously. The New Zealanders actually played in fancy dress. From there a few countries had low-key domestic tournaments. The first World T20 was so unimportant that India didn't even send a full strength team, and didn't originally want the tournament to exist.

But when Misbah ul-Haq scooped a ball straight in the air just as he was about to win the final for Pakistan, he turned this fun new format into a behemoth. When India won that tournament, India took T20 seriously. That meant creating a franchise-based cricket league that would hurtle a conservative not-for-profit sport into the free market.

Teams had owners. Teams were from cities, not counties or countries. Players were bought at auction. Cheerleaders were trucked in. Fireworks were bought en masse. It was, as Lalit Modi called it, cricketainment.

Most Test cricket fans still look down on the IPL, but for a cricket fan, it is something that should be experienced at least once. It is like a megachurch of cricket; you are not so much there for the religious wisdom, more the feeling of actually being there. It's not so much a celebration of cricket, but a celebration with cricket.

•

An eternal queue lines up at gate 9, Chinnaswamy Stadium, Bengaluru. Near the gate are police officers with sticks: cane for the men, plastic for the women. They punish any queue-jumpers. There aren't enough police officers, though, as the queue won't die. It goes beyond the bridge, past the tax office, around the corner and down the road.

The face-painters run at punters with their paint at the ready. More as a threat than a service. One, wearing a Kings XI Punjab shirt, is a Marcus Trescothick fan. He does a more-than-ok Mark Nicholas impersonation.

There are as many bootleg shirts, hats and flags as the eye can see. All are of questionable quality and cheap, but extremely enthusiastically sold.

The queues are literally around the corner. The crowd is full of middle-class Indian kids. But the crowd has everything. There are hipsters, people who take selfies, name brands, women with such immaculate make-up it seems almost fake, grumpy grandfathers, random tourists, entire families, the cool girls, the nerdy guys, businessmen and excitable young kids. The IPL brings in a crowd that Test cricket could only dream of, although they would probably look down on them anyway.

The first person to touch your groin at the ground does so fleetingly just inside the gate. People have to get in to see the game. Someone has already lost a wicket. It's a fleeting touch rather than a secure pat-down. The second person to touch is at the stand. They too have a backlog of people, so they check there are things in pockets – there are – and that is all they want to know. At the third touch point, the security guard pats once and then moves the queue on forcibly. At the fourth, the guard thinks everyone there has been checked so many times he barely touches at all. Four security checks, but no actual checking. At Mumbai, you will get a proper body scan. At Eden Gardens, you will line up for even longer, and then someone will forget to do a security check on you.

The scoreboard tells little. Kolkata Knightriders (not a homage to David Hasselhoff apparently) are batting, but there is no record of who batted before, or which bowlers have overs left. The scoreboard ignores highlights, lowlights, or anything worth seeing again. It does have words like 'awesome', 'devastating' and 'Oh!'. The cricket exists right now, or it doesn't exist at all.

A man presses a button that plays a Spanish horn, the crowd cheer. Another man counts down, back from an ad break, the crowd counts down too. The cheerleaders occasionally cheer for the wrong team, no one seems to notice. The commentators get cheered as much as the players.

It is a spectacular spectacle, but there is something that feels almost megacult-like. If you've been correctly brainwashed, this is the single greatest moment of your life, but for some, it's just a bunch of noise over a cricket match.

The first innings is completed, and then the world boss enters. Chris Gayle gets a reaction that no foreign cricketer would have ever received away from home. Most home cricketers would never receive this. The hometown DJ cranks up the music, but it's nowhere near as loud as the cheer for Gayle. Gayle is not from Bangalore. He's not Indian. He's just a professional cricketer plying his trade. But the fans treat his entry like they would for one of their greatest national icons.

There is a slight lull as he gets his eye in, then Gayle hits a six, and it's like every single person in the ground hit a six.

From then on in, the chant goes up, 'we want a six', an English chant, for a West Indian cricketer in India starring in an American-style league. Gayle hits another six. Gayle is ending this match, occasionally his cross-batted shots look like they will demolish the stands he hits them into. A pull shot leaves his bat and just seems to disappear.

There are times when Gayle is so in control, it's hard to tell the difference between him and a player having a net. This is one of those times.

•

The image of Gayle range-hitting is much like the old footage of Sonny Liston hitting a heavy bag. It sticks with you for life. In Sri Lanka one time, knowing that the press and locals were watching, Gayle went from just hitting big sixes, to trying to clear local buildings. After each ball,

Gayle would stop, watch how far it went, make an appropriate noise, and then laugh and face up again. When he just hit a normal length 85-metre six, he hit a corrugated iron roof at long on. It made a cracking sound. And everyone at the practice facility reacted when he hit it. For the next few minutes he just aimed at it. He's hitting a cricket ball 85 metres with a checked punch to try and hit a target to make people go 'oooh, awww'. Gayle is the World Boss.

The photos he puts online are life versions of the sixes he hits. They are of the nightclub he owns, or at least, him with women in his nightclub. They are of him topless, or him topless with women who are virtually topless. Him in jacuzzis, or him in jacuzzis with women. Him with his massive guns flexed, or him flexing his massive gun arms for women.

At times there are no women, just gold suits, cigars, five-star hotels, first-class flights, all of the time with him claiming to be the World Boss.

None of this would be possible had he just stayed playing for the West Indies. These are all the trappings of success that the IPL, and then other T20 competitions, brought him. You cannot be a West Indian cricketer only and be a millionaire, be this famous, be this bling. There is no money in it.

In the 20 years that followed their glorious 20 years, the West Indies players have gone on strike, twice. Other teams barely play them. Occasionally someone in cricket will say, 'Cricket will never be strong unless the West Indies is strong', but as Tony Cozier once said, 'no one really believes that, most believe that cricket will be strong as long as money is made'.

To play an ODI for his country, Chris Gayle will get less than $1000. He will play it in a meaningless series, without much interested from anyone. The IPL has made him a millionaire. It has made him a worldwide brand. He is an aspirational role model to a new kind of rich and hungry India. And he is, what the West Indies as a cricket nation have been left with, a hero for hire.

In this match at Bangalore, Gayle does much the same, but with slightly longer breaks between the sixes. He hits another six. The crowd chants 'RCB', 'RCB'. Gayle has just won the match for the Royal Challengers Bangalore. Gayle is the World Boss, but he's hardly the West Indies boss anymore, as he's often not playing for them for one reason or another.

This is cricket's new financial existential crisis. Players have over the years occasionally played in professional English leagues ahead of playing for their teams. But never this many, and never at the same time. Tests have been cancelled, or made essentially meaningless as the big players just have bigger pay cheques to collect elsewhere.

That is what has happened to the West Indies, this limbo between playing for their cricket team, and travelling the world actually getting paid what their talent is worth. At Bangalore, Gayle had a full ground. Massive support. Millions of dollars. At Bangalore, he is a legend.

Back in the West Indies he plays in front of barely anyone. The home fans are disappointed in the current team and he gets paid barely anything. And no one sees him as good as Headley, Sobers, Richards or Lara.

During the last 20 years, the West Indies has been as terrible as they once were magnificent. The West Indies cricket Board turned to a man, Allen Stanford, to save their cricket. But it turned out that Allen Stanford, or Sir Allen Stanford at the time, was a massive con artist who had set up a $7 billion ponzi scheme, which has earned him 110 years in jail. Their victory in the World T20 of 2012 was another false dawn. The West Indies might never be great again. There is a chance that, one day, cricket will continue without the West Indies as a Test nation. The greatest we've ever had, gone forever.

Chapter 59

THE RISE OF INDIA

CRICKET'S MONEY CHANGED many things. Especially in India. In 1992 cricket in India was shown on the public broadcaster, Doordashan, who demanded about US$10,000 a day from the cricket board to do so. They thought they were doing cricket a service. The Board of Control for Cricket in India had to fight to get cricket from them and sell their rights to other broadcasters.

When India play a home game today, the broadcaster pays US$6 million. That could be for a Test against Zimbabwe (only kidding they have not hosted Zimbabwe in over 10 years) or a T20 against Australia.

While Australia was building one of the best empires in cricket, India went about owning the whole planet of cricket.

India first began by simply gathering votes. Cricket revolves around a voting system from the major boards. With only the special few Test nations getting votes, India's job of getting votes onside from the other nations was reasonably easy. England and Australia had allowed other teams to have a vote, but maintained a veto.

It was never actually used. But the mere idea of it incensed many cricket fans and boards around the world. Many board members thought the veto was a form of cricket racism to keep them down. India used the idea of the veto, and the fact that England had always run the game and Australia was their thuggish ally, to pick up votes of their Asian counterparts. Then South Africa, West Indies, Zimbabwe and when they were given Test status, Bangladesh.

India proved no different than England, or even Australia, before them, and used their new voting bloc to control the game for their own interests. But, by 2008, India was no longer just a smart operator, they were the richest cricket board that had ever existed, and had they wanted to, could have bought all the best cricketers and owned all formats of cricket. Instead, they just borrowed them for the IPL.

But the need for a voting bloc grew less, as all India had to do now was say to another country, come with us, or you will miss out on a tour. Modern cricket's economy meant that boards made a little money from Australia and England touring; they made a lot of money when India did, and a lot from the ICC tournaments. So India not touring, or even making the tours smaller, could mean millions in lost revenue.

So eventually England, India and Australia joined forces to form a new holy trinity. India, Australia and England joined forces, and while cricket fans were kept in the dark, and cricket officials were left just as clueless, these three nations planned their takeover of cricket.

By 2013, it was clear that all future ICC tournaments would be hosted in Australia, England and India. These three teams now played each other on an endless loop, piling tours and series on top of each other in order to milk as much money as they could. England played so much cricket that the best team they had developed since 2005 was brought to its knees by their workload – but the ECB made a great deal of money.

Some of this money was put to great use. Women's cricket was developed in all three countries, and all of them had professional cricketers. England also developed disabled cricket and blind cricket. Australia paid their cricketers over a quarter of their revenue. India set up a pension scheme for all retired first-class players as a brilliant safety net for their players.

But cricket is not about these three teams, cricket is about everyone, and these three boards did not care about cricket outside of their own country.

In January of 2014 an ICC draft was leaked. It was a document that was written by three boards. It was a plan for the takeover of cricket. They tried to write it off through leaks to the English media as merely a draft.

It was a draft that would give them more money, over 50 per cent of ICC revenue, more power, the top job rotated between the three major nations, and more everything. No future Test teams would get a vote, even if they happened to pass their new, and almost impossible, qualification system for Tests.

They also limited the number of teams in the World Cup to only 10, and pretended to give a few extra spots in the World T20. They said cricket wouldn't be an Olympic sport, because England would lose three weeks of summer every four years, despite the good it could do for women's cricket, disabled cricket and cricket around the globe.

Cricket had been taken over. The men in power had spent years trying to own it, and now, due to the economies of India, Australia and England, they could take it over. Australian and English officials told the other Test nations that if they didn't do as India wanted, India would walk out of the World Cup. It was a bluff, it was nonsense, and by February 2014, it was official.

And India had more and more reasons to be prideful. Since their 1983 World Cup win, India had continued to improve as a cricket nation. Their nation was also growing economically and in political importance. Their cricket team was just a part of that, in the bigger picture. But to many Indians, their cricket team was the public face of that. The heart of that. Part of their inevitable rise to 'India, superpower'.

In 2001, when India hosted Australia, it wasn't just a Test series, it was a team that had won its previous 15 Tests. Coming to India, where Australia hadn't won since 1969, Australia really expected to keep on winning. India really expected to beat them at home.

Australia started by bowling India out for 176. This was the tour when Matthew Hayden's professionalism shone through, and his preparation came in handy when Australia had collapsed to 5/99. In the next 32.1 overs, he and Adam Gilchrist put on 196 runs. Australia's cricket was a machine intent on destruction. Australia then went straight out there and bowled India out for 218, and Hayden slapped 28 off 21 to win the match by 10 wickets. Australia started the second match by whacking 445, Hayden slapping 97 this time. Then India were bowled out for 171.

The Australian machine was all conquering, and the final frontier was not even a speed bump.

This was halfway through the three-match series. Australia had won 16 and a half Test matches at this point. Matthew Hayden looked like an impossible mountain to climb. Gilchrist had made a bombastic century. Steve Waugh had made a grittier one. And all the Australian bowlers were taking wickets.

Australia enforced the follow-on. Over 200 teams in Test cricket have enforced follow-ons. On two separate occasions, Australia had lost to England after doing it. There was no reason to believe this would go differently.

There are certain batsmen who can do hard things better than other batsmen can do easy things. For instance, not all batsmen leave the ball well. Even some of the greats can do it in a kind of awkward manner. VVS Laxman could play a cover drive out of the leg side rough better than many great batsmen leave the ball.

No one as beautiful as VVS should be judged on stats. He's not a man who deserves to be put into a spreadsheet. His batting was poetry.

At Kolkata, he was promoted to number three after the first innings. India was just gambling on form, gambling on hope.

Australia first tried to take his wicket driving. He drove, they took no wicket. Australia then tried to take his wicket pulling. He pulled, they took no wicket. Australia then tried to take his wicket with slower balls. He waited, they took no wicket. Australia then tried to take his wicket with ring fields. He pierced, they took no wicket. Australia then tried to take his wicket in the rough. He smashed, they took no wicket. Australia then tried to take his wicket in the slips. He middled, they took no wicket. Australia then tried to take his wicket by giving up. He batted, they took no wicket.

VVS made 281. When India started the follow-on, they were 274 behind. VVS beat the follow-on. There was an inside edge from maybe Gillespie, and an outside edge off probably McGrath. There was a close call for a run-out, and some odd pull shots through midwicket, and one almost back to the bowler and one that went through mid-off. But that was the closest he came to losing a wicket.

VVS had taken the world's most potent attack – Glenn McGrath, Jason Gillespie and Shane Warne – and turned it into a eunuch.

By the end, Steve Waugh used every player on his team other than himself and wicketkeeper Adam Gilchrist. Waugh had one of the greatest bowling attacks in cricket, and he was bowling Justin Langer.

VVS didn't just beat Australia; he beat their entire system. He beat their will. He beat their ego. And he did it in such a way that Australia had to give up. They were little more than a collection of 11 puddles as VVS played shots that human beings shouldn't be able to play.

At the other end, he had Rahul Dravid. Dravid only made 180. They only put on 376 together.

Rahul Dravid will never get the respect he deserves. There were too many other players in the same period who were as important, or more important to India than him. Sourav Ganguly was the leader who gave them confidence. Virender Sehwag gave them runs at speeds that Test cricket shuddered at. And VVS Laxman gave them Kolkata 2001. Dravid was the best number two India ever had.

Australia had enforced the follow-on and lost by 171 runs. Now three teams had enforced the follow-on and lost. Australia will never enforce the follow-on again without their fans feeling nervous.

The streak of Australia had been ended by VVS. Australia lost the next Test too, and the series.

Chapter 60

ONE MAN, ONE BILLION FANS

Vvs was often the hero. Dravid as well. In India Harbhajan tormented Australia. Virender Sehwag was so good someone formed a religion called Sehwagology. And Kumble managed to make a career from bowling deliveries with virtually no spin while his two biggest rivals spun it sideways, and he still took 619 Test wickets.

Then there was Sachin. His career started in 1989. The Cold War was still going. When Sachin started his career he played one-day cricket in whites. There were only eight Test teams. And the reverse sweep was still frowned upon.

His career lasted so long, that his last major match as a professional cricketer was playing for a team that didn't exist when he started, in a competition that didn't exist when he started and in a format of cricket that didn't exist when he started.

If there was any one cricketer you had to see, it was Sachin Tendulkar.

There have been others who have been important to their country's national psyche. Viv, Donald, Imran, to name a few. None has been as important to their country as Sachin has to his.

Sachin gave a billion people the feeling that one of theirs could be the greatest that ever lived. That changes a society. That changes everything. That is beyond cricket, beyond sport, that is about life. Pride.

In 200 years people will talk about the rise of India. There will be pictures of two men, Mahatma Gandhi and Sachin Tendulkar. One man who changed the way disenfranchised people went about taking down the oppressors, and a man who was dynamite off his pads. It won't make sense to them. And, it shouldn't.

Sachin is beyond common sense.

You can't argue with a Sachin fan, because you're not arguing with a cricket fan, you're arguing with a belief. Logic and common sense has no place.

A cricketer has stats. A belief has followers.

Sportsmen being called 'god' is a common thing. There is always a valid reason. But when a Sachin fan looks at him they actually see a god. That is something else. That is something different. When he touches a cancer patient, people really expect him to heal them.

A billion people know who Sachin Tendulkar is. And more than that, a billion people love and respect Sachin Tendulkar. There are people who retell their life through the timeline of Sachin Tendulkar. He is the first man bigger than the game since WG Grace created the game.

There are so many photos of him. There is one where he is pointing at the crest of his helmet after making a hundred. He is saying he is proud to represent India, but it might as well say, 'I built this'. There is another when he has the bat cocked, he is about to hit a ball through covers, behind him the crowd has already started to stand up, men are lifting for the applause before he's told them why. And then when he played his last Test, as he comes out of the change-room door, one shot catches an entire block of the crowd turning to watch him. Many hold their phones up, to capture a moment they will never truly be able to explain to anyone.

Those three photos are what Sachin Tendulkar has lived under. A prisoner of his own batting. The man who doesn't bat for a team, but for a giant fractured nation. A man whose every moment is for everyone else.

They have that chant for him. 'Sachin, Sachin'. A crowd full of people shouting that is just beautiful. They are shouting for Sachin. They are shouting for them. They are shouting for India. They are shouting for cricket. I once saw them do it when there was a shot on the big screen of him out the back of a change-room. Someone had just hit a six, but, 'Sachin, Sachin'.

I don't know what it's like to be Indian, so my Sachin is not a man of India, but a man of cricket.

In November of 2003, my life was not as I wanted it. I had not played my shots, I was a 23-year-old high school drop-out who wanted to be a writer, but wasn't one. I was in a dead-end relationship, dead-end job, and I had just come off a long-term illness. I was not in a good place.

The one good thing about my job was that I was a shift worker, which meant I was able to get down to the MCG to watch Victoria play. When I found out the Indians would be playing them, I wasn't going to miss that. The first day I couldn't get to the ground because of work. That day Sachin made 80 odd.

I knew better than most what it was like to watch shield games at the MCG. It was you, and almost not another living being in this amazing place, watching something you love. That's when I realised that I had to see Sachin there. I had seen him before, I would see him again, but I might never get another chance to be one of a handful watching Sachin bat.

A private viewing of God.

On day two I went down to see Brad Hodge bat. Brad Hodge once had a book written on him called *Brad Hodge: The Little Master* and he was a good bat. But no one has a religious epiphany watching Brad Hodge. And in that game, or to most people, he wasn't the little master.

On day three, the final day, my girlfriend decided to come. She was not a cricket fan; she did like drinking at one-day games, and somehow she convinced herself that this would be like that. I tried to assure her that the atmosphere would be different, but she wanted in.

As Hodge approached 200, I doubt there were 200 people there. India stopped trying early on day three. There had been a disagreement between both sides. Victoria was now going to bat until India was angry, and instead they batted until India lost interest. I could feel my girlfriend's irritation the moment she arrived. She wanted atmosphere, and instead it was whisper quiet, she went off to get drinks straight away. Virender Sehwag eventually took Hodge's wicket. And India came in to bat.

Sehwag came in and played big shots. Of all the crowd, no one more than my girlfriend, appreciated it. But he was soon out. This left Aakash Chopra and Sadagoppan Ramesh at the crease. This led to what happened to everyone who batted above Sachin in his entire career. The crowd, even their home crowd, cheered against them, not because they were rubbish, not because they were boring, but simply because they weren't him.

It was dead quiet in that ground. There were probably only a couple of hundred people in this birthplace of Test cricket; this heaving cauldron that can hold a hundred thousand people. But every conversation, every whisper, every thought, was about Sachin.

Ramesh and Chopra were hardly lighting the place up. They were both defining the word dour in what was obviously now nothing more than a net practice. The problem was I couldn't leave. What if a wicket fell straight away, I'd miss seeing Rahul. Or worse still, what if two fell, I'd miss Rahul and Sachin together. Or worse yet, what if one fell and Sachin came in at four.

Like most casual cricket fans my girlfriend knew little about any team that wasn't her own. Yes, she knew Sachin was good, but he wasn't batting, and she didn't care about waiting for him.

So I sat and waited. And waited. Waited.

The sun got hotter and hotter during this period. I could feel my skin burning. My beer was long past drinkable. My girlfriend was now breathing in purely sighs. Even some of the young Indian fans left the ground. But I stayed.

Ramesh went out, magically. I was there, and I was watching, but it seemed to just happen without a ball being bowled. As he walked off, the MCG stand's shadow started creeping out onto the surface. I swear in 30 seconds the whole place got a bit darker.

There were still about 150 people left at the ground. All our necks turned to the same place. The door of the Indian change-room opened, and then closed again, without anyone coming out. Then it swung wide open, as if moved by some magical force, and out walked a man with a gait that everyone, bar my girlfriend, could instantly tell was his just from the way he moved. We had all seen it so many times. He was walking down the stairs and out onto the MCG when a small kid from a few rows in front turned to me and said, 'Is that him?'

Rahul Dravid had entered the ground.

> My girlfriend and I saw a bit of Dravid batting, but as the shadows of my favourite ground, or place on earth, covered Dravid, even I knew it was time to leave the ground.
>
> That was the day I almost saw Sachin. And I remember so much of it. Just the hope, the chance, the daydreaming of how I might see him, that was enough. That was Sachin to me. And I suppose, that was Sachin to everyone.
>
> Sachin, Sachin.

MS Dhoni is a hero in India. He was the new India, perhaps their first truly modern cool player. He was a self-made man, not from a big city, but from a forgotten part of India. He batted, he kept, he captained, his way. There were times when it didn't seem like there was a delivery that could stop him from hitting a six, or stop him from being in control. In limited-overs cricket, it was if he alone had the schematic to the way the game was played.

The 2011 World Cup was in many ways India's coronation as a superpower. It never truly felt like another country would beat them. It was their tournament, in their home, in their sport. It was Dhoni who made all this possible.

By the time Dhoni took guard for the last time in the final, the game was over. But the crowd still looked tense. When he hit the last ball over mid-on for six, the ground screamed, India screamed with it. Their captain had delivered them a World Cup win at home, and done so, over the long-on boundary.

Sachin had only made 18. But it was his six, his victory, his reward. A lifetime of being India, and finally, India had given back.

Dhoni was the hero. But the loudest chant was still, 'Sachin, Sachin.'

My wife found cricket through her father. He had grown up in Sri Lanka. She had grown up in England. His favourite player was Sachin. Her favourite player was Sachin. Her father would come home from work and ask how Sachin had done. She would fill him in. They bonded over this. Her father died young. Sachin was her link to him.

Sachin was more than cricket. Sachin is cricket. 'Sachin, Sachin.' Cricket, cricket.

Chapter 61

AFGHANI MALIK

TAJ MALIK IS a leg-spinner. Taj Malik is a right-hand batsman. Taj Malik is a cricket coach. Taj Malik is a cricket selector. Taj Malik is a cricket administrator. Taj Malik is Afghanistan cricket.

In 2001 when Taliban fighters were fleeing their country as the US bombed them, Taj Malik went the other way.

Taj has some clothes, a cricket bat and a ball. He is coming from Pakistan, the country whose refugee camps taught him cricket. Al-Qaeda is still in his country. It's possible he is walking through an area that is housing Osama Bin Laden. Taj is on his way to Kabul, which the Americans had captured less than a month earlier. His dream is to start an Afghanistan cricket team and take them to the World Cup.

On Wednesday 18 February 2015, Taj Malik's dream came true. Taj Malik did it. He gave his country something amazing, a positive story during some of their darkest days. He's given them sporting heroes. He's given them victories. And he's given cricket to Afghanistan.

Michael Jordan. Lionel Messi. Mohammad Nabi. These are the replica shirts on the back of the Afghan kids in the crowd during their first game. Mohammad Nabi walks his team out onto the field. Mohammad Nabi walks his team into the World Cup. Afghanistan doesn't have to rely on imported heroes anymore.

Hamid Hassan is strapping. Other words do not do him justice. He has large shoulders. Large hands. Large pecs. Large glutes. He is an immense hunk of muscle. Hamid Hassan's headband bears the

Afghanistan colours. Stickers of Afghanistan colours on either cheek. He looks like a fast bowler. He bowls like a fast bowler. And when he completes his first ball, he has started Afghanistan's World Cup history.

The crowd cheer like mad. Another cricket journalist says, 'That's a big cheer for a dot ball.' It's not a dot ball. It's a wide. They have cheered a wide. Their wide. Their first wide in a World Cup.

Hassan is one of the many players in this side who was a refugee. His family did not encourage his cricket. He cites Rocky Balboa as a hero. Hassan is more of a hero than any made-up character.

When his body is fit, he is one of the fastest bowlers in the world. He once took a five-wicket haul in an ODI against UAE. This is his 25th ODI but only his second against a Test-playing nation.

Hassan starts very fast. He appeals like crazy against Tamim Iqbal. All the newsrooms in the world use the image of him appealing. This is a big story, this is a battered and beaten land, one that has been torn apart from internal and external sources, by communists, capitalists and terrorists. But here Hassan is, hands out, mouth wide open, a scream at the umpire. Hassan might be appealing, but he is also screaming that Afghanistan are in the World Cup.

Afsar Zazai was in the nets the day before, standing up and taking edges like a pro. His hands are quick, and soft. His footwork looks so sharp. He outshines many Test keepers. An assistant coach asks to give him some full ones outside off. 'No, full down leg.' He gloves them all perfectly.

The next day he is in mid-air. Diving. Flying. For a nick. The ball drops on him and he plucks it with his left hand. All cricket fans in the world swoon. But while he is still flying, the ball starts to come out, he clutches at it with his right hand. He keeps it in.

According to cricket writer Sid Monga, 'Afsar's family live in a small house with a temporary roof that can't offer proper protection from the snow.' His hands are his family's chance. His hands are magnificent.

Afghanistan have their first wicket in a World Cup, caught Afsar Zazai, bowled Mirwais Ashraf. In Canberra.

While Afghanistan play, cricket administrators are busy trying to justify their decision to make it all but impossible for Afghanistan to qualify for future world cups.

They do that as Shapoor Zadran runs in.

Shapoor is glorious, even in the nets. His run-up is almost double the length of his fellow bowlers'. His run-up is beautiful, his hair is beautiful, his action is beautiful, his follow-through is beautiful, his appeals are beautiful. Beautiful.

At one stage Shapoor bowls a quick short ball outside leg stump. The batsman misses it outside off stump. The keeper takes it in front of first slip's throat. Any cricket official who tries to limit associate cricket should have to face Shapoor on a bouncy wicket first.

When Afghanistan struggle they throw him the ball. He bowls fast around the wicket. It is Imran. It is Wasim. It is Shoaib. It is Shapoor.

The crowd chant. 'Shapoor, Shapoor, Shapoor'.

Two quick wickets fall to him. It is quick, it is skillful, it is fast bowling and it is Afghanistan cricket.

Shapoor has been around a long time. When Afghanistan played their first international against Oman 11 years ago, Shapoor was there. So were Asghar Stanikzai, Mohammad Nabi and Nawroz Mangal. Their first recorded match as a side was in 2001 when they played Nowshehra in the Quaid-e-Azam Trophy, Grade II, Pool B, Group I. Nawroz Mangal played in that too. Against Oman he made 101.

Nawroz has been a source of pride for 14 years. Before most of his countrymen knew what cricket was. He looks far older and wiser than the 30 years his profile says he is. He has been a captain, a leader, and a rock of Afghanistan cricket. When he enters in this match it's 3/3. He has been involved in more collapses than any batsman should ever be a part of. Today he tries hard, and stops the flow of wickets, but his 27 isn't enough.

Andy Moles, their coach, is trying to produce more players with the sensible nature of Nawroz. He talks of education, and he runs his net sessions like a schoolteacher. Moles once said, 'Sometimes you hear a boom go off somewhere when coaching in the middle. You see Black Hawk helicopters flying over the ground, going on missions and coming back. Like coaching in a war movie.'

They have come a long way from the Taj Malik days.

Taj Malik was Afghanistan's first coach. Taj is the embodiment of every club-cricket hero in the world. There is nothing Taj wouldn't do for Afghanistan cricket. He played coached, administered, smoked and bled for his team. And it was his team. Without Taj's passion and inspiration,

Afghanistan might not be here. He will teach kids on the street, or coach the national side. Taj is the man who walked back home from Pakistan to give his country cricket.

Taj once declared he would throw himself in the Atlantic if Afghanistan didn't win a lowly ICC tournament. When Afghanistan cricket grew, it outgrew him, but he planted it.

A braggart, and a dreamer. Taj is Afghan cricket. He is cricket.

Hassan is coming back on for this third spell. His pace has gone. Now his proper quick bowling is more fast-medium than fast. After seven overs he has taken no wickets, and conceded 41 runs.

Bangladesh has a massive partnership, their batting stars are just about to take the game away from Afghanistan. The first ball of Hassan's eighth over is a horrible full-toss, the next ball is a poor short ball, he looks slow and tired as Shakib Al Hasan picks up 10 easy runs. The third ball he finds a dot-ball with a yorker.

The fourth, with Shakib on fire, he bowls a clever slower ball. After he finishes the ball his big frame turns slowly around and walks back to the mark. His teammates come in to celebrate his first World Cup wicket. By the next over he has taken another, this time he pumps his fists and has that Rocky spirit in his eyes.

His pace is gone, his body is failing, he is off eight paces, and he is still fighting. The crowd scream 'Hassan'.

Samiullah Shenwari bowls seven balls, for two runs. Then he is taken off. He is a leg-spinner who has been told three times he is running on the pitch. Afghanistan has overcome war, poverty and devastation, but even they can't beat the laws of cricket. With the bat Shenwari looks good. Of all the Afghanistan top order he is the most composed, scores the easiest and moves towards a comfortable half-century.

But he goes for a second run, when there is not quite a second there. Brilliant fielding from Sabbir Rahman fires the ball back to the keeper and Shenwari dives. He lands in the turf. His face is down. He doesn't get up. The replays are looked at by the third umpire. Shenwari's body language is even more conclusive. He is out. He has run on the pitch, and then been run out. Shenwari's run is over.

Shenwari leaves Mohammad Nabi at the crease, and little else.

Afghanistan needs practically 10 an over, but the crowd is cheering for Nabi.

In the book *Second XI*, Tim Wigmore recounts this tale. 'In May 2013, Nabi's father, a wealthy car salesman, was abducted from his car in the city of Jalalabad. For more than two months, his father's whereabouts were unknown, despite a concerted effort by the government to find him.'

Nabi's father was found just before he had to play World Cup qualifying matches against Namibia in Windhoek. Nabi smashed 81 not out off 45 balls. Then he took 5/12.

Today Nabi makes them chant his name. When they have no hope, he scores at better than a run a ball, he hits boundaries, his fans say, 'Nabi, Nabi, Nabi'. His final shot is one of a man who knows he can't get them home.

Nabi leaves the ground with a defeated shrug.

Before the game young kids hold a flag in the shadows of the former MCG scoreboard. Their job is to take it out onto the ground. A simple gesture that has been done many times in this World Cup.

The Afghan crowd scream as their flag is taken onto the ground.

A man wearing an Afghanistan shirt, with his face painted in his country's colours, is quiet. Around him are flags and his colours. There is another man painted from his waist to his hair in Afghan colours. Others are in replica shirts, branded World Cup shirts, homemade Afghanistan flag shirts and traditional Afghan clothing. It is a typical cricket scene. But as that flag moves from under the old MCG scoreboard out onto the ground, the quiet man's eyes start to well up.

He's crying. He's smiling.

This is just a flag ceremony. Just a cricket game. Just an ODI. Just a World Cup. But for Afghanistan, this is their chance, their hope, their everything.

Afghanistan lose. Their fans leave the ground with the same face that losing fans all over the world have. That look of emptiness once the hope has gone. A few hug each other. One shouts, 'Well done, Afghanistan,' at no one in particular.

Then a song starts. It is 'Joy Bangla'. A song of hope and of a new beginning about Bangladesh coming out of war and into brighter days. Bangladesh's cricket is finally coming to their better days. The Bangladeshis sing along as their players do a victory lap. A few Afghan fans dance along as they leave the ground.

It's not their song. It's not their win. It will forever be their day.

In 2009 Afghanistan lost a match in ICC World Cricket League Division Three. There were few in the ground. The games weren't telecast around the world. The cricket world largely ignored it. But Hassan came off the ground crying. Documentary-maker Leslie Knott, part of the team behind *Out of the Ashes*, asked Hassan why. 'I have seen people die and I have not shed a tear. But there is something about cricket that gets me here [pointing to his heart]. Cricket is our chance.'

A chance cricket didn't want to give them. This might be their last World Cup. Cricket has told Afghanistan it doesn't want it. The ICC has already announced the next two tournaments are for 10 teams only. The Test-playing nations don't care about the associates.

While Afghanistan was qualifying for the World Cup, Mr N Srinivasan – the man whose IPL team threw matches, which were fixed by his son-in-law, who ran the team – was being made the head of worldwide cricket, the chairman of the International Cricket Council. Those who ran cricket had made their choice.

Chapter 62

SPECIAL GAME, SPECIAL PLACE

A T THE SAMPATH Bank headquarters in Colombo there is a round-faced man smiling happily wearing a polo shirt with the bank's logo on it. He is being felicitated. He is a finger-spinning maestro. He is a World T20 winner. And this man, Rangana Herath, is also an employee at the bank.

Not in a ceremonial way. Herath actually works at the bank. Doing things that people in banks do. He probably has his own coffee mug there. When Herath sees the Sri Lanka cricket schedule, one of his first calls is to his bank manager to ask for leave to travel to the tour. Just like Dennis Lille and Fred Spofforth before him.

Herath worked there when he made his comeback to Test cricket in 2009. Herath worked there while he took more Test wickets than any other bowler in 2012. Herath worked there even while he was ranked the second-best Test bowler on earth.

James Anderson doesn't work in a bank. Every part of his life was part of a plan to make him a better cricketer. James Anderson is England's all-time leading wicket-taker. Anderson has had every advantage possible over Herath and has never been ranked higher than the sixth-best Test bowler on earth.

Sri Lanka Cricket is currently in debt. An exact amount is unknown. It was at one stage supposed to be US$70m. That is to pay for new stadiums to replace the old stadiums that were in some cases not that old. This led them to not pay their players.

According to Forbes, MS Dhoni was worth US$30m in 2013. He captained the side that Sri Lanka beat in the World T20 final. In sport, money does buy wins. Internationally, less so. But Sri Lanka is playing cricket off the field in a way that the other countries haven't done for decades. Their support staff is short of people, undertrained, and at times seemingly not able to do their own research. They rely on the touring journalists for a lot of things that cricket board staff would usually do. They are not professional.

On Sri Lanka's west coast, north of Colombo, there is a town called Chilaw. There is an ancient Hindu temple in Chilaw that was once visited by Gandhi. Every year they have the Munneswaram festival. It was once famous for pearls. And they have a first-class cricket team: the Chilaw Marians Cricket Club.

Shaminda Eranga comes from Chilaw.

Like many in Sri Lanka, the cricketers from Chilaw are largely invisible inside the system. They are not from a big town. There are Test-quality cricketers playing on the streets of the Hikkaduwa right now who will never play with a hard cricket ball in their life.

Eranga was not playing first-class cricket. He was not in the system. He shouldn't have made it at all. He didn't own bowling boots. But like his seam-bowling partner Nuwan Pradeep, he made his way to a fast-bowling competition.

He bowled fast. But five guys bowled faster. Somehow the sixth-fastest bowler in that completion was picked for Chilaw Marians Cricket Club. Five years later he would clean bowl Brad Haddin with his second ball in international cricket.

Eranga is the closest thing Chilaw has produced to a pearl in a very long time.

The 2011 World Cup felt like perhaps the most inevitable result ever. Sri Lanka was the second best side. They proved that.Three years later the World T20 was in Bangladesh. India played Sri Lanka again. Sri Lanka had lost two of the three previous World T20 finals and the two previous World Cup finals.

Sri Lanka has never won a major world championship in another sport. They have no Olympic gold medalists. They don't play in the football World Cup, or the rugby World Cup. Their national sport is volleyball, but they're not the best at it.

When India batted in the World T20 final, they scored well, and then their two biggest names in limited overs cricket came in. They have won World Cups and World T20s before. They have been given a great platform.

Sri Lanka decide to bowl full and wide. It's a clear tactic. Not from robotic data analysis, but from smart cricket brains. It's been done against these two before. This time, Sri Lanka do it magnificently, and India's final big bang doesn't happen. Sri Lanka bat. Kumar Sangakkara is joined by his closest friend, Mahela Jayawardene. They have played together for a lifetime. They have never won anything this big. Mahela looks effortless. Kumar looks focused.

Mark and Steve Waugh shared a womb, and many change-rooms, but they are nowhere near as close to each other as Kumar and Mahela.

At a sponsor event, Sangakkara was asked to look like he was dressing Jayawardene, for the sort of standard embarrassing athlete photo opportunity. What was already awkward enough was made more so by the fact that people already question how close they are. There is already erotic fiction written about the two of them. Sri Lanka is already awash with them as a pair. Want to be as happy as Kumar and Mahela are, drink a Coke and share in their good times. Want to look as smart as they do, get some Emerald suits and you too can look this smooth. Want a great-tasting crab meal, eat at the Mahela and Kumar's restaurant, the Ministry of Crab, and wear the same bibs they wear.

The cricket public perception of the two is often quite clear. Jayawardene is seen as the cherub-faced batting wizard, often smiling and happy to be doing what he does. Sangakkara is seen as a modern-day cricket intellectual of impeccable morals who will one day be the spirit of cricket's professor emeritus.

It's not really true; Jayawardene can get as angry as Ricky Ponting on a bad day. And it's quick, Hulk quick, often reacting with anger before he has even fully grasped what has happened. The cherub face is replaced with this snarling beast. Yelling is done, handshakes are ignored, and he lets everyone in the area know exactly how he feels.

Sangakkara is so smart and eloquent that he has managed to cultivate a statesman role when, in truth, he is a hard-ass, son-of-a-bitch cricketer who would be just as likely to psychologically destroy you as talk about the great cultural mix in world cricket. He once tricked Ahmed

Shehzad into thinking a throw was coming in so he could make Shehzad dive to save himself. In actual fact the throw was miles away. Shehzad hurt himself, Sangakkara laughed. His sledging of Shaun Pollock at the 2003 World Cup is still one of the greatest monologues recorded from a pitch.

'Lots of pressure on the skipper here yeh? [said in a decent enough South African accent] gonna let his whole country down if he fails. Oh man, The weight of all these expectations here, the weight of the country chaps ... 42 million supporters right here, depending on Shaun.'

It was perhaps even better than his spirit of cricket lecture, which *The Guardian* described as, 'scathing attack on the endless political power-struggles that bedevil Sri Lankan Cricket'.

The cherub-and-gentleman vibe is nowhere near accurate and actually sells them short of what they really are: fierce, determined, passionate cricketers who want to win.

They played a whole career together; they have fought every step of the way. They had batted as best friends, brothers, for a lifetime, they had held their small nation on their back, and they carried Sri Lanka to the second ever World Championship win in history.

Mahela is dismissed, Kumar stays in until the end.

Thisara Perera comes in to join him. Perera bowls and bats like he could only come from Sri Lanka. His final shot could be played on any beach in the land.

The Sri Lankan cricket board may be in debt, they may not be able to pay their players at times, but they have just beaten the richest cricket team in the history of the world.

Twenty-four days before his felicitation at the bank, Herath took 1/23 in four overs as Sri Lanka won the World T20.

Herath has been in Test cricket since 1999. He invented and pioneered the modern carrom ball. He disappeared back into first-class cricket and the bank, and was in club cricket in England when he was picked for his comeback.

There are no billboards in Sri Lanka with his face on them. He's not famous like Kumar, Mahela, Lasith Malinga or Angelo Mathews. Even Ajantha Mendis is sponsored by chicken sausages.

Sri Lanka was given two Tests against England for 2014. They simply didn't have a big enough TV market to demand more. The series before, they hosted only two Tests against England, because a third would have clashed with the IPL, and they might have lost their star players.

Everywhere Sri Lanka looked, a superpower was squeezing them.

In the first Test Herath is poor with the ball. Despite brilliant hundreds from Mathews and Sangakkara, England dominates the match. On the last day of the Test all Sri Lanka needs to do is bat out 90 overs with all 10 wickets in hand.

There are nine fielders out on the ground but they are casting 36 shadows.

It seems like there isn't a single gap on the infield that doesn't have a fielder covering it. The leg side has more bodies than blades of grass. All hands on knees, waiting for a mistake.

There are six balls left. There are two wickets left.

Broad goes wide around the wicket and fires it in short at Herath, he jumps out of the way, but the ball takes his glove, he walks while England appeals. No one notices, Herath included, that his glove was off his bat. That is until the many, many replays come up on the screen. He walked for a not out.

Now out comes a man with a two-and-half line Wikipedia entry, uncoached action, often-untucked shirt, a homemade haircut reminiscent of a member of the band Poison and a Test bowling average of 72.83. On the scoreboard they call him Fernando, everywhere else he's called Pradeep.

If you replaced Nuwan Pradeep with a puppy in the field, it wouldn't cause much more damage. While he is naturally athletic, quick and looks like he belongs, he seems to read the ball like it's Baudelaire untranslated.

He seems to have walked into this situation by accident. They don't even know his name and he's walking out to save his country against their former colonisers.

Pradeep is marinated by Broad first ball with a bouncer that is only there to get him where he needs him. Pradeep is little more than a piece of meat in front of the stumps. Four balls left. Next delivery is short of a length, quick and moves away, Pradeep should be given a medal for even getting that close. Three balls left. He middles the next one, as much as he could ever middle a ball. Suddenly he's a batsman.

But the next one is too fast, too straight and it's not for the likes of him. He's instantly given out, but he reviews it before umpire Paul Reiffel has fully given it.

So does Eranga at the non-striker's end, and perhaps every single Sri Lankan alive. England is celebrating at deep point, the BBC has already tweeted the victory. But somehow Reiffel missed the huge chunk of wood hitting the ball. And DRS saves Sri Lanka. Nuwan Pradeep has one ball to face.

In the first innings, Pradeep faced a short ball that he clearly didn't see. His face started to turn and his bat wafted in general self-defence, the ball smashed into his shoulder, this twisted and crashed his whole body that fell uncontrollably and ended with him smearing the stumps with his bat. It was embarrassing, viral and he would never ever live it down.

One more ball.

Nuwan Pradeep, or Fernando, the competition winner, leans forward with absolutely no certainty at all. It's quick and straight from Broad. The ball takes the edge, and goes straight for second slip, Chris Jordan, England's best slipper. It's quick and low, like a plane flying under radar, and Jordan picks it up as clean as you can in the slips.

On the half volley.

Eranga clutches at the air, Pradeep, still in the pose of the shot, looks around confused. He's not even sure if it has been caught. England is silent. He has done it. He saved them by inches. He survived the five toughest balls of his life. Sri Lanka goes 0-0 into the second and deciding Test.

Eranga bowled well to start the second Test, but he couldn't break through. There was some swing, but not enough. Even the second new ball did nothing for him. Then finally, he found some form, when the game already looked beyond Sri Lanka, and took four good wickets.

But Sri Lanka still shouldn't have been in the game. Their captain, Angelo Mathews, brought himself on, and for the first time in Tests Angelo took more than two wickets. He took four. England still ended up 108 in front. When Sri Lanka was 66 runs in front, Angelo came in to bat. They survived till dusk, they came back at dawn, and he and Mahela attacked. There is a short ball from the fast bowling of Liam

Plunkett that Angelo doesn't even bother going back, he just stands on the front foot and smacks it past the sweeper at point. It's a shot that won't stop ringing in England's ears all days.

After lunch, Herath is on 2, and is determined to get out. The first ball he faces he throws and misses. Angelo says nothing. Herath chases the next one as well. Angelo has a quick word. Herath slogs even harder. Angelo walks down the wicket and has a very stern word. Herath leaves the fourth ball. He will stay with Angelo for virtually all the session.

Angelo pulls a four. Cook has six men on the boundary. Angelo flicks a four. Cook has seven men on the boundary. Angelo cuts a four. Cook has eight men on the boundary. Angelo spits a four. Cook puts every single man onto the boundary. Cook doesn't even bring them in when Angelo is on 99. There are just not enough fielders to stop Angelo. It was biblical. Off his bat came a plague of locusts. You will know his name is Angelo when you feel this innings upon you.

It was an innings that won a session, a day, a Test and a series. Angelo the savior. Angelo the everything. Angelo the rock. Angelo the sword.

Thanks to the sword, Sri Lanka was in the game. But even in the second innings, Eranga bowled the worst he had in the series. At Lord's he was the pick of the bowling; in the first innings at Headingley he inspired the comeback. But when his team really needed him to help win the game in this innings, he couldn't get it right. He lost his line and length. He didn't make people play. He was too short. The only time he looked good was when he just tried to knock Joe Root's mouth off. That didn't work either. Then when he took a wicket, that of Jordan, he also overstepped.

Eranga's first 23.4 overs were just not great. It was probably mostly luck that he received the last over. Dhammika Prasad had bowled the second last over. Herath could not out-fox Anderson. Pradeep looked spent. And Angelo Mathews had lost his first innings magic.

Eranga was just the man who was left.

Sri Lanka feel like they don't get the credit they deserve. They feel that when they win, the opposition is blamed for being poor. Or the home conditions helped them. At Headingley, they started one of the great comebacks in modern Test cricket. Their captain played one of the great knocks of modern Test cricket. They were on the verge of their first ever series win in England.

Their first major series win outside Asia for almost 20 years.

And the next day the cricket world talked about how the other captain had a shocker.

Before the tour they lost their coach to the opposition. While it was on, they have been accused of breaking the spirit of cricket. Their spinner was accused of breaking the laws of cricket. Their bowlers were pop-gun and a glorified county attack. Their batsmen were suspect against the moving and short ball. They would be bombed by the short ball. They were sent in to be annihilated here. They felt under siege.

They almost always did.

This is not the strongest team Sri Lanka has brought to England. They've had Murali, Dilshan, Jayasuriya and Vaas to bring before. This team has two all-time greats, one potential great, and the second-best spinner they have ever had.

It also has Nuwan Pradeep and his bowling average of 72.78. It has Dimuth Karunaratne, who is immune to going out early, or making runs from his starts. Lahiru Thirimanne, who stopped believing runs existed. And Prasanna Jayawardene, who looked a spent force with bat and gloves.

Mahela Jayawardene never made a hundred. Herath never took a five-for. Nuwan Kulasekera was dropped after the first Test. But people kept stepping up.

James Anderson was playing for England by the time he was 21. You can see his face on the back of buses in London. He's had every advantage you get playing for a rich cricket board. What he eats, how he trains, what his spare time is spent doing. He has been psychologically tested. He has been groomed in every way to be as good as he can at what he is paid to be. He has won games with the ball all round the world. He's saved games with the bat.

On 4 June 2014, Anderson faced 54 balls with the knowledge that any mistake and his team would lose a Test, a series, become a joke. Yet he played almost every ball well. Stoically. Until Sri Lanka very nearly gave up.

No fast bowler has ever bowled as much in Test Cricket as James Anderson did in the six years leading up to this Test. He was a professional cricketer, but he was an ECB commodity, a part of their financial planning. Just another workhorse bowler bowling until he bled. This time not for gentleman captains, but for gentleman administrators.

Anderson looked tired, he often did these days. On the 55th ball, a world-class professional sportsman was bounced by the sixth-fastest bowler from the North Western Province and caught by a chubby slow guy from Kurunegala.

The pearl and the bank clerk.

These amateurs have beaten the new professionals. They had beaten a system that was rigged against them by politics and financial muscle.

Sri Lanka is a special place. Cricket is a special game.

Chapter 63

ONE DAY AT THE ADELAIDE OVAL

O<small>N 3 DECEMBER 2014</small> Phil Hughes was laid to rest. Michael Clarke gave his eulogy and quoted his favourite line: 'dig in and get to tea'. On 9 December 2014, Australia hosted India at the Adelaide Oval. Michael Clarke was captaining his country.

Some of the same teammates and friends who rushed to Phil Hughes' side, who were at his funeral, were now playing in a Test match that had almost been turned into a wake for him.

Cricket Australia tried to find the balance between being respectful and over-the-top in their tribute. They had Hughes' Test number 408 written on the field and on the shirts. The players wore special armbands with PH on them. They made Hughes 13th man; since the Lord's Ashes Test of 2013, Hughes had often been the 13th man. Now there was no other choice.

The players stood to pay their respects. Players from both sides looked to the sky. Some looked upset. Virat Kohli looked as he often did. It might have been a moving moment, but Kohli was focused on something else. That first Test as captain. And when Kohli was focused, there was little that could change that.

The ground was filled with the voice of Richie Benaud. You didn't often hear Richie at the ground. So from the speakers, he sounded like the Voice of Cricket.

But it was a broken Richie, older and upset, sounding like he never had before. It was a relief when he finished; the sadness from every word was unbearable. And what followed were 63 seconds of applause.

The fans had turned up early, very early. They were eager to pay their respects. To see what would happen next. To help cricket heal. Strangely for Adelaide, most of them didn't head out the back of the members' to drink. They watched the cricket. Cricket Australia and the crowd had played their part, but in truth, the game now needed to start healing itself. This was right in Hughes' new hometown. On his pitch. A Test he could have played in.

'There it is,' said Ian Healy on Channel 9.

Nineteen balls. That was how long it took. There had been yorker length. Full length. Length length. Back of a length. And then nothing. The pitch map just had this unofficial demarcation in it: the Philip Hughes respect zone. Starting at roughly 63 inches from the batsman.

This Test couldn't start until a bowler hit the middle of the pitch. Until that first bouncer was bowled in an aggressive way and handled in a safe way. The rest was fidgeting.

Mohammed Shami and Varun Aaron both started around the wicket and bowling full, in some sort of premeditated bad plan. It wasn't short, it wasn't intimidating, and it wasn't good.

After five legal balls and three Warner boundaries, Aaron stood mid-pitch the way bowlers do when the over won't end and the fielders are still collecting the ball. Fast bowling 101 suggests the next ball should be a bouncer. Escape the over, and let the batsman know you're angry. Would cricket remain as we knew it?

Aaron flew in and bowled a back of the length ball that was pushed into the covers for one.

Six more bowling-plan balls from Shami, full and non-threatening.

Then ball 19. Around the wicket. Quick. Angled straight at Warner. Full enough to hit something. Short enough to hit something precious. Warner is coming forward. He sees the ball late. His head hurriedly drops. His feet struggle for balance. The bat stays up. The ball flies over the right shoulder. Warner can't see it. It lands in Wriddiman Saha's glove. Safely, from a cricket and life perspective.

Ian Healy almost sounds excited at the bouncer; the crowd ooohs. They were caught by surprise as much as Warner. Then they applaud.

It's a long applause; it's not an ovation, and no one seems to be standing. It comes from every part of the ground, and it sounds pure. There seem to be no idiots yelling, whistling or booing. Just sustained applause for cricket and a thank you to Aaron for delivering their cricket back.

Warner twiddles his bat. Aaron steams back to his mark. The crowd starts chatting. The replays are shown. The Test has started.

Aaron follows up with another bouncer. Warner tries to smash it. It could be Richardson to Trumper. Larwood to Bradman. Adcock to Sutcliffe. Lillee to Richards. It's just a bouncer, not even a good one.

Sean Abbott comes on at the SCG in a Shield game. Abbott is the man who delivered the fateful ball to Hughes. Just a regulation bouncer that killed his friend. At the SCG, a few minutes later, Abbott bowls a bouncer his fifth ball; it also goes through to the keeper.

Shane Watson comes in and is bounced straight away by Ishant Sharma. It was only a few days earlier when Watson was talking about struggling against the short ball in the nets. Now he is facing one. You can see Watson take his eye off it. You can see him turn his head. You can see the potential for disaster. You can see the back of his head. You can see the ball going towards the unprotected zone. You can see the ball going past. You can see the men on the hill who are cheering each bouncer. You can see Warner looking unfussed from the non-striker's end. You can see it all in a way you never saw before.

You can see that cricket goes on.

Warner will stop on 63 to celebrate the new landmark, that of Phil Hughes' last innings being stopped on 63. If, in cricket lore, 87 is the Devil's number, then 63 is God's number. The bouncer belongs to neither; it belongs to cricket.

That sends us on a live cricket memorial. It was touching, amazing and seemingly never-ending. Warner remembered Hughes on 50, 63 and 100. Michael Clarke did it on 37, but hit a boundary to skip 63. Steven Smith did it on 50, 63 and 100 as well. Ryan Harris, Nathan Lyon, Mitchell Johnson and Peter Siddle all did so when taking their wickets.

There was looking at the sky. Raising the bat at the sky. Standing by the number. They pointed at the number. Touching the arm band. Patting the 408 on the heart. Raising the ball to the sky. Kissing the armband.

Black armbands have been too prevalent in recent cricket history. They were worn after terrorists attacked the Sri Lankan team. And when

Andy Flower and Henry Olonga wanted to protest their government's regime. These were for the victims of a dictator and terrorists. The ones in Hughes' honour were for a victim of cricket.

The crowd cheered when the total went to 408 as well. It was as if the 63 seconds of applause from day one would never end.

Then a noise. Hearts skipped. Some players heard the same sound they had at 2.23pm, 25 November on the SCG. The crowd went silent.

'Woooooooooaaaaaaah!' James Brayshaw practically howling. He loses himself in commentary; he is paid to be loud and blokey. 'Struck.' He's barking excitedly. 'Right on the helmet.' But then Brayshaw realises the moment. This isn't just another accurate bouncer. Brayshaw tries to dial back; it's not three weeks earlier, it's 63 not out time.

Brayshaw's commentary is echoed throughout the crowd. Woah, then quickly silenced. By the time the ball hits the ground the crowd is already going silent. It feels like you can hear the ball hit the ground, this heavy thud. It's the last noise that registers for a while.

Mitchell Johnson walks down to Virat Kohli. His head is leaning to one side. He's trying to see underneath the helmet. He's trying to see if Virat is ok. His walk is quick and worried. There is no aggression. He needs to get down there. He needs to know Virat is ok. Johnson's eyes aren't fixed in a terrifying stare; they're terrified.

Australian fielders turn up from everywhere. Chris Rogers puts a hand on Kohli. So does David Warner. Brad Haddin comes in as well. Kohli was at Hughes' funeral, and is now surrounded by worried Australian fielders, and mourners. The same fielders that Faf du Plessis referred to as a pack of dogs. The same men who then howled at du Plessis like wild dogs. The same men who told James Anderson to prepare for a broken fuckin' arm.

The same men; but not the same. Not now.

They stood around for support, not for sledging. The arms weren't broken, they were rubbed. Mental disintegration had gone; it was replaced by cricket unity. Two teams, one family.

Virat Kohli had his helmet off for all of six seconds.

He was shaken up; his head was hit by something at 90 miles per hour. He was surrounded by well-wishers. Worried looks from each and every one of them. But, had the same thing happened, and Johnson gone straight back to his mark, Kohli might have been ready to face without any delay.

That couldn't happen, not for this hit, not at this time. Kohli pushes away his batting partner Che Pujara. Kohli nods at Clarke. Kohli waves the umpires back. Maybe he is in shock. Maybe he is trying to posture. Maybe he doesn't want to be seen as the victim.

Johnson turns, and despite the fact that Kohli is ok, Johnson is not.

Clarke runs over to ruffle his hair. Then puts his hands on his shoulders. Johnson looks like someone who has just seen something he shouldn't have. He tries to act busy, walk past Clarke. A stop at the crease to check his footmarks. Maybe trying to trick himself into forgetting the last ball. The last fortnight. All of it.

The ball before, he had tapped the 408 on his shirt. He couldn't forget. It was in his eyes. It was on his face. It was on his mind. It is on his mind. Mitchell walks back to his mark. It feels like a long hard walk. It was. It is.

Mitchell is not bowling at full pace. His terrifying pace is gone; part of that is because of what happened to his friend.

Like Aaron, Kohli just got on with the cricket. It wasn't a surprise. Virat's father died while his son was playing in a Ranji trophy match. Kohli was the not-out batsman overnight when his father passed. Virat still batted the next day. He made 90.

The Indians may have been fumbling, dropping and missing balls in the field. Their bowlers may have had trouble with line and/or length. They might have bowled around the wicket, roughing up the pitch for off-spinners, despite not having one. Their batsmen might have given away starts. But they were playing cricket.

Kohli was playing something else. Something special. He hit a cover drive that should be put in the Louvre. Off his pads he was virtuoso Virat. When they went short, he handled it. When they went full he punished it. He was all business in one of the most personal Tests ever played.

At 100, there were no gestures for Hughes. He was full of fire and brimstone. He swung his bat around like a sword. He was inspiring his team; threatening his team. Showing them what passion really is. This Test meant a lot to so many people, but regardless of Hughes, it meant just as much to Kohli. He pointed to his damaged badge like a warrior who had conquered an army.

Clarke also did no special gesture for his hundred. He could barely lift his bat. Clarke was overcoming his back injury, his hamstring injury and his heart. His innings was full of the sort of determination the Australian public had once accused him of not having. He was the first Australian batsman to make a hundred after being retired hurt. And probably the first to give a eulogy of a teammate right before making a Test hundred.

Two giants of the game, moving cricket forward in different ways.

On the rare occasions when there were no moments to applaud at the ground, they found them in the Shield games. Ed Cowan made two emotional hundreds in Hobart, both for him, Tasmania and his mate Phil.

The SCG had something even more remarkable. There is no way we can ever really know what Sean Abbott was going through. Hughes was on every TV, newspaper, magazine, radio show and website in Australia. There was no way Abbott could exist in this country right now without being reminded of it. Even Elton John gave a shout out to Hughes and Abbott during a set.

Other players who didn't even deliver the ball had to miss their Shield games as they were too upset. Abbott played. Maybe he just had to. Grief doesn't come with a strict set of guidelines; you just get through it. Abbott bowled through his. In his first over Abbott had bowled a bouncer, and later he took wickets. Everyone was pleased for him, pleased for cricket.

That seemed like nothing when he ran in to bowl in the second innings against Queensland. This magical collection of six deliveries. A short wide one. A couple that kept low. A ripper outside off. A quick yorker. And the brute. It jumped up into the glove that was moving into a defensive position towards the throat before ending in slip's hand. Every single delivery seemed to be a gift from cricket. Unless you were the batsmen who faced them.

When Abbott's figures hit the big screen at Adelaide oval 6/14, the crowd applauded. So did Warner. So did cricket.

Bouncers were ok. Hits were ok. Abbott was ok. Cricket was ok.

The whole thing was nice. Indian reporters and fans were shocked that this was the Australia who had spent years bullying and sledging their players, who now openly wept, cared for the opposition's safety and stopped to celebrate a mate so often.

The amnesty lasted 10 sessions. During the second session of the fourth day, the birthday balloon outside Adelaide Oval for Hughes finally hit the ground. In a perfect world, it might have floated there forever. Cricket doesn't live in a perfect world. It never has.

On the field Kohli brought cricket back down to earth. Kohli's decision to send off Chris Rogers was aggressive, unfriendly and kind of bizarre. Australia was setting a total; they were in front; it was Chris Rogers and he swept a ball to a fielder. It was like sending off your uncle in a backyard game. Why you would walk beside Rogers doing an angry chicken-dance send-off was anyone's guess.

Then Aaron shouted 'c'mon' in the direction of Dave Warner when he was dismissed. But it was a no-ball. Warner walked back and shouted 'come on' at Aaron three times. He then aggressively left the next ball and did it again.

It was in no way like the man who cried into his captain's shoulder on day one.

Later, Warner and Kohli ended up next to each other as Smith and Rohit Sharma were also involved. It was ugly. It was aggressive. It was also cricket. The two teams weren't playing a memorial game in Hughes' honour, they were playing a Test. Tough. Ugly. And not always right.

Clarke's body finally gave up completely, and he was taken off to hospital. And it was Kohli standing between Australia and happiness.

Kohli was dogmatic. Kohli was dominant. Kohli was floating above the crease like a supernatural being. It would be an understatement to just call it batting. Mitchell Johnson broke an entire team here last year. In the space of two balls, Kohli had smashed him, smiled at him, and then laughed as he bowled a wide.

There are some innings that look like they can't be ended. Kohli's looked like he refused to believe there was an ending. When you bat like this, when you lead like this, when you believe like this, it should end with you being carried on the shoulders of your teammates.

Kohli should have been brought down by a ball of the century. The world's best-ever run-out. A catch of the purest athleticism. Something fitting of the innings. But it wasn't.

The ball was short. Really short. It should have been a drifting ripper that sliced through the gate. It should have. It wasn't. It was so short Lyon would have been disgusted with his effort. The ball should have been heaved into the Mark Ricciuto stand. It should have been annihilated by Kohli's mere existence. It should have. It wasn't.

It clanged against his bat like a shopping trolley hitting a car. It floated out accidentally towards Mitchell Marsh. It should have been taken quite easily. It should have. It wasn't. Marsh went the wrong way. Then his hands went the wrong way. And in the end he fell to the ground like a toppled animal and caught it like it was his first-ever catch.

Kohli bent over at the waist. He never left the crease. He clutched at the blade of his bat. In both innings he had been king of the crease. Now he was trapped there by disappointment. And he couldn't even hold the bat properly.

His grief was like no one else's in the whole Test. It was purely for the win. Not for a friend. Not for a cricketer. But purely for Test cricket. He had taken his side within sight of a great away win in one of the great Tests. And then he'd made one mistake. He stayed there for such a long time it looked like he might never leave that crease.

It was utter devastation. But finally, for the first time in a few weeks, devastation of the right kind. A captain losing the match with one mistake. A poorly executed shot. A cricket tragedy. Not a tragedy.

When the Australians took the last wicket they followed Brad Haddin who ran manically across the field. They ended up next to the 408. This was a perfect cricket moment. The perfect Test. The perfect celebration.

After stumps a band out the back of the members' played 'Throw Your Arms Around Me' by Hunters and Collectors.

At the post-match press conference Michael Clarke said, 'There's a chance I might never play again.' Virat Kohli said he was 'getting to terms with how life goes on every single day'.

Cricket had overcome everything thrown at it. When Phil Hughes died, it was one of the first times cricket had been the villain and not the hero. It couldn't bring Hughes back, but in Adelaide, cricket healed itself.

It was the perfect Test. It was another Test. It was a Test.

Test cricket dug in and got through to tea.

It always does.

Thanks to ...

My wife, kids and parents for allowing me to disappear during our holiday and write. And all the other times you let me write. Also all the Kimbers, Ahamats and their affiliates. Joel 'Big Daddy' Kimber, Simon 'The Professor' Spehr and Todd 'Tidd' Spehr for getting me started in the first place. The Campbellfield and Coburg Cricket clubs. Hardie Grant, especially Pam, Michael and Rihana. Gideon Haigh, Chris Ryan, David Studham, Subash Jayaraman, Andrew Samson, Sam Collins, Andy Plowright, Andy Zaltzman, George Dobell, Osman Samiuddin, David Hopps, Sambit Bal, Dan Brettig, Alan Gardner, Andrew Fidel Fernando, Andrew McGlashan, Alex Winter, Raf Nicholson, Simon Lister, George Binoy and Leslie Mathews for their words, nonsense and help along the way.

Also a special shout out to all those who responded to my desperate late night tweets. You are all the unofficial researchers of this book. Legends. All of you.

So many books and articles were consulted for this it would be almost impossible for me to name them all. I have, where possible, tried to drop the name of the books and websites I have used. But there are certain people and organisations that deserve a second special mentioning. Malcolm Knox, John Major, Osman Samiuddin, HS Altham, Richard Boock, Martin Williamson, Ramachandra Guha, Gideon Haigh, CLR James, *Wisden*, the MCC Library (both of them) and ESPNcricinfo have all done amazing things for cricket.

All of cricket's historians. And by all I mean everyone from those who pedantically update Wikipedia, to illegal Youtube uploaders, caustic bloggers, timeless essayists, jobbing journalists, fanatical redditors, methodical chat roomers, anal tweeters, story-telling commentators, and all the unloved authors way back to John Nyren. You are all the reason cricket has an amazing collection of historical documents. Cricket should be proud that so many people have spent so much of their time not just watching and playing, but writing and talking.

Special thanks to Grandpa, Nan and Bonga Bonga for teaching me how to tell a yarn.

About the Author

Jarrod Kimber was born into a family of cricket fundamentalists in the north of Melbourne. He slept with many cricket bats, skipped school to watch tour games, wrote a sitcom set in a cricket club, and played cricket on turf, matting, synthetics, backyards, roads and even against a brick wall and a stocking on a clothes line. He owns seven Victorian Bushranger shirts (over 70 ODI shirts from around the world), backpacked around the '03 World Cup and left Melbourne in 2008 to become a cricket writer in the UK.

He has written three books: *A Year of the Balls*, *When Freddie Became Jesus* and *Australian Autopsy*. He was also co-director and writer of the documentary *Death of a Gentleman*. He is the global cricket writer for the world's largest cricket website, ESPNcricinfo. He was formerly the editor of the magazine *Spin Cricket*. He has commentated for ABC Grandstand and appeared as a talking head on BBC, Talksport, NDTV, 3AW, SABC and CNN.

In his career he has covered cricket in India, Australia, New Zealand, South Africa, England, Ireland and Sri Lanka. In the last five years he has seen 61 Tests, a World Cup, two World T20s, shield cricket, big bash, IPL and women's internationals. His favourite meal was a fish curry out of a massive cauldron in Eden Gardens. He was once choked (sort of accidentally) by a security guard at the WACA, was called the 'most hated man in cricket' by a powerful cricket administrator, and ghost-wrote sledges for a county cricketer.

He provided the cover photo of a P. Diddy album, is a high school dropout, uses a Charlie French bat, bowls ineffectual leg-spin and lives in South London with his wife Miriam and sons Zachariah and Ezekiel.